OUT AMONG THE
WOLVES

OUT AMONG THE
WOLVES

CONTEMPORARY WRITINGS ON THE WOLF

EDITED BY
JOHN A. MURRAY

Whitecap Books
Vancouver/Toronto

To the memory of Charles William Murray, Sr.,
and to Helen Louise Murray

Managing editor: Ellen Harkins Wheat
Editors: Linda Gunnarson and Carolyn Smith
Book and cover designer: Cameron Mason
Cover photograph by Victoria Hurst/First Light

Printed in the United States of America

Canadian Cataloguing in Publication Data

Out among the wolves : contemporary writings on the wolf

Includes bibliographical references and index.
  ISBN 1-55110-100-9

  1. Wolves.   2. Wolves—North America.   I. Murray, John A., 1954–
QL737.C22095   599.74'442   C93-091537-2

"[I warn you of] the Evening wolves, the rabid and howling Wolves of the Wilderness [which will] make . . . Havock among you, and not leave the Bones till the morning."

—Cotton Mather
Frontiers Well-Defended, 1707

"In the wolf we have not so much an animal that we have always known as one that we have consistently imagined. We embark then on an observation of an imaginary creature, not in the pejorative but in the enlightened sense— a wolf from which all other wolves are derived."

—Barry Lopez
Of Wolves and Men

CONTENTS

PREFACE

THERE ARE MANY REASONS for assembling an anthology of contemporary wolf writings. For one thing, no such collection has been prepared before. For another, you and I have the good fortune to live in what posterity may well call "The Decade of the Wolf." After centuries of persecuting and misunderstanding wolves, American society has begun to reexamine long-held attitudes and adopt a more enlightened and tolerant view of predators. As a result, conservation and restoration programs for the wolf, unthinkable as recently as the early 1970s, are now commonplace. At this writing, red wolves again run wild in eastern North Carolina, gray wolves have repopulated northern Montana and northern Washington, gray wolves will probably soon be restored to Yellowstone National Park, and Mexican wolves may be released on the White Sands Missile Range in southwestern New Mexico. If these and other events proceed successfully, wolves could be considered for other suitable locations, such as Olympic National Park in Washington, the central Sierra Nevada in California, Grand Canyon National Park in Arizona, Big Bend National Park in Texas, the Gila Wilderness Area or the Gray Ranch in southwestern New Mexico, the Weminuche Wilderness in Colorado, and perhaps a location or two on the northern plains in the Missouri River drainage. Wolves are not that hard to live with, as residents of northern Minnesota and Canada, not to mention Italy, Greece, and Spain, have known for quite some time.

Canadian readers will, of course, be more familiar with the wolf in the wild than American readers. Wolves are currently found throughout Canada, from the Pacific Coast to the Atlantic Coast, from the international border with the United States to the barren arctic islands of the far north. Canadian wolves occupy about 80 percent of their historic range in the country. The species became extinct in Nova Scotia and New Brunswick by 1870 and was eliminated from Newfoundland by 1911. Popular wolf-viewing areas in Canada include Algonquin Provincial Park in Ontario, Riding Mountain National Park in Manitoba, and Banff National Park in Alberta.

Even in areas in which they are relatively plentiful, however, wolves are losing habitat to agriculture and urban sprawl. This is

particularly the case in southern Quebec and Ontario. Various agencies and private associations still offer bounties for documented wolf
kills, and in 1993 the Yukon Territory announced it would commence
a controversial wolf control program (similar to the one proposed and
then withdrawn in Alaska in 1993). The overall population is estimated to be between 50,000 and 65,000 individuals, as compared to
less than 1,300 in the contiguous forty-eight states of the U.S. As in the
U.S., the major challenge facing Canadians is to conserve large, discrete units of wilderness where the wide-ranging packs can conduct
their affairs undisturbed by humankind.

People always ask me how they can help save controversial species
such as the wolf. They say it is not enough to read books and rent the
Dances With Wolves video, and they are right. There are at least several
ways you can become directly involved. First, support through membership and donations those conservation organizations that are
actively leading the fight for wolf preservation; these include such
groups as Defenders of Wildlife, the Audubon Society, the Sierra Club
(particularly the Sierra Club Legal Defense Fund), the Nature
Conservancy, and the Wilderness Society, among others. It never
ceases to amaze me how much influence a determined band of
people who pool their resources can have in this world.

Second, do everything you can to preserve habitat. If you've been
to Great Smoky Mountains National Park or Rocky Mountain National
Park or even North Cascades National Park recently, you know how
serious the problem of growing population and shrinking wildlands
has become. When people say we have enough national parks, don't
believe them. Believe your eyes. Look at those filled-to-capacity camp-
grounds, those crowded trails, those mobbed bison and elk standing
by the road. There are plenty of wild areas now in private ownership
(waiting to be privately developed) and plenty of funds available (the
Federal Land and Water Conservation Fund) to purchase them. And
one more thing—don't support that new ski development on national
forest land (we have enough ski areas going bankrupt), that new
mountain valley subdivision (there goes some more deer and elk
winter habitat), or that new dam (say good-bye to a river).

Third, speak out. Don't talk only with your friends and preach to
the converted. Try to convince people who don't agree with you that a
wolf, or a mountain, or a desert is worth saving. Wave this book at
them. Once you have their attention, turn to the Edward Hoagland or

the Barry Lopez or the Jan DeBlieu selection, read some of that eloquent prose aloud, and see if that doesn't move them. One of the
axioms of political science is that a vocal minority is always more powerful than a complacent majority; remember that a relatively tiny lever
and fulcrum can move a boulder that has rested comfortably in one
location for 10,000 years. An idea whose time has come in the hands
of a few good people can move the world.

Fourth, vote. Before voting, of course, check the history of your
candidate for legislative or executive office. Most of the conservation
groups will be happy to share these public records with you. Your
elected officials will ultimately make those decisions that affect your
life—whether your children hear a wolf pack howl one cold
September night in Yellowstone's Hayden Valley or whether you must
tell them, sadly, that once there were wolves but a small group of men
killed them off and then another, even smaller group made certain
they never returned again. Once your candidates (or maybe not your
candidates) are elected, write letters and make telephone calls to their
district or state offices every time you agree or disagree with them.
Don't let them forget you, or your concerns.

Fifth, support science education in the public schools. How many
of us still remember that field trip to the natural history museum,
where we saw the wolf pack hunting caribou in the northern Alaska
diorama; or that field trip to the city zoo, where we saw the wolves restlessly pacing from one side of their enclosure to the other; or the
times that the "wolf man" hired by the school every year brought his
wolves to the gymnasium and showed us what these largely misunder-
stood animals were all about? Part of supporting education also means
supporting your public television station with a generous donation
during pledge week. Their stellar programs—including the award-
winning "Nature" series and the Marty Stouffer "Wild America" seg-
ments—have probably done more to change public opinion on a
massive scale than anything else.

I have many thanks to give. My education on the subject of wolves
began in 1986 while researching and writing the wolf chapter for
my book *Wildlife in Peril: The Endangered Mammals of Colorado* (1987).
I would be remiss if I did not acknowledge those debts again—to
Glen Kaye, chief park naturalist at Rocky Mountain National Park;
Dave Stevens, park biologist at Rocky Mountain National Park; Judy
Sheppard of the Colorado Division of Wildlife; Sandy Binker of the

Colorado Woolgrowers' Association; and Bob Ralston of the Colorado Cattlemen's Association. More recently, my friends at Denali National Park have greatly facilitated my study of the subarctic wolf: Ralph Tingey, George Wagner, Bill McDonald, Tom Griffith, Russ Berry, Ken Kehrer, Ralph Cunningham, and Fred Dean. Many thanks to park naturalist Rick McIntyre, with whom I spent long hours watching wolves in that glorious summer of 1990 when the Toklat pack denned so close to the Porcupine Forest that we saw them hunting nearly every day. A special thanks to Montana writer Rick Bass, who joined me for a memorable photo safari in Denali in 1990 (who could ever forget the storm that flattened our tents?); to California writer David Rains Wallace, who hiked with me up the Savage River, where we found old wolf scat and fresh wolf tracks and watched four grizzlies for an hour; and to writer Paul Schullery of Yellowstone National Park, who mailed a huge packet of wolf information that kept me busy reading for a week. Montana cinematographer Bob Landis points out wolves to me in Denali each summer. One of my oldest and dearest friends—Jimmy Miller—accompanied me on some incomparable hikes through Alaskan wolf country in 1991 and once again proved himself the ultimate bon vivant.

The book would not have been possible without the enthusiastic cooperation of authors, agents, and publishers, and I thank them all for their assistance. Thanks again to Alaska Northwest Books editors Marlene Blessing and Ellen Wheat, who also worked with me on *The Great Bear: Contemporary Writings on the Grizzly* (1992) and who energetically supported this project from the very beginning.

Finally, I would like to extend my heartfelt gratitude to my mother and father for their constant encouragement over the years; to my son, whose birth taught me more about nature than all those years climbing the mountains; and to Fen, for sacrifices and kindnesses too numerous to list.

—John A. Murray
Fairbanks, Alaska
July 14, 1992

OUT AMONG THE
WOLVES

1. THE EAST FORK OF THE TOKLAT PACK

ADOLPH MURIE

IN FRONT OF OUR CABIN AT EAST FORK RIVER, ON May 15, 1940, wolf tracks were seen in the fresh snow covering the gravel bars. The tracks led in both directions, but since there was no game upstream at the time to attract the wolves, it appeared that some other interest, which I hoped was a den, accounted for their movement that way. I followed the tracks up the bar for a mile and a half directly to the den on a point of the high bank bordering the river bed. In contrast to the Toklat den, which was located in the woods in a flat patch of timber, this one was 2 miles beyond the last scraggly timber, on an open point about 100 feet above the river where the wolves had an excellent view of the surrounding country. Apparently a variety of situations are chosen for dens for I was told of two others which were located in timber, and of a third which was in a treeless area at the head of a dry stream.

Foxes had dug the original den on the point, and wolves had later moved in and had enlarged a few of the burrows. It seems customary

"The East Fork of the Toklat Pack" is taken from Adolph Murie's The Wolves of Mount McKinley, *originally published in 1944.*

in this region for wolves to preempt fox dens. Former Ranger Swisher, who had found at least four wolf dens, said that all of them had originally been dug by foxes. There are many unoccupied fox dens available so it is not strange that they are generally used by the wolves. The soil at the sites is sandy or loamy, at least free of rocks, so that digging is easy. Only a little enlarging of one of the many burrows is required to make a den habitable for a wolf. Although the adult wolves can only use the enlarged burrow, the whole system of burrows is available to the pups for a few weeks. This advantage is incidental and probably has no bearing on the choice of fox dens as homes.

When I approached this den a black male wolf was resting 70 yards away. He ran off about a quarter of a mile or less and howled and barked at intervals. As I stood 4 yards from the entrance, the female furtively pushed her head out of the burrow, then withdrew it, but in a moment came out with a rush, galloped most of the way down the slope, and stopped to bark at me. Then she galloped toward the male hidden in a ravine, and both parents howled and barked until I left.

From the den I heard the soft whimpering of the pups. It seemed I had already intruded too far, enough to cause the wolves to move. As I could not make matters much worse, I wriggled into the burrow which was 16 inches high and 25 inches wide. Six feet from the entrance of the burrow there was a right angle turn. At the turn there was a hollow, rounded and worn, which obviously was a bed much used by an adult. Due to the melting snow it was full of water in which there was a liberal sprinkling of porcupine droppings. A porcupine had used the place the preceding winter. Its feeding signs had been noted on the many nearby willows. From the turn the burrow slanted slightly upward for 6 feet to the chamber in which the pups were huddled and squirming. With a hooked willow I managed to pull three of the six pups to me. Not wishing to subject all of them to even a slight wetting, and feeling guilty about disturbing the den so much, I withdrew with the three I had. Their eyes were closed and they appeared to be about a week old. They were all females, and dark, almost black. One appeared slightly lighter than the other two and I placed her in my packsack to keep for closer acquaintance. The other two were returned to their chamber and I departed.

After my intrusion it seemed certain that the family would move, so the following morning I walked toward the den to take up their trail before the snow melted. But from a distance I saw the black male curled up on the point 15 yards from the entrance, so it was apparent that they had not moved away after all. In fact, they remained at the den until the young were old enough to move off with the adults at the normal time.

On a ridge across the river from the den, about a half mile or less away, there were excellent locations for watching the wolves without disturbing them. There was also a view of the landscape for several miles in all directions.

Between May 15, when the den was discovered, and July 7, when the wolves moved a mile away, I spent about 195 hours observing them. The longest continuous vigil was 33 hours, and twice I observed them all night. Frequently I watched a few hours in the evening to see the wolves leave for the night hunt. Late in the summer and in the early fall after the family had left the den, I had the opportunity on a few occasions to watch the family for several hours at a time.

So far as I am aware it has been taken for granted that a wolf family consists of a pair of adults and pups. Perhaps that is the rule, although we may not have enough information about wolves to really know. Usually when a den is discovered the young are destroyed and all opportunity for making further observations is thereby lost.

The first week after finding the East Fork den I remained away from its vicinity to let the wolves regain whatever composure they had lost when I intruded in their home. On May 25, a few days after beginning an almost daily watch of the den, I was astonished at seeing two strange gray wolves move from where they had been lying a few yards from the den entrance. These two gray wolves proved to be males. They rested at the den most of the day. At 4 P.M., in company with the black father wolf, they departed for the night hunt. Because I had not watched the den closely the first week after finding it I do not know when the two gray males first made their appearance there, but judging from later events it seems likely that they were there occasionally from the first.

Five days later, a second black wolf—a female—was seen, making a total of five adults at the den—three males and two females. These five wolves lounged at the den day after day until the family moved away. There may have been another male in the group for I learned that a male had been inadvertently shot about 2 miles from the den a few days before I found the den.

Late in July another male was seen with the band, and a little later a fourth extra male joined them. These seven wolves, or various combinations of them, were frequently seen together in August and September. Five of the seven were males. The four extra males appeared to be bachelors.

The relationship of the two extra males and the extra female to the pair is not known. They may have been pups born to the gray female in years past or they may have been her brothers and sister, or no blood relation at all. I knew the gray female in 1939. She was then traveling with two gray and two black wolves which I did not know well enough to be certain they were the same as those at the den in 1940. But since the color combination of the wolves traveling together was the same in 1940 as in 1939, it is quite certain that the same wolves were involved. So apparently all the adult wolves at the den in 1940 were at least 2 years old. In 1941 it was known that the extra male with the female was at least 2 years old for he was an easily identified gray male which was at the den in 1940. The fact that none of the 1940 pups was at the 1941 den supports the conclusion that the extra wolves at the 1940 den were not the previous year's pups.

The presence of the five adults in the East Fork family during denning time in 1940 and three in 1941, and three adults in the Savage River family, suggests that it may not be uncommon to find more than two adults at a den. The presence of extra adults is an unusual family make-up which is probably an outcome of the close association of the wolves in the band. It should be an advantage for the parents to have help in hunting and feeding the pups.

Wolves vary much in color, size, contour, and action. No doubt there is also much variation in temperament. Many are so distinctively colored or patterned that they can be identified from afar. I found the gray ones more easily identified since among them there is more individual variation in color pattern than in the black wolves.

The mother of the pups was dark gray, almost "bluish," over the back, and had light underparts, a blackish face, and a silvery mane. She was thick-bodied, short-legged, short-muzzled, and smaller than the others. She was easily recognized from afar.

The father was black with a yellowish vertical streak behind each shoulder. From a distance he appeared coal black except for the yellow shoulder marks, but a nearer view revealed a scattering of silver and rusty hairs, especially over the shoulders and along the sides.

There was an extra fullness of the neck under the chin. He seemed more solemn than the others, but perhaps that was partly imagined by me, knowing as I did that many of the family cares rested on his shoulders. On the hunts that I observed he usually took the lead in running down caribou calves.

The other black wolf was a slender-built, long-legged female. Her muzzle seemed exceptionally long, reminding me of the Little Red Riding Hood illustrations. Her neck was not as thick as that of the black male. This female had no young in 1940, but had her own family in 1941.

What appeared to be the largest wolf was a tall, rangy male with a long silvery mane and a dark mantle over the back and part way down over the sides. He seemed to be the lord and master of the group although he was not mated to any of the females. The other wolves approached this one with some diffidence, usually cowering before him. He deigned to wag his tail only after the others had done so. He was also the dandy in appearance. When trotting off for a hunt his tail waved jauntily and there was a spring and sprightly spirit in his step. The excess energy at times gave him a rocking-horse gallop quite different from that of any of the others.

The other gray male at the den I called "Grandpa" in my notes. He was a rangy wolf of a nondescript color. There were no distinctive markings, but he moved as though he were old and a little stiff. Sometimes he had sore feet which made him limp. From all appearances he was an old animal, although in this I may be mistaken.

One of the grays that joined the group in late July was a large male with a light face except for a black robber's mask over the eyes. His chest was conspicuously white. He moved with much spring and energy. The black mask was distinctive and recognizable from a distance.

The other wolf, which joined the group in August, was a huge gray animal with a light yellowish face. In 1941 he was mated to the small black female which had no young the preceding year.

All these wolves could be readily distinguished within the group but some of the less distinctively marked ones might have been confused among a group of strange wolves. The black-faced gray female, the robber-masked male, and the black-mantled male were so characteristically marked that they could be identified in a large company.

2. THINKING LIKE A MOUNTAIN

ALDO LEOPOLD

A DEEP CHESTY BAWL ECHOES FROM RIMROCK TO rimrock, rolls down the mountain, and fades into the far blackness of the night. It is an outburst of wild defiant sorrow, and of contempt for all the adversities of the world.

Every living thing (and perhaps many a dead one as well) pays heed to that call. To the deer it is a reminder of the way of all flesh, to the pine a forecast of midnight scuffles and of blood upon the snow, to the coyote a promise of gleanings to come, to the cowman a threat of red ink at the bank, to the hunter a challenge of fang against bullet. Yet behind these obvious and immediate hopes and fears there lies a deeper meaning, known only to the mountain itself. Only the mountain has lived long enough to listen objectively to the howl of a wolf.

Those unable to decipher the hidden meaning know nevertheless that it is there, for it is felt in all wolf country, and distinguishes that country from all other land. It tingles in the spine of all who hear wolves by night, or who scan their tracks by day. Even without sight or sound of wolf, it is implicit in a hundred small events: the midnight whinny of a pack horse, the rattle of rolling rocks, the bound of a flee-ing deer, the way shadows lie under the spruces. Only the ineducable tyro can fail to sense the presence or absence of wolves, or the fact that mountains have a secret opinion about them.

My own conviction on this score dates from the day I saw a wolf die. We were eating lunch on a high rimrock, at the foot of which a turbulent river elbowed its way. We saw what we thought was a doe fording the torrent, her breast awash in white water. When she climbed the bank toward us and shook out her tail, we realized our error: it was a wolf. A half-dozen others, evidently grown pups, sprang from the willows and all joined in a welcoming mêlée of wagging tails and playful maulings. What was literally a pile of wolves writhed and tumbled in the center of an open flat at the foot of our rimrock.

In those days we had never heard of passing up a chance to kill a wolf. In a second we were pumping lead into the pack, but with more excitement than accuracy: how to aim a steep downhill shot is always confusing. When our rifles were empty, the old wolf was down, and a pup was dragging a leg into impassable slide-rocks.

We reached the old wolf in time to watch a fierce green fire dying in her eyes. I realized then, and have known ever since, that there was something new to me in those eyes—something known only to her and to the mountain. I was young then, and full of trigger-itch; I thought that because fewer wolves meant more deer, that no wolves would mean hunters' paradise. But after seeing the green fire die, I sensed that neither the wolf nor the mountain agreed with such a view.

SINCE THEN I have lived to see state after state extirpate its wolves. I have watched the face of many a newly wolfless mountain, and seen the south-facing slopes wrinkle with a maze of new deer trails. I have seen every edible bush and seedling browsed, first to anemic desue-tude, and then to death. I have seen every edible tree defoliated to the height of a saddle horn. Such a mountain looks as if someone had given God new pruning shears, and forbidden Him all other exercise. In the end the starved bones of the hoped-for deer herd, dead of its own too-much, bleach with the bones of the dead sage, or molder under the high-lined junipers.

I now suspect that just as a deer herd lives in mortal fear of its wolves, so does a mountain live in mortal fear of its deer. And perhaps with better cause, for while a buck pulled down by wolves can be replaced in two or three years, a range pulled down by too many deer may fail of replacement in as many decades.

So also with cows. The cowman who cleans his range of wolves does not realize that he is taking over the wolf's job of trimming the herd to fit the range. He has not learned to think like a mountain. Hence we have dustbowls, and rivers washing the future into the sea.

WE ALL STRIVE for safety, prosperity, comfort, long life, and dullness. The deer strives with his supple legs, the cowman with trap and poison, the statesman with pen, the most of us with machines, votes, and dollars, but it all comes to the same thing: peace in our time. A measure of success in this is all well enough, and perhaps is a requisite to objective thinking, but too much safety seems to yield only danger in the long run. Perhaps this is behind Thoreau's dictum: In wildness is the salvation of the world. Perhaps this is the hidden meaning in the howl of the wolf, long known among mountains, but seldom perceived among men.

3. TIMBER WOLVES

SIGURD F. OLSON

I COULD HEAR THEM PLAINLY NOW ON BOTH SIDES OF
the river, could hear the brush crack as they hurdled windfalls in
their path. Once I thought I saw one, a drifting gray shadow against
the snow, but it was only a branch swaying in the light of the moon.
When I heard the full-throated bawling howl, I should have had chills
racing up and down my spine. Instead, I was thrilled to know that the
big grays might have picked up my trail and were following me down
the glistening frozen highway of the river.

It was a beautiful night for travel—twenty below, and the only
sound the steady swish and creak of my snowshoes on the crust. There
was a great satisfaction in knowing that the wolves were in the country,
that it was wild enough and still big enough for them to roam and
hunt. That night the wilderness of the Quetico-Superior was what the
voyageurs had known two hundred years before, as primitive and
unchanged as before discovery.

Some months before, I had had the same kind of experience on a pack trip in the Sun River country of Montana. In the bottom of a canyon I saw the fresh track of a big grizzly in the soft muck beside a glacial creek. Although I did not see the bear, I knew it was nearby. Those tracks changed the country immediately for me. From that moment on, it was the land of Lewis and Clark, the land of the mountain men of the last century, a valley of the old west.

The river ahead narrowed down to where two points of timber came out from either bank, and as I approached, I sensed instinctively the possibilities of attack. I was familiar with the wolf lore of the Old World, the packs on the steppes of Russia, the invasion of farms and villages, and had I believed the lurid tales of our early settlers and explorers, I might have been afraid. To the best of my knowledge, however, including the files of the U.S. Fish and Wildlife Service, for the past twenty-five years there has never been a single authenticated instance of unprovoked attack on man.

But still there was a feeling of uneasiness and apprehension, and I knew that if the animals were concerned with anything but satisfying their curiosity, the narrows would be the place for a kill. A swift rush from both points at the same time, a short, unequal scuffle in the snow, and it would be all over. My bones would go down with the ice in the spring, and no one would ever hear the story and no one would be able to explain.

As I neared the points of spruce, I could almost hear the crash of heavy bodies against windfalls and brush. Weighing a hundred, even as much as a hundred and twelve pounds or more, timber wolves are huge and powerful, can bring down a caribou or a moose, have nothing to fear on the entire continent but man. This was not the first time I had felt they were playing their game of hide-and-seek with me. On other lone midwinter expeditions I had sensed that they were close—a hunch perhaps, but as instinctive a reaction when in their immediate range as though I had actually seen them. I knew, as I hiked along that night, that I was being watched, a lone dark spot moving slowly along the frozen river.

That very morning I had seen where they had pulled down an old buck on the ice of a little lake, seen how they had run the deer to exhaustion and then sliced at his hamstrings, his flanks, and his throat, seen the long crimson spurt where they had ripped the jugular, seen the bits of mangled hide on the snow. He had been large and his horns were broad and palmate, but in the trampled bloody circle where he had made his last stand, he had not lasted long. He might have died slowly of starvation or disease, but he died as he should when his time had come, fighting for his life against his age-old enemies, dying like the valiant warrior he was out on the open ice.

The wolves had not eaten much, only the entrails and the viscera, but they would return, I knew, to satisfy themselves again. Such was the habit of their kind until we interfered with poison and trap and taught them caution and fear. When that happened, they learned to leave the carcasses after the first feeding and killed more than they would have normally. That kill was part of the age-old cycle of dependency between the wolves and deer. The predators, by the elimination of the old, the weak, and the diseased, improved the character of the herd and kept the younger and more virile breeding-stock alert and aware of danger. The deer provided food when there was no other source, when the heavy snows hid small rodents, the fish and snakes, grubs and berries and birds that gave the wolves sustenance during all other seasons of the year. There on the ice was evidence of the completed cycle, and, though all kills are gruesome things, I was glad to see it, for it meant a wilderness in balance, a primitive country that as yet had not been tamed.

In the narrows the spruces stood tall and black against the sky. The shores there were only a stone's throw apart. I must walk straight down the center, must not run, must not break my pace; and suddenly I was aware that, in spite of reason and my knowledge of the predators, ancient reactions were coming to the fore, intuitive warnings out of the past. In spite of what I knew, I was responding to the imagined threat of the narrows like a stone-age hunter cut off from his cave.

Then, far ahead, way beyond the dangerous points, two shadows broke from cover and headed directly down the river toward me. I stopped, slipped off my pack, and waited. Nearer and nearer they came, running with the easy, loose-jointed grace that only the big timber wolves seem to have. A hundred yards away they stopped and tried to get my wind; they wove back and forth, swaying as they ran. Then, about fifty feet away, they stopped and looked me over. In the moonlight their gray hides glistened and I could see the greenish glint of their eyes. Not a movement or a sound. We stood watching each other as though such meetings were expected and commonplace.

As suddenly as they had appeared, they whirled and were off down the river, two drifting forms against the ice. Never before had I been that close, possibly never again would I see the glint in timber wolves' eyes or have such a chance to study their free and fluid movement. Once more came the long howl, this time far back from the river, and then I heard them no more.

A little later I pushed open the door of the little cabin and touched a match to the waiting tinder in the stove. As I sat there listening to the roar of it and stowing away my gear, I realized fully what I had seen and what I had felt. Had it not been twenty below, I would have left the door opened wide so as not to lose the spell of the moonlit river and the pack ranging its shores.

After I was warmed through and had eaten my supper, I stepped outside once more. The river was still aglisten, and the far shore looked black and somber. An owl hooted back in the spruce, and I knew what that meant in the moonlit glades. A tree cracked sharply with the frost, and then it was still, so still that I could hear the beating of my heart. At last I caught what I was listening for—the long-drawn quavering howl from over the hills, a sound as wild and indigenous to the north as the muskegs or the northern lights. That was wilderness music, something as free and untamed as there is on this earth.

Although thrilled to hear them once again, I was saddened when I thought of the constant war of extermination which goes on all over the continent. Practically gone from the United States, wolves are now common only in the Quetico-Superior country, in Canada, and in Alaska, and I knew the day might come when, because of man's ignorance, the great grays would be gone even from there. Just before leaving on my trip up the river I had seen a news story about the killing of six timber wolves by airplane hunters in the Rainy Lake country. The picture showed them strung up on the wing of the plane and the hunters proudly posed beside them. As I studied that picture and the applauding captions, I wondered if the day would ever come when we would understand the importance of wolves.

Knowing the nature of our traditions of the old frontier and the pioneer complex that still guides our attitudes toward wildlife, I realized that it might never come. We still do not realize that today we can enjoy the wilderness without fear, still do not appreciate the part that predators play in the balanced ecology of any natural community. We seem to prefer herds of semi-domesticated deer and elk and moose, swarms of small game with their natural alertness gone. It is as though we were interested in conserving only a meat supply and nothing of the semblance of the wild.

It was cold, bitterly cold, and I hurried back into the cabin and crawled into my sleeping bag in the corner bunk. Beside me was my pack and in a pocket my brush-worn copy of Thoreau. I took it out, thumbed through it by the light of the candle.

"We need," he said, "to witness our own limits transgressed and some life pasturing freely where we never wander."

4. SCHOOL DAYS

FARLEY MOWAT

BY MID-SEPTEMBER THE TUNDRA PLAINS BURNED somberly in the subdued glow of russet and umber where the early frosts had touched the ground cover of low shrubbery. The muskeg pastures about Wolf House Bay were fretted with fresh roads made by the southbound herds of caribou, and the pattern of the wolves' lives had changed again.

The pups had left the summer den and, though they could not keep up with Angeline and the two males on prolonged hunts, they could and did go along on shorter expeditions. They had begun to explore their world, and those autumnal months must have been among the happiest of their lives.

When Ootek and I returned to Wolf House Bay after our travels through the central plains, we found that our wolf family was ranging widely through its territory and spending the days wherever the hunt might take it.

Within the limits imposed upon me by my physical abilities and human needs, I tried to share that wandering life, and I too enjoyed it immensely. The flies were all gone. Though there were sometimes frosts at night, the days were usually warm under a clear sun.

ON ONE SUCH WARM and sunlit day I made my way north from the den esker, along the crest of a range of hills which overlooked a great valley, rich in forage, and much used by the caribou as a highway south.

A soot-flecking of black specks hung in the pallid sky above the valley—flocks of ravens following the deer herds. Families of ptarmigan cackled at me from clumps of dwarf shrub. Flocks of Old Squaw ducks, almost ready to be off for distant places, swirled in the tundra ponds.

Below me in the valley rolled a sluggish stream of caribou, herd after herd grazing toward the south, unconscious, yet directly driven by a knowledge that was old before we even knew what knowledge was.

Some miles from the den esker I found a niche at the top of a high cliff overlooking the valley, and here I settled myself in comfort, my back against the rough but sun-warmed rock, my knees drawn up under my chin, and my binoculars leveled at the living stream below me.

I was hoping to see the wolves and they did not disappoint me. Shortly before noon two of them came into sight on the crest of a transverse ridge some distance to the north. A few moments later two more adults and the four pups appeared. There was some frisking, much nose smelling and tail wagging, and then most of the wolves lay down and took their ease, while the others sat idly watching the caribou streaming by on either side only a few hundred feet away.

I easily recognized Angeline and George. One of the other two adults looked like Uncle Albert; but the fourth, a rangy dark-gray beast, was a total stranger to me. I never did learn who he was or where he came from, but for the rest of the time I was in the country he remained a member of the band.

Of all the wolves, indeed of all the animals in view including the caribou and myself, only George seemed to feel any desire to be active. While the rest of us sprawled blissfully in the sun, or grazed lethargically amongst the lichens, George began to wander restlessly back and forth along the top of the ridge. Once or twice he stopped in front of Angeline but she paid him no attention other than to flop her tail lazily a few times.

Drowsily I watched a doe caribou grazing her way up the ridge on which the wolves were resting. She had evidently found a rich patch of lichens and, though she must have seen the wolves, she continued to graze toward them until not twenty yards separated her from one of the pups. This pup watched her carefully until, to my delight, he got to his feet, stared uneasily over his shoulder to see what the rest of the family was doing, then turned and slunk toward them with his tail actually between his legs.

Not even the restless George, who now came slowly toward the doe, his nose outthrust as he tasted her scent, seemed to disturb her equanimity until the big male wolf, perhaps hurt in his dignity by her unconcern, made a quick feint in her direction. At that she flung her head high, spun on her ungainly legs and gallumphed back down the ridge apparently more indignant than afraid.

Time slipped past, the river of deer continued to flow, and I expected to observe nothing more exciting than this brief interlude between the doe and the wolves, for I guessed that the wolves had already fed, and that this was the usual after-dinner siesta. I was wrong, for George had something on his mind.

A third time he went over to Angeline, who was now stretched out on her side, and this time he would not take "no" for an answer. I have no idea what he said, but it must have been pertinent, for she scrambled to her feet, shook herself, and bounced amiably after him as he went to sniff at the slumbering forms of Uncle Albert and the Stranger. They too got the message and rose to their feet. The pups, never slow to join in something new, also roused and galloped over to join their elders. Standing in a rough circle, the whole group of wolves now raised their muzzles and began to howl, exactly as they used to do at the den esker before starting on a hunt.

I was surprised that they should be preparing for a hunt so early in the day, but I was more surprised by the lack of reaction to the wolf chorus on the part of the caribou. Hardly a deer within hearing even bothered to lift its head, and those few who did contented themselves with a brief, incurious look toward the ridge before returning to their placid grazing. I had no time to ponder the matter, for Angeline,

Albert and the Stranger now started off, leaving the pups sitting disconsolately in a row on the crest, with George standing just ahead of them. When one of the youngsters made an attempt to follow the three adults, George turned on him, and the pup hurriedly rejoined his brothers and sisters.

What little wind there was blew from the south and the three wolves moved off upwind in a tight little group. As they reached the level tundra they broke into a trot, following one another in line, not hurrying, but trotting easily through the groups of caribou. As usual the deer were not alarmed and none took evasive action except when the wolves happened to be on a collision course with them.

The three wolves paid no attention to the caribou either, although they passed many small herds containing numbers of fawns. They made no test runs at any of these groups, but continued purposefully on their way until they were almost abreast the niche where I was sitting. At this point Angeline stopped and sat down while the other two joined her. There was more nose smelling, but Angeline got up and turned toward the ridge where George and the pups still sat.

There were at least two hundred deer between the two groups of wolves, and more were coming constantly into view around the eastern shoulder of the transverse ridge. Angeline's glance seemed to take them all in before she and her companions began to move off. Spreading out to form a line abreast, with intervals of a couple of hundred yards between them so that they almost spanned the whole width of the valley, they now began to run north.

They were not running hard, but there was a new purposefulness to their movements which the deer seemed to recognize; or perhaps it was just that the formation the wolves were using made it difficult for the herds to avoid them in the usual way by running off to one side. In any event herd after herd also began to turn about and move north, until most of the caribou in the valley were being driven back the way they had come.

The deer were clearly reluctant to be driven, and several herds made determined efforts to buck the line; but on each occasion the two nearest wolves converged toward the recalcitrant caribou and forced them to continue north. However, three wolves could not sweep the whole width of the valley; the deer soon began to discover that they could swing around the open wings and so resume their southerly progress. Nevertheless, by the time the wolves were nearing the ridge, they were herding at least a hundred deer ahead of them.

Now for the first time the deer showed real signs of nervousness. What had become an almost solid mass of a hundred or more animals broke up into its constituent small bands again, and each went galloping off on its own course. Group after group began to swerve aside, but the wolves no longer attempted to prevent them. As the wolves galloped past each of these small herds, the caribou stopped and turned to watch for a moment before resuming their interrupted journey south.

I was beginning to see what the wolves were up to. They were now concentrating their efforts on one band of a dozen does and seven fawns, and every attempt which this little herd made to turn either left or right was promptly foiled. The deer gave up after a while, and settled down to outrun their pursuers in the straightaway.

They would have done it, too, but as they swept past the clump of willows at the end of the ridge a perfect flood of wolves seemed to take them in the flank.

I could not follow events as well as I would have wished because of the distance, but I saw George racing toward a doe accompanied by two fawns. Then, just as he reached them, I saw him swerve away. He was passed by two pups going like gray bullets. These two went for the nearest of the two fawns, which promptly began jinking. One of the pups, attempting too sharp a turn, missed his footing and tumbled head over heels, but he was up on the instant and away again.

The other pups seemed to have become intermingled with the balance of the deer, and I could not see what they were up to; but as the herd drew away at full gallop the pups appeared in the rear, running hard, but losing ground.

A single fawn now began outdistancing its pursuers too. All four pups were still running flat out, although they no longer had a chance of overtaking any of the deer.

What of the adult wolves meanwhile? When I swung my glasses back to look for them I found George standing exactly where I had seen him last, his tail wagging slowly as he watched the progress of the chase. The other three wolves had by now returned to the crest of the ridge. Albert and the Stranger had lain down to rest, after their brief exertions, but Angeline was standing up and watching the rapidly retreating caribou.

It was half an hour before the pups came back. They were so

weary they could hardly climb the ridge to join their elders, all of whom were now lying down relaxing. The pups joined the group and flopped, panting heavily; but none of the adults paid them any heed.

School was over for the day.

5. THE CUSTER WOLF

ROGER A. CARAS

AS FROM A LONG SLEEP, THE LITTLE WOLF—THE white one, last of five to be born in the cave beneath the great tree stump—struggled into consciousness. Exhausted from the pulling and crushing, worn out from the first great battle for survival, the little blind animal felt the air rush into his lungs, felt the strangeness of dry air against his nose and throat. Then he slept.

Not much more than a handful of fur, still soaked with the fluids of birth, the small creature felt the joy of movement, experienced the first ecstasy of freedom. Even as he slept his legs twitched and his head turned from side to side. After a few minutes the cub awakened, his whole being possessed with a desire he had not experienced before. There was a gnawing, a need to be filled, a need to press his muzzle and gums against something. He had to suck.

Instinctively he twisted and turned, trying to use his legs that were now free. Finally, driven by the strange mounting need, he crawled on his flat belly toward the source of heat, felt the fur, nuzzled it, searched through it. Something pressed against him, trying to push him back from the fur and warmth, but he struggled mightily against his littermates until he reached his mother's body. His nose found a hard little nipple and greedily he pressed himself to it, took it into his mouth and began working his gums. The rich, warm fluid poured into his mouth and he choked. Fighting back against his brothers and sisters, and fighting the great choking at the same time, he finally cleared his throat and mouth and sucked again. This time the fluid flowed properly, and for the first time in his life he swallowed. The aching in his guts stopped. The little white cub had won the second battle of his life. Here, in the hole beneath the ground, he would survive.

SOMETIME DURING THAT first day the wolf cub had a second great awakening. Strange sensations registered on his growing consciousness. With his nose pressed against the fur on his mother's belly, he received an impression that quickly shaped itself into his first memory. The next time he sought the source of warmth and food, there was no need to press into the fur to know that he was close. For now his nose directed his movements. He had the power of scent.

There were other things in the cave besides the fountain of warmth and milk. Something caressed him, cleaned his fur and made it smooth. This was the good feeling, the feeling that went along with the one that stopped the hurting in his belly. Each time he ate, he slept, and when he awakened he felt new strength in his legs. His muscles were filling out and he began to show a measure of coordination. Each time he tried a movement now it came easier. Soon he could crawl to his mother, over and across his struggling littermates, without difficulty. Hour by hour the strength came, and hour by hour the world formed into a reality.

For twelve days, the wolf cubs lived in a world of total darkness. There was no day, no night, only the need to fill their stomachs and the need to sleep. There was the warmth when they were near their mother, and the cold when they weren't. There was that which felt good, and that which felt bad. The great struggle was to achieve the one and fight off the other; as the hours and days progressed, the fight developed from an unconscious one to a conscious experience. Theirs was a completely elemental world composed of life-essentials.

On the thirteenth day a strange thing happened to the cubs. They kept turning their heads involuntarily toward that part of the cave from whence the cold air came. A strange magnet seemed to draw their attention toward the opening. Then, as their sealed eyes slowly began to open, a new sensation was given to them. Suddenly, quite suddenly, there was a light time and a dark time. At first, there was little to be seen, little that could not be recognized better by sound, touch, taste, and odor. Soon, though, there were things that could be separated from others by sight. When the large wolf—the one that did not offer the milk—returned to the cave, when his great form filled the mouth of the tunnel, it could be known because the light was cut off. Indeed, the first visual knowledge the cubs had was of the coming and going of their parents.

Now the world was very real. It could be tasted (by the end of the first week any foot or tail that came close was gummed and mouthed endlessly); it could be smelled; it could be heard. And now, it could be seen.

For four long weeks the cubs were restricted to their tight little world beneath the tree stump. Smells and even some muted sounds drifted toward them from the mouth of the tunnel as their parents moved in and out of the blinding light, but any move in that direction by a cub brought a warning growl from one or both parents. Those cubs that ignored the growl the first few times quickly learned that a law existed that governed their lives.

One morning both parents left the cave together. The cubs could hear them outside whining, making little calling sounds. Hesitantly they stumbled and rolled over each other toward the sound. Suddenly the father loomed in the light, walked over them, bowling their round bodies against the sides of the tunnel. He turned in the end chamber and began pushing from behind. One against the other, the cubs were tumbled and pushed until they were at the mouth of the tunnel. One by one they felt the searing pain as the hot light crashed against their eyes and blinded them.

Strange odors, strange sounds unheard before, and hot light bombarded them. They whined and turned to re-enter the safety of the tunnel—all but one. The white cub stood alone at the entrance, his forelegs stiff, braced against the world. A baby cry, an approximation of a growl, filled his throat.

Meanwhile, the parents picked up the other cubs in their jaws and gently carried them to the flat place in front of the tunnel mouth.

Individually they were retrieved from the tunnel to which they tried desperately to return and were carried again to the world outside. The white cub stood braced until he too was scooped up and carried to the flat place. Tumbled together, cowering as the world exploded its new sensations against them, the cubs huddled and whimpered, each trying to hide under the others. The suspicion and fear with which they reacted to the new world was infectious and the small, round bundle of white fur that was Lobo whimpered with the rest.

After the first fearful minutes, a new sensation, a new need filled the cubs. They were curious. Despite their fears, despite the threat of the bird sounds in the trees and the wind sounds, they began to investigate. Hesitantly, each turned from the group and began to seek the secrets of this strange new world. Each new sound electrified them and sent them tumbling toward each other. Slowly they became oriented and their curiosity, a passion that would be with them for as long as each lived, took over. Proudly, the parents stood off to the side and watched the awakening.

Within a matter of hours the cubs were rolling in their tumbling games on the flat place. New sounds continued to distract them, but the terror was gone. This was the world to which they belonged. Once the white cub—Lobo—wandered off from the rest and heard the warning growl. Ignoring it, he continued toward the new smell that lured him. Suddenly his father loomed over him and the great mouth closed on his neck. He was jerked off the ground and roughly dropped back among his littermates. This was not the gentle carrying, but a stern punishment for not heeding the warning growl. In the few days that followed, the punishment became more severe, the teeth bit harder into the scruff, and the cubs learned that the warning growl was absolute.

Each day a signal—half whimper, half soft, rumbling growl—told the cubs that they might go to the flat place. And each day a quick growl told them to return to the tunnel. Outside they were allowed to investigate, to move off in new directions for a brief time; the warning growl told them when to stop and turn back, when to lie down, when to follow. Day after day the cubs learned to respond more quickly, came to know more signals, more directing sounds.

There were good times with the grown wolves as well. The tan male would lie down among them in the warm sun and invite them to torment him. They chewed and they snarled, they crawled on him and bit his ears. Patiently the male wolf tolerated their antics; but when he gave his warning signals, compliance must be immediate.

The mother, too, demanded total obedience. Her teeth were sharp, and the press of her great paw was painful on the neck. Together, the parents completed lesson number one in the education of the cubs.

Often the father moved off and was gone for hours at a time. When he returned he would deposit great smelly chunks of meat at his mate's feet. With a satisfied sound in her throat, the female would lie down and gnaw at her food while the male went off with the cubs for the tumbling and fighting games. One day (the cubs' thirty-fourth day) the father brought a small strip of meat to where the cubs were playing and dragged it before their noses. The white cub grabbed at it and began to shake his head, flopping the piece of meat back and forth. The little black female grabbed the other end and began to pull. A mighty tug-of-war was mounted and there was much baby snarling. The harder the white cub pulled, the deeper he sank his needle-sharp baby teeth into the meat.

Suddenly a juice flowed into his mouth and he let go of the prize, sending his sister tumbling end over end. He walked over to where she had dropped the meat and pawed it. He whined and cocked his head from side to side, sniffed it, and ran over toward his father, who was basking in the sun watching the antics. Arching his back, the white cub again stalked the prize; stiff-legged he jumped and rolled over it. Again he bit at the meat. The juice was strange and he ran to his mother and began to suck until the milk had washed the strange taste from his mouth.

Each day their father brought the cubs strips of meat to play with, and each day the games with them grew fiercer. There was the tugging, the pulling and the snarling. The meat could be charged, it could be run with, it could be torn from the grasp of another. But always there was the juice, the taste that came full and rich to the tongue. After a few days the taste was no longer strange. One by one, the cubs learned to gnaw on the prize once it was won from the others. Each time the supply of meat was bigger until there was enough for all.

After a few more weeks—about ten from the time of the birth— the cubs were eating a little meat each day. They still relied to a large measure on their mother's milk, but it was no longer enough. On some days great chunks of raw meat were carried to them by their father within his stomach; arching before them, he would retch the meat up, still fresh, still rich with the juice. On other days there would be a whole animal—a prairie dog or a squirrel—still in its fur. But before such prizes could be ripped apart and eaten, there must be the games; for the meat with the fur still on offered the greatest opportunity for the fighting play.

Always the eyes, the great yellow eyes of the parents, were on them. Always they were watched and often they heard the sound signals, the growls and low throat rumbles, to which they responded. Everything they did had a lesson behind it. In their eating, in their playing, in their very existence, the lesson was always there. One day, while they all lay about the flat place sleeping in the sun, the father leaped abruptly to his feet. The hairs along his back and neck stiffened and his back arched. Motionless he stood with his ears erect and his front legs braced. Suddenly he whirled and growled deeply—the warning sound. There was no allowance in the sound this time, no permissiveness. The female shot toward the mouth of the tunnel and echoed the warning. The cubs stumbled toward her, frolicking over and under each other in mock play. A second time the growl came and the father bit hard on the flank of the small tan male who was slower than the rest. The parent wolves rushed the cubs down the tunnel, herding them into the far chamber. The bodies of the adults blocked the passage, the female on the inside, the male pressed flat near the tunnel entrance, motionless, waiting.

A strange sound began to fill the world. A great thumping resounded through the tunnel and small bits of earth, the dust of the dried walls, filtered down. One of the cubs began to whine and a harsh grunt from the mother cut him short. Terrified, the cubs huddled in the chamber until the great rhythmic pounding faded off. The white cub felt the strange excitement of danger, felt the electricity that ran through his parents; he tried to crawl forward to where his father lay frozen, but a snarl from his mother sent him back to the others.

For the rest of the day the cubs were kept in the tunnel. Their movement was severely restricted and any effort to begin playing was cut off with a growl. For hours they lay in the chamber, until their mother finally came back and stretched out, allowing them to feed.

They dropped off to sleep after filling themselves, the great adventure of the day soon forgotten.

The white wolf, the one we call Lobo, did not know that he had had his first encounter with his one and eternal enemy: man.

6. LAMENT THE RED WOLF

EDWARD HOAGLAND

I

GAS RATIONING IS IN ORDER, THE ENVIRONMENTAL Protection Agency suggests. What will young people do? Ordinarily a fuel shortage accompanies a war, when they have various surrogates. It's not really that driving equals living dangerously, however. People drive more dangerously in the Alpes-Maritimes than in America, and in Italy a car itself perhaps can represent more precisely a man's own personality—at least, to hear the honking, it seems so. When I was living in a village in Sicily, the padrone of the lemon groves lying all around would wake up the populace after midnight with the peremptory note of his Ferrari's horn as he sped home. He was signaling to have his front gate opened, and to hasten the job, began a tattoo of toots right as he entered town. But distances, not speed, characterize American driving: trailers, campers and the like.

"Lament the Red Wolf" is taken from Red Wolves and Black Bears *by Edward Hoagland. Copyright © 1976 by Edward Hoagland and reprinted by the author's permission.*

References mentioned in the Hoagland selection are listed in Red Wolves and Black Bears.

Or a retired couple, as their first project, will set out to tour from coast to coast, reserving a motel room each morning four hundred miles ahead. Youngsters, above all, start off, having the breadth and complexity of the continent to familiarize themselves with.

Geography has glamour in America. The whole excitement of driving here implies some opposite new place to reach, and other nationalities like us for this. The English, arriving in Boston, promptly want to head for Arizona to meet the Navajos. Thomas Wolfe celebrated the cross-country railroad, the auto's smoky, rumbling precursor; and how Walt Whitman would have loved to drive, finally to run plunk up against the shining Pacific. Although there used to seem to be no need to go beyond the sea—whichever sea—because almost everybody's ancestors had crossed over from the other side, those two grand bulky oceans, separated by such a spread of miles, did much to mute for us the sadness of the end of the frontier.

What is ominous is that we know that once they have been instituted, alterations and restrictions in the scope of life are never quite relaxed. Actual rationing may not come to pass, but in the meantime the spontaneity of travel has become a privilege, not a right; a freedom that was traditional has been pinched off. It would be easier to assent to the call for a return to the simple life—long walks, and so on—if we hadn't already made so many localities uninhabitable, on the theory that everybody who lived in them could pop onto the freeway and drive someplace else for a day off. Nixon, jumping into his jet or speeding along the thruways near San Clemente to let off steam, was only a souped-up version of the rest of us.

I have driven clear from east to west and west to east half a dozen times, and yet this closing of the open road strikes me as an immediate personal loss. When my native iconoclasm builds up in me until I want to knock people's hats off, I pile into my car and drive away with the window open, and soon find myself singing "God is good, God is great!" at the top of my lungs into the roaring wind, looking out at the tire recaps along the highway in Pennsylvania—then, two days later, at alligators, which are the spitting image of tire recaps, in the watery Louisiana woods.

This trip I was wolfing, though. I had a hand-cranked siren in the trunk that wolves will answer to, and a wolfish, lunging husky along, whose beastly nostrils at my ear and boisterous snuffles from the back seat kept the car from becoming completely a car. I'd been to

Minnesota to see how the black bears manage, because there is some hope for them, and now I wanted to have a look at an officially endangered species, and while I was at it, perhaps at the animal which in America is the worst off, Texas's red wolf. Even with the crush in the world, some creatures do thrive—the scavengers and compleat omnivores like possums and coons, and beasts that move into a disrupted habitat by preference, like cottontails and ground squirrels. Others, more conspicuous—the arrowy, showy predators and hearty herd creatures like buffaloes and prairie dogs—or animals that are too single-minded or delicately attuned, haven't much chance. One's interest swings back and forth between the two groups.

Conservationists assume that a day will come when we will all want to pick up the pieces—that if only they can hold onto such living entities as the green turtle and the right whale for a little while longer, the consensus of civilized opinion will swing behind them. It is a questionable assumption, and so the gloomier, more visceral individuals go instead on the hunch that something may happen whereby finally the saved animals will inherit the earth. This isn't sensible, is misanthropic, and is a view they keep to themselves, but the most vivid observation to be made about animal enthusiasts—both the professionals who work in the field and, in particular, the amateurs—is that they are split between the rosiest, well-adjusted sort of souls and the wounded and lame. (More professionals are rosy, more amateurs are lame.) Animals used to provide a lowlife way to kill and get away with it, as they do still, but, more intriguingly, for some people they are an aperture through which wounds drain. The scapegoat of olden times, driven off for the bystanders' sins, has become a tender thing, a running injury. There, running away—save it, save it—is me: hurt it and you are hurting me.

Wolves are well suited to cupping any wounds that we wish drained. Big and concise enough to command the notice of any dullard, they are aggressive, as the wounded themselves wish to be aggressive. Once passionately persecuted, in just the kind of turn-about which people relish, a wolf can now be taken to represent the very Eden we miss, and being a wolf is thought to be the best at what it does in a world which demands that any creature to receive attention must be the "best." Although in fact red wolves are inferior to other wolves at wolfish deeds, their name "red" adds a cachet, concealing their ineptitude from everybody except their friends.

Luckily for me, the scientist working with these little wolves, Glynn Riley, was not under contract to the *National Geographic,* or otherwise operating under the notion that he should hoard his findings. On the other hand, he wasn't a certified scientist either, but a trapper who simply had interested himself and learned more than the degree-bearing scientists had been able to. This meant, in the first place, that he was suspicious of any writer from the big city because of the campaign of the urban humane societies against the leg-hold steel trap—a threat to his livelihood, as he conceived it, which loomed importantly to him, if not to me. Also he felt none of the curiosity in chatting with me that the full-fledged *National Geographic* biologists are likely to reveal, even as they hold back the yarns and lore they plan to jot down for their own profit at some future date. One can wheedle considerable information from them sideways, so to speak, and it is not as lonely with the *National Geographic* biologists because the rapport goes both ways, whereas after a week or two with a trapper, one begins wishing that maybe he'll ask a question about New York City.

Instead of growing less susceptible to the debilitations of solitude, as I get older I am more so. It's a peculiar life; Tuesday hurrying along Sixth Avenue in New York, Wednesday, after a flight, exploring Dog Canyon in the Big Bend country near the Rio Grande, startling the vultures off a lion-killed deer in a dry streambed overhung with black persimmon trees. To drive the distances involved helps cushion the switch, but then one runs out of gumption that much sooner at the site one has come so far to inspect. More than once I've had to dash away from scenery that was unimaginably lovely because I knew my time was up, that if I lingered, my mind, like Cinderella's, would soon be crawling with transmogrified mice. I've had crying jags and such, once in the room which serves as office for water pollution control for the Louisiana Department of Wildlife and Fisheries, headquartered in Baton Rouge. It was an appropriately empty, watery spot for crying, and funny because to actually deal with water pollution in Louisiana would require an office suite the size of the Pentagon. I'd spent a clutch of weeks with four French-speaking fur trappers in the Cajun salt marshes that front the Gulf in the southwestern part of the state, and now after my contact man here in officialdom got through arguing his budget request for the ensuing year, we were to set off on a night trip by skiff so that I could stay awhile with several freshwater trappers in the cypress–tupelo gum tree swamps between the Mississippi River and Lake Maurepas. I couldn't stem the tears.

Air travel and the telephone, too, make for hysteria. A few spins of the dial and we can talk to almost anybody in the world, and in towns like Hackberry or Buras, Louisiana, or Alpine, Texas, at the first strong pinch of loneliness I've known that I could jump into my Hertz Ford and hop a plane for home. The trouble is, at home I've often wanted to catch a plane for Alpine—to be back in Dog Canyon again listening to the javelinas yap and fuss; then, uneasy there, might want to streak for Philadelphia. A friend of mine does let this panic take possession of him. His acquaintances in Hawaii, Los Angeles and London hear from him, the times being rough and events going badly. Since he is an endearing chap, they say yes, he can come, and await his next move. He's reassured by all the invitations and calls or writes his other friends to tell them he is going to Hawaii, London, Los Angeles or Mexico City. He calls the airport for fare and timetable information, but in the end, more frequently than not, relaxed at last by the show of affection, he goes nowhere at all.

In Minnesota, Lynn Rogers, the bear expert, had been rather guarded with me, as though he were feeling vulnerable himself and did not welcome the possibility that somebody else might get a handle on him which properly ought to be his. By contrast, Glynn Riley had no suspicions of me as a lay psychologist, didn't care what I thought of him and wasn't concerned with the riddles of motivation. Instead, he was alert to the good name of his profession, and while he told me freely about his boyhood, his screw-ups in school, and courting Pat, his wound-up, stringbean wife—she has a certain flash and dazzle to her eyes and hair, and used to fold herself into the trunk of his car to get into the drive-in movies when they were kids—with the equanimity of a man at peace with himself, he would do this only on his own front porch. Never would he let me bounce about the country with him on his regular rounds, as Rogers had, checking traps and palavering with the ranchers, lest I see a trapped creature and write of its struggles. I couldn't convince him that an exposé of trapping was very low on my list of priorities; I'd seen plenty of trapping and knew that if the fellow wasn't one of a kind, like Riley, he was probably by now a grandfather who wouldn't be around by the time the controversy resolved itself. Similarly, the trapper employed by the wolf scientists in Minnesota, an old-timer who catches the wolves that they can't, won't let anybody else watch how he works. If he is in his pickup with one of the Ph.D. candidates, he will drive past a likely trap site, giving no sign that he has noticed it, and stop a hundred yards beyond, leaving the young man in the truck and walking back to set the device with his back turned, lest at this late date these doctoral scholars, discovering his secrets, might desert their latter-day vocation for the sake of becoming a master trapper and compete with him.

In spite of being thin-skinned, Rogers had liked lecturing on bears and appearing on television and in the papers, but Glynn Riley had let me drive down to see him solely in the hope that I might pry loose from the Bureau of Sport Fisheries and Wildlife in Washington his appropriated funding, and more too, so that he could put radios on the wolves and hire a spotting plane and someone to help him. As I had seen, they were being as slow as a taffy-pull up there, but he was also sick of blathering to newspapermen—sick of their errors, ignorance, perfunctoriness, misemphasis—and though I explained that letters might accomplish what he wanted,* that I had hopes of doing more with the wolves than merely publicize them, he remained correct with me, not to be cozened.

The dog-wolf family is thought to have originated in North America, migrated to Eurasia, where the gray wolf defined itself as a prodigy of the Northern Hemisphere, and then returned. Some biologists think that red wolves may be descended from a primitive wolf that stayed in North America during this diaspora and were hounded into the southeast lip of the continent by the returning grays. Others speculate that they are an offshoot of a worldwide race of primitive wolves of the early Pleistocene which have disappeared elsewhere; or, on the contrary, that they are a product of the devious ice-age geography blocked out by the glaciers which did so much differentiating among animal species. Another theory is that the red wolf sprouted from a common ancestor with the coyote in the Pliocene, and is not directly from the gray wolf's line. Coyotes, like Old World jackals, are "brush wolves" that became miniaturized for pursuing smaller prey in broken country where a hefty predator might not operate as well. They can put up with hotter temperatures—ranging into Central

---

*Sure enough, writing to Washington, I did elicit the funding he had wanted, but along with the funding came a supervisory bureaucracy, which pleased him less.

America—but not with the deep snows and freezes that arctic gray
wolves know.

Red wolves are short-coated and long-eared, with stilty, spindly
legs for coursing through the southern marshes or under tall forests.
They have the neck ruff, almond eyes and wide nose pad of other
wolves, but not the massive head and chest, and so their angular ears
and legs seem to stick out plaintively. Anatomically their brains are
primitive, almost foxlike among the canids, and they have impressed
naturalists as being rather rudimentary animals, fragile in their social
linkups, not very clever, unenterprising and almost easy to trap.
Besides the pacing gait that they share with larger wolves and a flat
dash, they bound along like modest rocking horses, standing up on
their hind legs to peer over a patch of tall weeds. They are an unem-
phatic, intermediate sort of animal, behaviorally like wolves, ecologi-
cally more like coyotes. They howl like wolves, not like coyotes, and
snarl when threatened instead of silently gaping the mouth, as coyotes
do. They scout in little packs, unlike coyotes, which have stripped
away a good deal of the pack instinct for better secrecy in crowded
country and better efficiency at gleaning small game. A grown male
weights about sixty pounds, midway between a coyote's thirty or forty
and a gray wolf's average of eighty pounds; but skinny as he is, the red
wolf can live on a coyote's diet of cotton rats and marsh rabbits, and
whereas a gray wolf needs about ten temperate square miles to feed
himself—coyotes can get along as densely distributed as one every
square mile—the red wolf again is in between. Five square miles sup-
plies his food, and ten to forty is enough to stretch his legs and psyche
with other members of the pack, about half what a pack of Minnesota
timber wolves requires.

The earliest observers—William Bartram in 1791, and Audubon
and Bachman in 1851—were definite on the subject of a smallish,
darkish, long-legged wolf inhabiting the region from Florida to what is
now central Texas, and north to the Ohio River. It was primarily a
forest beast, piney in its affinities. The first government biologists of
this century, men like Vernon Bailey and Edward Goldman, backed
up the idea of a specifically southern wolf still more strongly, although
the animals on the eastern seaboard had been exterminated already,
and were gone everywhere east of the Mississippi by the 1920s. They
did range the Ozarks and the river bottoms of Louisiana and the
East Texas prairies, but because some of these latter had started

hybridizing with an invading legion of coyotes, a body of opinion claimed that red wolves might never have existed at all except as hybrids of a coyote–gray wolf cross, or maybe as local grays, colored to suit the climate, in much the way that "white" wolves developed in the north. Since gray wolves possess such a fastidious sense of self that a cross of the sort would be a rarity, the rival proposition was offered that though red wolves might have existed as a true species at some point, they'd crossed themselves into extinction even before white men arrived.

Wolves are special beasts, so variable genetically that they partly live on disguised as dogs. Dogs, too, dance attendance on a breadwinner, cheerfully accepting the ups and downs of life with a master just as wolves stick with the pack, and bark and rush at an intruder close to the "den," otherwise marking their passage through life semantically with squirts of pee. If dogs were to inherit the earth they would quickly turn into wolves again; and coyotes carry the flag for wolves most directly, becoming bushy-necked and wolfish in appropriately remote surroundings, or little more than wild dogs when they live close to a city. Indeed, gray wolves would need only a nod from the voters to get a foothold in corners of their old range—Maine, for instance. Brought in, they would soon be at home, parceling up the timberland wherever the human populace is thin, until the deer found themselves in a density of two or three hundred per wolf.

But red wolves are so far gone by now—none has been photographed in the wild since 1934, and they are considered present in pure form in only two of Texas's two hundred and fifty-four counties—that the main effort to protect them involves not only shielding them from human intervention but from encroachment and dilution by coyotes. This situation is unusual. The rarest breeds of ferret, parrot, and so on, even manatees and prairie chickens, depleted in numbers though they are, seldom require protection from other animals, and it is this peculiar rattle-headedness—that these last wolves will so amenably let a coyote mount them—which has called into question their right to be regarded as a species. Mostly the museum scientists, such as Barbara Lawrence of Harvard, rather than the outdoor workers, have been occupied with challenging them, but recently a formidable young taxonomist at the University of Kansas, Ronald Nowak, with a friend named John Paradiso from the National Museum in Washington, has computerized a much larger body of evidence than Lawrence's and has taken up the cudgels for them. The current majority view is to return to the belief that *Canis rufus* (called *Canis niger* for a while, but scientific names sometimes change more frivolously than common ones) is indeed a discrete creature, only lately decimated.

Nearer the East Coast, there were no other predators to replace the wolves when they had been killed off, but west of the Mississippi, coyotes from the plains slid in as soon as the shattered packs stopped defending an area. Coyotes could withstand the poisoning and trapping campaigns better, and the hard logging that the settlers did among the old-growth trees actually benefited them by breaking down the forest canopy. According to the evidence of skulls in the National Museum, the red wolves of Missouri, northern Arkansas and eastern Oklahoma met their end in good order as a species, not mating with the coyotes as they were superseded. (It is a textbook theory that a true species is supposed to preserve its racial purity even more stubbornly in a border area under pressure.) But around the turn of the century, on the Edwards Plateau of central Texas where the same blitzkrieg of white settlers from the East was followed by an invasion of coyotes from every other direction, the demoralized red wolves for some reason began to accept coyotes as their sexual partners, and in the delirium of catastrophe created with them a "Hybrid Swarm." This "Swarm" thereupon moved eastward slowly, as ordinary coyotes were doing anyway at every latitude clear into Canada—and naturally was irresistible. Bigger, "redder" than coyotes, with such a piquancy of wolf blood already, these hybrids absorbed the wolves of Texas's Hill Country and Big Thicket all the more readily. They bred with true wolves and true coyotes and wild-running domestic dogs (even a few escaped pet dingos)—anything they met and couldn't kill—becoming ever more adaptable, a shoal of skilled survivors in a kind of canine Injun-territory situation.

The beaver trappers in the West had hiked out of the mountains and switched to hunting buffalo when the beaver were gone. The buffalo hunters were soon wolfers as well, and bounty-hunted them for a living after they had run through the buffalo. They sold the skins and paved the mudholes in their roads with heaped wolf bones, so many thousands were killed. Throughout the 1800s strychnine was the poison used. Then a drastic potion, sodium fluoroacetate, known as "1080," was introduced, and by the 1940s, a device called the "getter gun," which when implanted in the ground fires cyanide gas into the animal's open mouth when it pulls on a trigger knob baited with

scent. From 1915 on, most of the wolfers were employed by the
U.S. Biological Survey, which under the umbrella of the Interior
Department eventually metamorphosed into the Bureau of Sport
Fisheries and Wildlife. Thus by a piece of bureaucratic irony the same
corps responsible for reducing the Midwestern red wolf to its final
extremity is now the agency in charge of trying to preserve it. Even
some of the personnel have been the same, which gives credence to
the frequent complaints of calculated foot-dragging that conservationists have made.

To a taxonomist who looks at skulls of the period, the record now
seems plain as to how succinctly coyotes supplanted wolves in the
hardwoods bottomlands along the Mississippi and in the Ozark
Mountains. But the salaried wolfers naturally preferred to continue to
see themselves, like the old-timers, as dealing with wolves, and so they
kept on totting up an annual kill of thousands of "red wolves" in the
official tabulation. As late as 1963, 2,771 were reported to have been
done away with in the federal program of control. The year before,
however, an obscure dissenter, Dr. Howard McCarley of Austin
College, Texas, had published his contention that many of these were
either coyotes or hybrids, and that the red wolf was nearly gone. Once
his discovery was confirmed, the received opinion among biologists,
who had taken so cavalier a view of *Canis rufus* until then, reversed
abruptly to the notion that the creature may well have existed, but no
longer. Since there was nothing to be done about it, the poisoning
was allowed to continue, even in the Texas coastal counties where in
fact a few survived, till 1966. Fortunately two Ontario scientists, taking
the matter more seriously than most of the Americans, journeyed
about one summer in the meantime playing recorded wolf howls in
wild places and listening to the answers that they got—sundry barking
mutts, coyotes and coydogs. They were privately financed and soon
ran out of funds, but they did learn that while McCarley had been
right about the broad belt of territory he had studied, down on the
muggy coast between the Vermilion River in western Louisiana and
the Brazos in Texas a tiny remnant of voices were answering their
Canadian wolves in kind. What with the lengthy delay in publishing
these findings in a recondite journal (like McCarley's, earlier), and of
bringing them to the attention of the federal specialists, not until
1968 was an organized recovery effort initiated, and not until 1973 was
enough money provided to really begin. The scientific method

depends upon a scoffing skepticism on the part of rival investigators to puncture a weak argument, but one reason why the biologists did not do more for the red wolf is that so many of them dillydallied while they scoffed.

PART OF THE APPEAL of Southeast Texas is that some of its residents tend to deprecate the charms of the place. They'll say that the landscape is mosquito-bitten and unlovely, the colors washed out, that a tourist who wants scenery ought to move on. For a hundred years an army of Texans have believed themselves to be a Chosen People on the grounds of their good fortune. . . . Many people have believed that they were Chosen, but none more baldly than the Texans. Standing one evening in the Chisos Basin, an old Apache stronghold which is probably the pearl of the western section of the state, I must have looked affected by the colors because I heard a Dallas fellow drawl behind me, "Well, you think you'll buy it?"

Minnesota had seemed fairly familiar—bleaker and flatter than northern New England, wilder than around my home in Vermont, but not more so than northern Maine, which has a moose herd three times the size of Minnesota's and a wilderness region three times as large. Lakes were interspersed through a balsam fir and white pine forest, and the natives had that clamped-down modesty cold weather brings, because you can't cultivate too grandiose an opinion of yourself when a three-foot snowfall at any time for half the year may shut you in. In Isabella, Minnesota, there was an individual called The Pig Farmer because of his supposed smell, who when the spring floods came would slosh around in two feet of water in his swamp cabin, eat cold food, and sleep in a wet bed instead of bothering to move to higher ground. Maybe nobody else can be as glum as a Great Lakes Finlander, but near my house in Vermont is a barn with a whole cavern smashed in it which the farmer himself fashioned one night by driving his bulldozer against the wall when he heard that his youngest son, too, was going to leave the farm.

People who are bundled up much of the time, with stacks of firewood half the size of the house, and the sense that things will most likely go wrong if they haven't already: this is the America which stretches next to the Canadian boundary from the Atlantic Ocean to the Great Plains. The warm-weather rain forest of the Pacific might alter even a woodsman's outlook substantially, and, otherwise, the Rockies will give him big ideas, but what happens where the plains begin is that all of a sudden there are no trees. *No trees!* People started wearing big hats not simply because the brims were shady and wouldn't catch in the branches, but to help break up the landscape. It was a vast change, and in a huge country without forests to enforce a different perspective, many of them got to feeling big in the britches as well as in the head. Indeed, the big got bigger. Whereas in the woods that fellow with the swamp shanty and two cabbagey acres owns everything the eye can see, on the prairie it takes a rich man to feel so proprietary.

Down in Texas, the hats, the vistas and the britches, the distances to be ridden, were more expansive still. To be thirsty in Texas was a powerful thirst. The rich grew filthy rich, but before that the Indians, whom the Texans dispatched with an implacable efficiency that was the envy of Indian-haters everywhere, had included some of the continent's stiffest tribes. Not only Apaches, but Comanches, and not only Comanches, but the Attacapas and Karankawas of the Gulf Coast, who in the early years were rumored to enjoy a man-bake as much as a clam-bake, eating a castaway's buttocks and arms right in front of him as he died.

The "Kronks," as the white men were wont to call the Karankawas (or, in an earlier, more authenic spelling, "Carancahueses"), were a robust people described as standing almost seven feet tall, with slender hands and feet, sensitive faces, and hair to their shoulders, with snake rattles tied in it and bangs in front, who swam superbly and cruised between the islands and sandbars of Galveston Bay in little fleets of dugout pirogues. They communicated with smoke signals— Ys and Vs, diverging, curling, spiraling columns or twin zigzags—and employed a six-foot cedar bow with a three-foot goose-feathered arrow. Two families might travel together in a pirogue with a small deck at either end and the baggage heaped in the middle, erecting at night a single shelter of skins thrown over poles on the beach. They worshiped the sun, and on ceremonial occasions blew the smoke of a fire in seven sacred directions. They had a personalized god named "Pichini" and a dread god "Mel," in whose grim celebrations they played a dismal-sounding stringed instrument five feet long, which bellowed like an alligator. For gayer festivities they had a tambourine made from a tortoise shell and a reed whistle. They talked in whistles and sign language as well as words, and counted on their fingers,

going from the pinkie to the thumb, which was the "father." They
were a voluptuous people, the women grabbing for the penis of an
enemy's corpse. It was said that they masturbated a good deal, and
their name Karankawa was generally translated as "dog-lovers,"
because of the horde of voiceless dogs they kept, though their detrac-
tors claimed that the love went to even further extremes. The Lipan
Apaches called them "those-who-walk-in-water" because they shot fish
while wading, rather than from a boat. The Tonkawas called them
"the wrestlers" because they liked to wrestle and were good at it. They
wore a breechclout of Spanish moss, with a wreath of palm leaves as a
hat and perhaps a cock partridge's feather behind one ear. They slept
wrapped in deerskins and kept their firesticks in a skin bundle, used
wooden spoons and fishbone needles, and red and black pots with
conical bottoms that would stand upright in the sand. They ate
seafood and every kind of meat, from buffaloes to skunks and rep-
tiles—nursing their children for years to shelter them from this rough
diet. The children, their foreheads sometimes flattened as a form of
decoration, played with wooden dolls, and the adults tattooed blue
circles on their own cheeks, and lines from eye to ear or parallel lines
descending from the mouth. With vermilion they accentuated their
eyes and striped themselves red and black and white, unmarried girls
with the simplest, thinnest line, but married individuals decorating
themselves with flowers, birds and animals, and hanging colored
stones and conch shells from their ears and the wings of the nose.

The Karankawas smelled of alligator grease, which was their chief
protection from the bugs. After the whites had outgunned them, they
hid in the thorn-brush thickets and behind the endless screen of man-
high roseau cane. Since they had fought against the Comanches and
Jean Lafitte's pirates, as well as against more orthodox settlers, and
since they had numbered probably only about four hundred warriors
when La Salle first landed on the Texas shore to establish a fort in
1685, they were all gone before the Civil War, when settlement really
started. The last canoeful of able-bodied men deliberately paddled for
the open sea during a storm, the legend goes, and the few women and
children left begged their way on foot along the coast to Mexico.

WOLVES, TOO, WERE a force that molded early Texas, and the opti-
mists would claim that if we can just hold onto a smattering of them,
when the time comes that people want to pick up the pieces we will

have them around as a force to observe once again. The difficulty is that though there are as many buffaloes alive as the buffalo reserves can hold, buffaloes are not a force any more; indeed, buffaloes not in the millions may not *be* buffaloes. Neither are Big Brown Bears a force, nor Mounted Indians. That former midcontinental prairie community of mounted Indians, gaudily iconic big brown bears, and buffaloes and rattlesnakes and eagles and gray wolves that once existed centering around what is now Nebraska and Wyoming represents our idea of the pre-white New World better than the coastal or woodland aboriginal cultures do, and we all turn a bit sorrowful, reading of the buffaloes shot by the millions for their tongues, of whole dramatic nations of Plains Indians starved or served up smallpox or ridden under the ground. Yet we wouldn't then and wouldn't now have had it any other way. What could we have possibly done with all those goofy buffaloes besides shoot them right off? Land of opportunity, land for the huddled masses—where would the opportunity have been without the genocide of those Old-Guard, bristling Indian tribes?

A pause is necessary when speaking in defense of wolves for some mention of their fearful destructiveness. The settlers had good reason to be afraid of wolves, the same reason that the Indians had for howling to each other when they surrounded an isolated cabin: wolves digging under a dead man's cairn to wolf down his spoiling remains, wolves disemboweling the family cow, feeding on her thighs and abdominal fat, burying their heads inside her, although her entrails lay unbroken and she was still alive and watching them. When wild game was no longer available, wolves killed the new livestock prodigiously—such stupid, lavish, feasty beasts presented to them on a tray. They soon cast off their wilderness inhibition against killing too much to eat; there was no sating them, and for a cattleman no living with them—at least the big buffalo lobos. It was either them or him. No honest-minded naturalist can peer at a caged wolf without recognizing in the old sense its wicked air. That sharp and fabled nose hooding the teeth, the bright eyes all the more dangerous for being downcast, the uncannily tall legs and twitching ears—these, with its lugubrious howl, were what the pioneers feared.

The first settler straggled into the wilderness with a single-shot rifle, leading a couple of mules, with a crate of brood hens on the back of one and two piglets in a sack to balance the load, some seed corn, potatoes and soldier beans, and dragging a long-suffering cow with a half-grown bull at her heels which the fellow hoped might manage to freshen her again before he butchered it. In the north, he settled in a beaver meadow where a little wild hay grew, and planted his potato peelings, living off boiled cowslips, sour dock, dandelion greens, Indian turnips and goldthread roots in the meantime. In red-wolf country, he lived in a hot hut with a scrap of cloth hanging across the door hole to fend the mosquitoes off, and saw his cattle, too, turn gray with malaria or bog down dead. He was afraid of wolves. The prairie was theirs, not his, and if they swept through in cavalry style, mocking his gun, and killed his mules, he was in a bad way. If they killed his cow, his children would have no milk; if they drove the deer out of the neighborhood and killed his chickens and hogs, the whole family might starve. A bachelor mountain man, wrapped in hides, here today and gone tomorrow with a pack of curs, could afford to be more nonchalant; he had no kids wandering alone along the stream-bank poking at the muskrats with a stick, and if he stretched his lungs at night he could holler from his bedroll louder than the hooting packs. When he shot a deer he tied his neckerchief to it to keep the wolves away until he lugged the last of it to camp. Still, sometimes these self-sustaining hobos were the ones who reported the attacks; the wolves were hunting something else and in their speed and hap-piness (they have been seen to jump up on the rump of a running moose and briefly ride there) happened to blunder on the man and turn toward him. In Kipling's *Jungle Book,* wolves were "the Free People."

A real wolfer lived for his wolves, trailed them for days, smelling their pee and fingering their toeprints to distinguish the bitch from her mate, slept out in order to waylay them on the trail, and when he'd shot them both, walked from his hiding place to scalp them and strip off their skins in an act quick as sex, leaving the white frames grinning in the grass. That yodeling, streaking wolf—he strung up snares that yanked it into the air and kept it hanging there, upright as an effigy, choking, kicking, till he came in the morning and hugged and punched it and cut its throat, or bound its jaws with barbed wire and carried it home across his horse to tie to a tree in the dooryard to tease for a week.

Here in littoral Texas the pioneers found an old-growth forest of large sweet gums, elms, loblolly and longleaf pines, hackberry trees and beech and oak. Wild violets and blackberries grew where the trees gave out, and then the prairie extended toward the sea: bluestem bunch grasses, Indian grass, gama grass and switch grass, with blue-bells and milkweed spreading blue and white during the spring and buttercups and Indian pinks under these, the terrain broken by occa-sional sand knolls covered with yaupon and myrtle brush where the wolves denned and hid out. Next came a marsh of spunkweed, cat-tails, cutgrass and the same spartina that the colonists on the Atlantic shore had fed to their livestock. A bayshore ridge fronted the Gulf, beyond which the wolves and pioneers and Indians crabbed and beachcombed, collecting stunned redfish by the wagonload after a storm. Wagonloads of oysters, too; and in the bayous mullet seethed among gar, catfish and bullheads. Out in the tides were weakfish, black drum, channel bass, gafftopsail cats, sand trout. Summer was the fishing season; in the winter everybody lived on wildfowl and game. Prairie chickens could be caught by hand when they got drunk on fer-mented chinaberries; so could the geese when their wings froze together when the rain blew cold.   ·

There was yellow fever, and hurricanes that washed away entire hamlets, and influenza in the winds and hock-deep water that the cattle still stand in. The wolves fed on sick waterfowl from everywhere north to above Hudson Bay. They still eat sick birds, mainly cripples from the hunting months, which is when the ranchers make their tax money, charging ten dollars a day per hunter. Red-winged blackbirds and robins continue to flock in million-bird masses, and blue and snow geese arrive from Canada by the tens of thousands, along with teal, gadwalls, canvasbacks, pintails, shovelers and widgeons. The fed-eral government has a bird refuge at Anahuac in Chambers County with two near Angleton in Brazoria County and one in Cameron Parish, Louisiana. The managers of these burn over the brush to plant millet and other goose food, and bring in cattle to keep the grass cropped green and short and to chop puddles in the ground with their hard hooves.

It seemed unbelievable that these last uncompromised wolves should have been discovered here in the salt marshes—next to Houston, Galveston and Beaumont, Texas's most industrial and popu-lated section—instead of in the piney woods and hillbilly thickets always listed as their home. Metro Houston grew by six hundred

thousand during the 1960s to a total of two million people, America's
third largest port by tonnage; yet the wolves had ranged within Harris
County itself and beside Galveston Bay and over in Jefferson County,
within sight of some of the new subdivisions, through intensively pro-
ductive rice fields, next to several of the state's earliest oil strikes, such
as Spindletop.

Oil wells pump like nodding grasshoppers, bird watchers creep
about on the lookout for avocets and phalaropes, and now that the
deer are mostly gone, the wolves chew on stillborn calves and the carcasses of bloated steers that died of anaplasmosis. It was the last place
the authorities had thought to look (for the debunkers, still a debat-
ing point), but the industrial buzz, the waterways and highways may
have served to delay the coyotes for a little while. The older wolfers I
dropped in on mentioned animals weighing ninety pounds or more
which they hunted half a century ago with their July and Goodman
hounds—roping them or clubbing them in the water when they took
to a bayou to escape the dogs. Nowadays the wolves altogether add up
to only one or two hundred sorry smaller specimens, because these
final marshes are so mosquito-ridden that a calf, for example, may
smother from the balls of insects that fasten inside its nose.
Heartworms kill or invalid the grown-up wolves, plugging up the heart
valves so that they suffer seizures if they run, and hookworms starve
the pups. Tapeworms, spiny-headed worms and sarcoptic mange
plague them indiscriminately, the spring floods drown their dens, the
summer heat renders them somnambulistic and the saw grass rips
their fur until their tails are naked as a rat's. In Chambers County
alone there are ten cattle ranches of better than ten thousand acres,
but the only cattle that can survive the bugs and watery winter footing
are an indigenous mongrel Brahma breed.

Still, the ranchers have built many windmill-driven wells that
bring fresh water to the wolves and other wildlife as well as to the
cattle. The U.S. Soil Conservation Service has constructed raised cow
walks above the standing water, and the oil companies have laid
oystershell-based roads running upon embankments which provide
the wolves with direct access nearly everywhere. Where the sand knolls
that used to be their safe haven have been bulldozed away, windbreaks
of salt cedar, huisache and Cherokee rose have been planted that ful-
fill the same purpose. Better still are the innumerable miles of canal

banks channeling water to the rice fields, in which a pair of wolves will excavate their various emergency holes to foil a flood or hunter, a practice which also cuts down on puppy parasites.

Rice farming has introduced a "horn of plenty," as Glynn Riley calls it, in the way of rodents. The fields stand fallow every third year, and when they are plowed and reflooded the rice and barn and cotton rats and gobbly mice and big and baby rabbits must scrabble out across the levees to another field in a frenzied exodus which the wolves attend delightedly—just as up north in dairy country, coyotes will follow a farmer's mower at haying time to bolt the running mice, or follow his manure spreader to eat the afterbirths which are included in the mess. But the wolves' best staple lately is another creature tendered up to them by man, the nutria. Nutria are furry water rodents five times the size of a muskrat, and locally more catholic in habitat and diet. Introduced from Argentina to Avery Island, Louisiana, in the 1930s by a Tabasco sauce mogul who dabbled in natural history, they escaped during a hurricane, and being tolerant of brackish water, made their way successfully along the edge of the Gulf and the Intracoastal Canal, reaching the Rio Grande around 1967. They are a resource in Louisiana—the pelts are worth four or five dollars apiece—but in Texas they are shot as pests because they burrow through the levees and breed exuberantly and eat a lot of rice. They leave fingery tracks—have delicate fingers which can pluck up a single grain of rice—though, when abroad, they are so clumsy that they have been a blessing to the beleaguered alligators as well as the red wolves. The gators grab them in the water and the wolves snatch them in the fields at night when they venture out to feed, and for the wolves there is a nice balance to it because whenever the water gets so high that the nutria achieve a degree of maneuverability, the dry-ground rats are in a panic.

In spite of this abundant provender, coyotes have now seized all but two of the last seven counties under study; there is talk of a "Dunkirk Operation" to salvage a few wolves and whisk them to some sanctuary island such as Matagorda (already teeming with coyotes)—or, as it soon seemed to me, there may be no hope. It may not matter much if we bear in mind the continentwide accomplishments of coyotes in resettling wild areas; these wolves have been grist for the mill, making them bigger and "redder." But such considerations did not temper my irritation at the officials I met who should have cared about what was happening and didn't. The arrangements of the national Wild Animal Propagation Trust to distribute red wolves for a breeding program among cooperating zoo directors had collapsed without getting started. A noted biochemist in Minneapolis who had been interested in doing blood protein studies of the species had been forced to quit for lack of funding. The State of Texas had made no move to resurrect the wolves from unprotected varmint status, or even to make legally permissible the little gestures of help that Riley was receiving from a couple of local enthusiasts. It was both sad and comic; he was entirely on his own—other federal agencies in the neighborhood, and even other chains of command within the Fish and Wildlife Service, seemed indifferent to the matter—yet, as a trapper, he had faith that here in Chambers and Jefferson counties his lone trapline could halt the tide.

Riley lives in the small town of Liberty, and grew up in Wortham in the East Texas brush not far away. His father did some trading in scrub horses and thin cows, and if there wasn't any money in the house it still was a good life for a boy. Now he's thirty-eight, calls his father Pappy and has that cowpoke look of not putting much weight on the ground when he walks. His face is trim and small, his body slim, his hair curly and neat and his voice mild. Like many wildlife men, he prefers being inconspicuous, and nature has given him the wherewithal. After a good supper he'll say that he's "full as a tick." He hasn't finished college yet, having dropped out several times, and is country-religious, so that although he is subject to more than his share of professional frustrations, if he is speaking bitterly and doing a slow burn, suddenly in midsentence he'll undergo a change and say of the other individual in an altered tone, "But bless his heart." "The good Lord gave the wolf forty-two teeth to eat with," he says in the same folksy way; and broadcasts wolf howls from his tape recorder on the telephone to callers. "Sounds like a pack of Indians." He says a mountain with a wolf on it stands a little taller, and that a wolf represents everything a man wants to be. "He's free, he's a traveler, he's always on the move, he kills his food. He's *worth* three hundred deer."

With none of the pained air of a late bloomer, Riley instead seems simply different in this age of Ph.D.'s, and himself suggests that someday his own head ought to be nailed on the wall at the Smithsonian Institution alongside the red wolf's. He is a first-rate trapper, has killed "a jillion" coyotes for the government, and therefore is as skilled at politicking with the old ranchers and trappers as any government agent is going to be. Since he is not a cosmopolitan man, his worst difficulty has probably been in dealing with what ought to be his natural constituency, the conservationists "up East," that redoubtable big-city crew of letter writers whom other scientists have rallied to the cause of the whooping crane, brown pelican, and what not.

From the start trapping has been his passion—on the first day of his honeymoon he insisted upon running his trapline—and he used to measure the tracks of the coyotes in Wortham against the sizable wolf tracks in Stanley Young and Edward Goldman's standard book, *The Wolves of North America,* discovering right as a teenager that these were no longer any variety of wolf, though everybody around still bragged them up as such. He knew of one old beech tree down next to the Trinity River which still carried the claw marks of a black bear that decades ago had climbed it, and knew an old hunter who as a boy had crawled into the briar jungle there after two hounds, thinking they had treed a squirrel, when, lo and behold, one dog jumped over his head to get away and he saw the bear sitting with its back against the tree, swatting the remaining pooch. Of course no bears are left in Texas now within six hundred miles for Riley to see, and his bitterest experience as a boy was when he had to sell his rifle and borrow a friend's one fall, in order to pay the landowner's fee, when he wanted to go hunting.

He loved the howling, the matching of wits, and went to work for the Bureau, eventually being put in charge of these last wolves because he'd grown so good at nabbing coyotes. He's in the position of knowing more about them than anybody else, yet watching a succession of schooled young men arrive to make their academic names studying the animal before it vanishes. They must turn to him for help, as do the cameramen and journalists who show up in Liberty, and he's evolved a quietly noncompetitive attitude, putting the fun of his work ahead of the rivalries of a career. He traps a few wolves to attach radio collars to, and traps calf-killing wolves when the ranchers complain, before they get caught in one of the mangling four-trap clusters that the ranchers set. (The old method was to drag a dead cow roundabout, strewing chunks of tallow laced with strychnine behind it.) Mostly, though, he traps coyotes, especially prophylactically along the edge of the Big Thicket where the middling tracks of the hybrid swarm already have met and mingled with the wolves' large pads.

WOLF AT WORK, says a sign in Riley's office. He claims he "probably would have amounted to something" if he hadn't become fascinated with wolves, but that the country "wouldn't be complete" without them. With people already wall-to-wall, he frankly couldn't comprehend why anyone who was enough like him to show up at his door in the first place would want to live in New York City for much of the year. He was uncomfortably amazed, and every morning talked to me at first as if he were seated in a dentist's chair—I being the dentist—so that his role in whatever I had in mind achieving for him professionally could be over and done with. My lunging husky did serve as a recommendation. Riley laughed at how very furry he was, although in Minnesota, where the dog had also served to break the ice with the predator men (everywhere he tended to offend the ranchers and the farmers), they would immediately begin to talk about a wolf pup they knew back in the bush that was about his size and shade of gray.

Another favorable factor for me was that I'd read some of the literature of this infant science of predator ethology. A poorly, skimpy showing it makes, on the whole—perhaps a good month's read—but few of the journalists who seek out these field men have bothered to look into it at all, and since the field men themselves are not readers outside the particular pocket of their specialty, they are impressed when somebody has taken the trouble. Besides, as boyish as I was (like Riley, I had the sense that these adventurous predators, just as they *eat* all other animals, somehow *contain* all other animals)—still trying morning and night to catch sight of a wolf, peering into the spoilbank thickets in the rice fields just as I had done thirty years before, speeding across the greasewood West as a youngster en route to Los Angeles on the Super Chief—by midmorning he would have managed to relax with me.

As kids both of us had climbed to many "caves," which usually proved just to be stains on the face of the rock when we reached them, but hoping to find some magic beast, a cougar or a wolverine, whatever the continent's legends might contain. So now in the evening he took me out to a coyote family's rendezvous, where with the siren we got them howling. Out wolfing again at dawn, we tried to provoke the soundless wolves, but instead it was the snow geese from white-wolf country, wheeling in platters by the thousands, that answered us. We saw coots in the ditches and an alligator so long it looked like two, half in, half out of the water, and more serrate and flat-looking than I'd anticipated. We saw fish popping in Oyster Bayou, and crabs and fat brown water snakes, and an armadillo with a tiny pointed head and papery ears; saw pelicans flying, and wavy lines of white ibises and cormorants, and roseate spoonbills like scoops of strawberry ice cream high in the air, and plenty of mink and otter tracks. Otters lope in a way that even in the form of prints communicates their speedy eagerness.

Riley himself walked rapidly, hunkering down to feel the depressions left by a wolf's toes. He bent right to the ground to smell its scenting station—a wolf's squirt smells milder, not as musky as a coyote's—to distinguish how much time had passed. The far-flung spatters were a diagram for him. He loves toes, hopping with his hands, his fingers in the toes, and never now encounters a wolf or coyote that he can't catch if he wishes to. Often he chooses not to, unless he wants to shift them around, but in any part of Texas he can envision the land much in the way that coyotes do, knowing where to find their prints and how to catch those toes. He's like a managerial cowboy, with wolves and coyotes for his cows.

His traps have toothless offset jaws, with a long swiveled drag to minimize the damage done. He attaches a bit of cloth steeped in tranquilizer for the wolf to mouth so that it will sleep. Sometimes, too, he removes a spring to weaken the bite, and adjusts the pan until the jaws close at a touch, so not the slender leg but the resilient paw is pinched. He boils the traps in a black dye, then coats them with beeswax, and has a shed full of dark-glass bottles of wolf, coyote and bobcat urine, with bits of anal gland chopped in, or powdered beaver castor and beaver oil—two universal lures from his old haunts along the Trinity—to sprinkle on a mudbank above the trap, although in fact the wolves are gullible enough to step into a trap lying open on the ground if it is placed well, and coyotes, though cleverer, are nearly as curious as they are clever, so that anything that stinks may draw some of them in.

Wolves scratch at a scent post after wetting it, whereas bobcats scratch beforehand, and neither is especially intrigued by the other's sign, but to trap either animal he employs the scent of an interloper of the same species. Wolves love to cross into the territory of another pack and leave their mark to razz the residents, like kids painting their colors on a rival school. Some of the feral dogs he traps run snapping at him, but wolves and coyotes are dumbstruck as he approaches, and after a bark or two will do anything to avoid offending him. Generally they hunch down, "sulling," facing away. I saw him bring a hybrid back and maneuver it into the netting of a holding cage, supplying a pan of water before he went to lunch. The coyote dipped its chin into the water to verify that it really was going to be permitted to drink, then held its head away from the pan until we left. He shoots these, saving the skull and skin and looking for any telltale vestiges, such as the placement of a certain vein on the rear ankle that red wolves bequeathed to the hybrids which neither gray wolves nor coyotes quite duplicate, or perhaps some feathers on the forelegs inherited from a stray bird dog. Or he may discover a coyote's little teeth set into a wolf's lanky jaw. The wear on the incisors will show its approximate age. Wolves have more forehead in their skulls than a coyote, and grays have more than reds, but dogs, which are dish-faced, have more forehead than wolves. Wolves boast big wide cheeks, big teeth and a proportionately lengthier, narrower braincase than coyotes or dogs, and the sagittal crest along the ridge of the skull where their powerful jaw muscles attach is more pronounced, but a dog's crest is higher than a coyote's. Coyotes, though, like wolves, have more space provided within the margins of the skull for their hearing organs than dogs do.

Wolves' hind legs usually swing in the same line as their forelegs—they single-foot, as foxes do—whereas dogs put their hind feet between the prints of their front feet and show a shorter stride. With his tape measure for checking tracks and a siren for censusing, Riley goes about looking at the feet of wolf-chewed calves to see if they had ever really walked or were born dead. If something did kill them, he sees whether they were pulled down by the ears, dog-style, or by the belly and the hams, as a proper wolf would. Everywhere he stops his truck to look at tracks—at the short feet of feral mongrels dumped sick originally from hurrying cars along the Interstate, at the wide feet of "duck dogs" lost during hunting season, and the big heelpad and long foot of a true wolf. For the record, too, he collects skulls and skins "off the fence," wherever the ranchers are still poisoning. When he catches notable beasts that please him—two black coyotes that I saw, for instance—he "transplants" them.

"You transplanted them to heaven?" I asked.

"No, no, somewhere that they're going to be real happy."

II

TEXAS ENCOMPASSES considerably less state-owned park and recreation land than New Jersey, and for its size, remarkably little federal
acreage too, because one of the terms of its annexation to the United
States was that the federal government acquired no public domain. Its
history has been all private enterprise, and whereas Florida and
Southern California have fetishized their sunshine, Texas has promoted the notion of space. Conservation legislation of any kind has
had a difficult time making much headway, and many a landowner
profits more from selling his deer to the hunters, at $250 per season
per man, than from his cattle. Minnesota's wolves range mainly on
government land, but Texas's live on private property, which means
that their fate is tied to the inheritance tax and the local tax rate on
land. If the ranching oligarchies fare badly, if their oil runs out or the
assessors decide to put the squeeze on them in favor of new industry
or summer development, or if a younger generation, coming into possession of the key spreads of property, wants to be rich in money
instead of open spaces and maybe live elsewhere, it will spell the end
of the red wolves.

In 1803 the U.S. purchase of Louisiana brought Anglo-American
settlers to the eastern border of what is Texas. In 1821 Mexico gained
her independence from Spain and the first Anglo colonists received
permission to cross the boundary and settle southward on the Brazos
under a Spanish-type "empresario" system, whereby one energetic,
commanding man was given a land grant on which he undertook to
establish upwards of two hundred families, exercising quasi-judicial
authority over them. This was a different conception of how to do
things from the homesteaders' democratic methods in the American
Midwest farther north, but within fifteen years the population of
Texas quintupled. By 1830 the government in Mexico City was trying
to forbid new Anglo settlements, to restrict immigration to Catholics,
and otherwise pinch off the fast-developing trade relations between
these Protestant citizens and their former homeland in the States.
The Texans' War of Independence followed in 1836, but the
emprasario method of settlement continued, and by the time

that Texas joined the Union in 1845, the population had again quintupled, to nearly a hundred and fifty thousand.

Thus Texas was annexed, but on its own say so—take us as we are—its land its booty, and fashioned in its infancy by Spanish-Mexican autocracy and in its adolescence by successful revolt and outlawry. In all the pulling and hauling there had been no Eastern-seaboard counseling, no older-brother leavening by Virginia and Massachusetts army generals who supervised the birth of other states, or by a moderating President and Congress in Washington. In quick order the Civil War began, in which Texas, a slave state, went with the South, deposing its elected governor, Sam Houston, who was a Unionist, in the process. More revolt, hard riding and bitterness through Reconstruction, until by the onset of the new century Texas's population had increased to three million, but the crest of settlement had included an embittered surge of Southern veterans—burnt-out families grappling for land to assuage their loss. The Mexicans had been bundled off or reduced to a serf class, the Indians done away with, the wildlife mostly extirpated, and in a pride-heavy, insular setting soon to be thoroughly lubricated with oil there was little influence to dampen the frontier swagger.

Booted boys and behatted giants fish from the boardwalk at Port Aransas, knifing the croakers that they catch with enthusiasm. Even Cokes look bigger in Texas; and eating habits remain Brobdingnagian, with funny consequences for the midriff. But in Odessa I went to a "rattlesnake roundup" advertised for the municipal coliseum, and found the entrance thronged with ticket holders. This seemed what I was after—the old Texas rite for ridding the calving range of snakes—except that the crowd turned out to be fans attending a rock concert. The "rattlesnake roundup" was way around in back inside an adjunct shed, with three cars parked at the door.

Texas is still a good place to be rich in. Money is the stamp of excellence, yet in the southeast sections a more rooted conservatism, involving the illusion of an old-family tradition, has been carried over from the states nearby. Since it is a conservatism essentially unburdened by the weight of tragic circumstance of the Old South, one needn't become a contortionist to imagine that this is indeed the good life. Part of a wolf-seeker's regimen is to visit these grand mansion houses, and everywhere he encounters gracious living in the form of magnolias and spacious acreage patrolled by black cowhands—

peacocks, guinea hens and fancy breeds of goose strolling the grounds, ten-foot alligators in private pools, pet deer in live-oak groves festooned with trailing moss. Quail and mourning doves, mimosas, pecans, orange trees, big-kneed cypresses, four cars in the garage, cool patios with iron grillwork, long lawns, little lakes, and girls and their daddies—girls so pretty Daddy doesn't quite know what to do with them.

These men of good fortune—men like Joe Lagow of Anahuac, and R.E. Odom, who lives across the Sabine River from Texas in Louisiana—glanced at my Vermont license plates, New York face and gray husky, and talked to me with caution. Lagow is a short jaybird of a man who serves as county commissioner and on a number of committees, and with his in-laws owns twenty-six thousand acres of snow-goose, red-wolf country. When I called to him across his aviary to ask if he was Joe Lagow, he swung around agreeably and said, "Yes, I'm what's left of him." Odom is younger and more reticent, even a little feline and courtly, in the Louisiana manner. We had tea in his jewel-box of a house, served by his white foreman. With his mother he owns a matchless spread of land in what is called Gum Cove, a luscious loop of grazing ground a few feet above sea level, enclaved within the badlands of Cameron Parish and reachable only by ferry across the Intracoastal Canal.

The time is past when Southern ranchers can be bamboozled into a reflexive show of hospitality, and various of these men gave me to understand, with conscious irony, that they were conservationists because they were conservatives and it would only be when new views took command that the ecology of their grasslands would be disrupted—smiling as they said this because of course a visiting Northern journalist was likely to represent those views. Nevertheless, the parade of exotic scribblers and photographers whom the environmental vogue is bringing to the door has started them thinking that the wolves that den on their mesquite knolls may be among the perquisites of wealth here on the Gulf; they've told their cowhands to quit killing them. It's the little operator, leasing pasturage for forty cattle that he has his hopes pinned on, who is still likely to put out traps, and if his few hundred acres happen to lie athwart a wolf run, it won't much matter how many thousands more stretch trap-free all around.

I went to Wolf Corner in Thompson, Texas, just beyond the

Houston city line, where a trapper named Charlie Grisbee has nailed up as many as thirty wolves or hybrids at a time. Grisbee wasn't home, but on his starchy lawn a wooden wolf was chasing a wooden family of ducks. It was a suburban sort of house interfaced with stone, all spruce and neat, with blue Pullman curtains in the windows of the garage. I'd asked whether Charlie was married and people had said very much so; they didn't think his wife especially liked his trapping, but that it "went with Charlie." A single twenty-pound coyote was hanging on the rack at the corner of a field next to the highway—attenuated-looking, rotting, twitching in the strong wind off the Gulf, with its head and tail hacked off, its rain-stained, rabbity fur and rabbity legs no longer distinguishable as those of a predator. In the grass for yards around were tibias, scapulas and backbone scraps, along with dewberries and Indian paintbrush, but some developers had now got hold of the field. I picnicked on the porch of a preempted farmhouse with a veteran fig tree for shade and honeysuckle all about.

In Danbury, in Brazoria County, I talked to Andrew Moller, among other old wolfers. Though Brazoria didn't bounty scalps, some of the fellows would deep-freeze what they caught and cash them in elsewhere. Moller is ninety-one. His grandfather jumped ship from a German whaler and bought land on Chocolate Bayou for five cents an acre, unfortunately sold off later. Once he was safely born, his father and his uncle had taken off for an adventure of their own, riding down the coast to Mexico for a couple of months, wading their horses across the many rivers they encountered at the mouth. And "in nineteen and eleven" he, a chip off the same block, had treated himself to a thousand-mile wagon ride around Texas, before paying thirty-five dollars for sixty cows, which over the next forty years he husbanded into a herd of fifteen hundred cattle. A traveling man, he mostly rented pasture for them. He trucked them to the Davis Mountains in West Texas, and to two decommissioned army camps in Arkansas and Oklahoma—unexpected long-grass pasturages on easy terms which he had hit upon during his hunting trips. . . . Once he bought a thousand mares at four dollars a head, all of them running wild—he had to catch them—but sold them for ten dollars a head to a bootlegger who pirated them across the Sabine to Louisiana undipped and uninspected. Two of his old hands visited him recently in Danbury. . . .

Using Walker hounds and Trumbulls, Moller caught little wolves in the nineteenth century when he was little and big ones when he grew up, till the barbed-wire fences were strung. A coyote, like a fox, will dodge into thick brush, he says, but a wolf "leaves the country." To catch him you first have to convince him that you are going to by running him ten miles through the sage and salt grass without letup. "Run a V on him" with other riders until his hind end wobbles and he hasn't gained a yard and begins to despair; then it may take another five or ten miles. Or if they could drive one into the Gulf of Mexico, they would keep roping him while he bit the ropes in two, until at last they drowned him. To run the wolves, even without a kill, kept the packs busted into isolated pairs which were less troublesome to the cattle, and generally Moller would catch the pups at the family rendezvous each fall. Sometimes, though, a varmint hunter would shoot a calf by mistake as it rose up suddenly in the grass. He'd had a couple of hog dogs as a boy that would chase any pup they came across, and with these he began wolfing on Chocolate Bayou, where the Amoco oil refinery now stands. In "nineteen and two" he was helping a trapper friend trail the wolves that hobbled off dragging the trap behind them, except it got to be such fun that they quit trapping and simply ran the creatures—ran them into swimming water where Moller would strip and grab a club and manhandle the wolf out to where the dogs could throttle it. Or he might rope it, haul it home to the hog pen and feed it cracklings and offal until his wife complained of the stink.

Moller is a well-set individual with pink coloring, a long face, a big pair of ears and nose, and a mellow voice. In 1895 eighteen inches of snow fell and half his father's cattle died. They skinned two hundred hides that week that fetched a dollar a hide in Galveston, both working as dollar-a-day cowboys afterwards, his father eating alligator tails and getting a dollar apiece for their hides too. Or they would paddle down Chocolate Bayou with four deer carcasses, put them on the city boat and trade them for a sack of green coffee in Galveston. In 1900 a hurricane blew down the house and washed away half the people who lived in the area, he says; one husband and wife held hands, grabbed hold of some driftwood and floated for thirteen miles.

The game was so plentiful—from cranes to doves—that on their hunts sometimes they couldn't hear the hounds for all the birds hollering. Sometimes, too, there were so many wolves about that when they went out after geese they couldn't creep close to a pond where a flight had just landed before some wolf would bound into the water to see whether any cripples were in the bunch, putting them all to flight. Moller captured the spring pups by riding up on a sand knoll where a lot of wolf tracks converged and prancing his pony around until its hooves broke through into the den. Then, on the following day, he'd jump the gyp-wolf (mama) there, and the day after that the pop. Once at the South Texas Wolf Hunters Association meet at the King Ranch, the Mexican hands had butchered a beef and hung it up for everybody to help himself, and brought out horses—the members had only had to bring along their own saddles. They all painted numbers on their dogs to score them in the chase, and Moller and a buddy stayed out late hounding a wolf until at last the creature "set his bucket down." He was exhausted, so they roped him, whipped the dogs away, and tied his mouth and carried him back across a horse, and at the big bonfire slipped off the ropes and heaved him into the crowd of wolfers to start the hunt all over again.

The cowhands close to Houston are mostly black, not Mexican, as they are towards the Rio Grande, or white, as in the bulk of Texas. . . . Since at least the work was manly in the old days, for some of them it may have been a tolerable sort of place to be a slave—alone on horseback hassling the cattle much of the day. It still would seem to add up to a better life than growing peanuts in Mississippi, although the shacks along the road look just as rickety as Mississippi's, and though many of the people one encounters have a peculiarly screwed-tight intensity to their faces—extraordinary faces that a traveler sees nowhere else in the United States—as if they had been scorched in a crucible, like black faces in Mississippi. Can it simply be the sun?

One morning I was chatting with a rancher who said he wanted to kill all the turkey buzzards in the sky as well as the red wolves. There are plenty of buzzards. We could count about fifteen standing about in the treetops and roosting on fence posts. Overnight the rain ditches had filled, the sky still smelled of rain, but as we visited, the sun broke through, lying at a cannon's angle, the kind of morning sun that made you answer to it, irradiating dead as well as living things. Greens bled into blues and reds, white was black and black was white: too much color and too bright. The wind, which had been chilly, began to heat. Then, in this incredible intensity of light, what the buzzards did, following some lead from an elder, was all at once to spread their wings, not in order to rise and fly, but holding them outflung to dry.

What we were witnessing was not unfamiliar. Everybody has seen pictures of a totem pole topped by a raven carved with its wings out-stretched, the Earth's creator, according to the maker of the totem pole. Ravens are the buzzards of the North. What we were privy to—fifteen buzzards spread-eagled, metal-colored in a violent sun—would have transfixed an Indian of the Northwest, would have provided a whole life's ozone to a woodcarver, a vision any warrior would have died for, if in fact his excitement didn't render him invincible. Fifteen images of the Creator in a rising sun would have propelled a great chief into his manhood after walking naked for a month; except we have no divine signs now.

I HAD SETTLED in Anahuac at a café-motel where the lady displayed her late husband's Yale diploma in the office as a talking point. She missed Arkansas, claimed it had been an awful mistake for them to have left Little Rock nineteen years before, and looked that Southern mixture of leftover hopefulness and untidy despondency—hard shoulders and forearms but vulnerable breasts and soft hands. She served a rueful menu of chicken-fried steaks and heavy catfish to lonely oil workers and roaming fishermen. I was discouraged, angry at the way the wolf project was on the back burner for everybody but Glynn Riley. In Washington there was a mixture of flutter and indifference—even to get information had required a personal visit—and over the years Texas's Parks and Wildlife Department has taken what might politely be described as a minimum of interest. (Their black bears were allowed to fall practically to the vanishing point before receiving partial protection.) The wolves' blood characteristics had been stud-ied not at a Texas medical center but in Minneapolis, and in Houston itself the concern, if possible, was fainter yet. The director of the Museum of Natural History, Dr. Thomas Pulley, an influential man, was not so much uninformed about the wolves as agin 'em. He hadn't exhibited the handsome skins that Riley had sent him, and liked to take the long view, speaking of man's impact on the world as related to evolution like the glaciers, belittling the notion of interfering as "causey, like preserving mustangs." He seemed bankerly in manner, a small-city, big-fish iconoclast with the mocking cast of mind that often develops in isolation, rubbing up against mostly laymen. He said that when he and his friends hunt deer they see plenty of coyotes.

The Houston zoo director, a civil servant, was not as self-assured. He had no wolves and agreed with me that though the zoos in San Antonio and Oklahoma City did keep one or two, it was incongruous that the only propagation program in the nation was way off in Tacoma, Washington. He said that to construct a "wolf woods" would cost only about seven thousand dollars, but that to raise such a piddling sum among the multimillionaires of Houston would be difficult because controversial, and so his efforts on behalf of disappearing species were devoted to the St. Vincent's parrot and Galápagos tortoise.

Riley carries hurt wolves to a veterinarian friend, Dr. Buddy Long, in the town of Winnie. Long pins together any broken bones (wolves will tear off a splint), administers penicillin and distemper shots and worms them. He is a man who "likes old things," and is the angel of Riley's program, having sunk thousands of dollars of his own modest funds into the work. He has a scrunched-together, matter-of-fact face, the mouth creased for smiling, and propagandizes as he makes his rounds among the cattlemen, several of whom still trap but who will telephone him when they catch something, if they don't like the idea of inviting a government man to poke about their property. The animal is a sad sight, clinched into a clutch of traps, with its feet mauled. Whatever toes are left he tends, or if the wolf is dead, he leaves it soaking in a tub for whenever the scientific community gets around to wanting to know what a red wolf looked like under the skin. At the time of my visit he had no legal authority to keep wild animals, and when the wolves he treated were ambulatory not a zoo in the country was prepared to take them, and so one night he'd leave the door of the pen open.

Long is a bit older than Glynn Riley, well settled in one of those delicious marriages that are a pleasure to catch sight of, and, as luck would have it, has been bolstering to Glynn. Through studying blood parasites he had become interested in the wolves, and now kept captives of his own in a big breeding arena. White on the lips and chin, with broad cheeks, narrow noses, a pointed attention and that skittery bicycling gait—whirling, almost fluttering, away from me along the fence—they were still jazzed up from the courting season, when they had chased each other all over Chambers County. Unfortunately this same month or two coincides with the calving season in the region, so that the ranchers see more of the wolves when they least want to.

Long took me wolfing along Elm Bayou, East Bayou, Onion
Bayou. A blue heron was eating baby alligators, though in a few weeks
it might be summering in one of the suburbs of Chicago. The geese in
their yapping thousands flew up from the fields around us; they would
soon be on the tundra. Long said that skunks are thick, and that
though a grown wolf would have enough sense to steer clear of a
rabid skunk, a blundering pup might get bitten and carry the disease
into the packs.

"Around here you can look farther and see less than anywhere in
the world," he said. But we inspected the "swimming holes" where the
stockmen swim their cattle across the Intracoastal Canal every fall,
then in the spring again, bringing them back to higher ground. We
saw the burros that they use to halter-break the yearling colts, tying
colt and burro neck to neck. He spoke about the problems of a cow
vet. "Sometimes they won't get well and sometimes they won't die." At
the fence gates we found wolf tracks. Now that the fields were drying
off for spring the baby rabbits were hopping from the nest, and the
wolves had scattered off the levees to catch them. Long said that
sometimes the wolves will run a ranch dog right through a screen
door, and twenty cattle through a fence, and pass the house again that
night, barking so as to rib the dog. When hunted, they will circle into
a herd if no other cover is close, and hamper the men from getting a
shot at them by sticking beside the cattle.

Among the many lice-chewed cattle we saw one fine high-horned
bull with a long dewlap, ears that hung down at a steep angle, a hump
big as a camel's and a penis like a rhino's. He was a pretty mouse
color, all the prettier for being so dangerous-looking underneath that
comely pelt. "That one would try to get in your back pocket with you,"
said Long as we negotiated the gate.

The only other strong ally of Riley's I was able to find in Texas was
Hank Robison, who sells cigarette lighters and ballpoint pens in
Houston. A lobbyist and crusader, he has worked to get the local
bounties removed. He lives in a workingman's district, has gold in the
front of his mouth, is self-educated and self-conscious about it, and
financially must live by his wits, he says. But posters of lions and tigers
stare off the walls of his small house; his blinds are dog-chewed. He
talks like a dogged cross between a crank and social worker and is a
fervid letter writer, keeping a file so that no officeholder can get away
with not replying to him. He has a flatly single-minded fighter's face,

taking you for where you stand, and when knocked down, obviously will not stay down, because his delight is just precisely to get up again. He camps in the Big Thicket on weekends and lives for his family as well as for wild animals, and yet in him I thought I saw what I notice in other enthusiasts and in myself: the injured man who recognizes in the running wolf his wounds.

Riley could comprehend a person preferring to live in the city if he liked going to the movies or had the money to eat in restaurants, but what he couldn't understand about the Eastern cities was the matter of muggers. Working with wolves, he wasn't afraid of muggers. "Why don't they clean them out of there?" Like Lynn Rogers in Minnesota, apparently he had a picture of himself walking down the avenues and, if he saw a mugger, punching him in the mouth. Of course, being familiar with firearms, he could adjust his image when I said that the mugger was likely to be armed, but he continued to presume that the solution lay in individual acts of heroism. What neither man could grasp was how *many* muggers there are.

Glynn has poisoned pocket gophers in East Texas and prairie dogs in West Texas, and out in Muleshoe in the Panhandle did rabbit counts for the Bureau, where he saw some odd spectacles: a badger and a coyote turning over cow chips in a partnership to eat the beetles underneath; an eagle snatching a duck from a windmill spillway. The eagles perched on the boxcars where feed was stored to spear the pack rats living underneath, and early one morning he watched a coyote filch a rabbit from an eagle, the coyote's chest fur shining nobly in the sun. Once in a while he'd drive a hundred miles or so to chat with an old wolfer who had shot the last gray Western lobos at their watering holes. One time the fellow had ridden here to the Gulf to dispose of a hog-killing red wolf: lay waiting for it behind the pen the night that he arrived, and when he heard the hog scream, shot the wolf, and the next day left—too many people here, not that big Western country. "We thought there'd always be another wolf. We didn't know they would ever play out," he told Glynn.

Riley's best thrill, when he has visited the study crew in Minnesota, has been to feel with his hands the outsized tracks the wolves make there in the fluffy snow. Gray wolves are real wolves in a way that red wolves aren't, and the black taiga wolves of the Yukon and the white arctic wolves are larger still. Someday he hopes to have a hand in studies of them all: jaguars too. He's a predator man and he wants size—dire wolf, cave bear! Then, because he was a novice on snowshoes, he began to make strange tracks himself, falling down and flinging out his arms. For days it was the joke in camp: *that's* where Glynn Riley from Texas fell down, and *there's* where he fell down again.

Like old-time trapping, Riley's is a lonely business. His best friend lives six hundred miles away in the Trans-Pecos town of Marathon, Texas. He's a mountain-lion hunter whom I'll call Mike Marfa, and the two of them became acquainted at what Marfa likes to call "rat meetings," where the varmint-control technicians of the Fish and Wildlife Service get together to talk shop, mostly about killing rodents and rabbits. But these two were men who had a penchant for pulling down a bigger creature, and, beyond that, were outdoorsmen with a vocation for it (Marfa likes to say that he's already caught enough coyotes to fill ten diesel trucks). When the two of them do manage a visit they can hardly contain their pleasure. They open the pungent brown bottles that Riley sets such store by, bobbing their heads like connoisseurs above the beaver oil and bobcat urine, two years in the brewing, though Marfa likes to tease Riley that it is where you put the trap, not so much what you sprinkle on it, that does the job.

Marfa is another man who knows more than many of the professors do who hold Chairs on the strength of their investigations into ethology, and sometimes comes back snorting from the symposia he goes to, saying he'd like to hear from the guy who *catches* their lions for them. For years he was the state's principal lion hunter, when the Bureau had a hundred and fifty trappers giving the coyotes a going-over. He was paid a little more and got up earlier too, he likes to claim, kidding Riley, and went out on muleback the whole day long, chasing after his hounds, instead of tooling about in a pickup truck like Riley and the rest, to prune the lions back to the edges of Big Bend National Park from a line which corresponded more or less to U.S. Highway 90. When I first met him he was on his way home from an excursion to Florida where he had demonstrated for the World Wildlife Fund that the Florida panther was rarer than Florida's wildlife officials had believed. His pack of mottled Walker hounds—a home brew he has bred and culled and whittled on over the years, and doesn't sell or swap or loan, he says, any more than a carpenter would his tools—were sleeping in a fresh pile of hay in the back of his truck, so placid after traveling so far that they spoke well for him. He and Riley took them for a run after bobcat along a bayou bank, but then, although Riley was eager to have him stay overnight and go to the Houston Fat Stock Show, which happened to be on that week, and although he himself was wistful about the possibility too, he said he had another twelve hours of driving ahead and didn't want to keep the dogs cooped up any longer than that. He's the type who scoops up every hitchhiker on the road, otherwise stopping nowhere, but compared to Riley, his mannerisms are gruff and harsh, and he is proud of going all day in the Big Bend desert without either water or food. Like so many other wildlife men, he was not in the Marines when he was a youngster and probably should have been. Where the bear man, Lynn Rogers, had made the burler's leap to city living in Minneapolis in the winter, Riley and Marfa had not. Riley had relinquished much of his hunter's spark, however, to a reflective attitude that suited his present work, but Marfa, whom Riley rather looks up to, was just as hot as ever; he had quit the Bureau and when he wasn't working on an experimental program to transplant mountain lions from the Big Bend country to South Texas, supported himself as a private lion hunter in the Big Bend region, and by trapping the last few lobo wolves down in the Mexican states of Durango and Chihuahua.

MARFA LET ME delve about with him a bit in his own territory, first wanting and then deciding that he didn't want a full-dress magazine article written about himself, but through both men I caught a sense of the cycle of wolf and coyote hunting.

The coyote is of course the "barking wolf," the Trickster of so many Indian tribes—a deity to the Chinooks and the Navajos, a subtle animal with a taste for the suckled milk in a lamb's stomach, for instance, which the simpler-minded bobcat does not share—the New World version of the jackal, and yet a creature so highly thought of that the pregnant women of certain Indian tribes would wear its testicles next to their stomachs to ward off difficulties. The fall is nonetheless the season when the guileless pups are dashing around; it is a chance to wipe out the year's crop while they are wet behind the ears, and was the season for the getter-gun until the getter-gun as a device was disallowed. Any witches' brew could be used to bait the knob—possum juice, rotted gopher, dead rattlesnake or frog—and since the pup took eight or ten leaps to die, more of the hunter's time was consumed in locating its little corpse in the brush than in any other part of the job.

In the winter the getters weren't as effective and the sort of guy without any particular skill who had coasted along in the fall by putting out a lot of them took a back seat to the serious trapper. Winter is the mating season, and the emphasis is on catching the adults as they hustle about, pissing at scenting stations and trailing one another. Sex is what interests them, not picking up the quaint and curious scents that getter-guns are baited with. The trapper, milking the bladders, cutting the musky anal glands out of the specimens he bags, creates some scent posts of his own or activates others—a turkey wing lying next to a sheep path—that the smarter coyotes will step up to. In a bog in Anahuac, the fellow might set his trap at the end of a footlog, with a wad of moss under the pan so that a raccoon's weight won't depress it.

In the spring and summer the animals lose interest in everything except their pups, and travel in a beeline between the den and hunting grounds. Trotting back full-bellied from a long drink at a spring, they may stop for a moment and piddle at the turkey wing or even investigate the outré smells on the bait knob of a "getter," but generally this is when the professionals hunt for dens. Den-hunting is a specialty, intuitive, distinct. The steel-trap men are condescending about the cyanide go-getter—a kind of scatter-shot method, a glib, perfunctory tool—and yet compared with trapping, den-hunting is downright purist and arcane. It's catching the animals alive, by hand, in their hidden home, and some predator hunters hardly bother to trap at all, killing a presentable quota of coyotes just by finding and digging up the year's new dens. Usually they ride, because a coyote fears a man on horseback somewhat less, and what the hunter looks for is a bustling hodge-podge of tracks that, as he studies them, begin to offer evidence of radiating from a given point which the coyotes have tried to conceal. Often the den faces southeast from a slight elevation, and he may try to call one of the parents toward him with a "squeaker" made from a piece of a cow's horn which emits a rabbit's squeal. If, having dismounted, he sees the coyote first and holds his fire until it scents him, he will have the benefit of its last quick anxious glance in the direction of the den to guide him on, before it takes evasive action. If the grownups attempt to decoy him he shoots them, then looks sharp for the first pup, which will streak for the hole as soon as it sights him. He tumbles about in the brush, grabbing the pups and clubbing them, or if they are very young he must dig, hooking them out from underground with a wire prong twisted on the end. If either parent has escaped him, he will bury a dead whelp with one foot exposed and set traps alongside it and by the den.

In sheep territory the javelinas root holes under the woven fences that coyotes also make use of, and this is where the ancient craft of snaring can be practiced. Then, by contrast, there are hunters who are primarily marksmen and shoot the creatures from a helicopter. But none of these systems will suffice after the less vigilant 70 percent of the population has been eliminated. There are always a few coyotes which flatten down instead of bolting when the helicopter makes its pass over the chaparral, and which keep their pups clear of the getter-guns. For these holdouts some studying is necessary; the animal becomes individualized, and a Riley or a Marfa becomes interested. Or they may meet an animal like Adolph Murie's blithe classic coyote in the valley of the Yellowstone which trotted toward him carrying a sprig of sagebrush in its jaws that it tossed up and caught and tossed and caught.*

When the Fish and Wildlife Service supervisors in San Antonio decided that the Big Bend mountain lions had had enough pruning, they set Marfa on a series of eccentric research labors, such as catching sixty coyote puppies "by Friday" for a sex-ratio study, collecting adults for a test of poisons, or gathering coyote urine and red-wolf skulls. (The number of red wolves killed in order to verify their existence as a species and then to train successive research cadres must surpass the number so far "saved.") Finally Marfa went into business for himself, charging the sheep ranchers $250 per lion, and more for the Sierra Madre lobos he has been capturing in Durango lately, working for the stockmen's association there. In some respects a wolf is more vulnerable than a coyote, because of the complexity of its social life and because it is bolder and therefore more accessible, but since it travels farther, in another way it is less so. These are "named" wolves, the last of their kind in an enormous spread of territory, in their way almost as endangered as Riley's wolves are, and correspond to the famous "outlaw" wolves of the American Great Plains a half a century

---

*Adolph Murie, *Ecology of the Coyote in the Yellowstone* (Washington, D.C.: National Park Service, Fauna Series Number 4, 1940), p. 38.

ago. Like them, they're quirky, lonely, queer, atypical beasts, final survivors because they have allowed themselves only the sparsest pleasures. Marfa carries a handful of traps as he rides his mule around for a period of days or weeks to spy out some small chink in the precautionary tactics of the wolf he is after—some stray indulgence by which it still tries to amuse itself that has escaped the notice of all the other trappers who have had a go at it. These Mexican lobos have short pretty heads, and you must know the length of the neck and stride in situating the trap.

One such wolf, "Las Margaritas," took him eleven months to catch, humbling him, he says, and in the meantime, it was claimed, slaughtering ninety-six cattle on a single large ranch nearby. The only entertainment left "Margaret" after so many narrow escapes in a lengthy career was killing steers, once she was safely inside a pasture. She was poison-proof because she fed at her own kills and nowhere else, and never a second time at one of them. Already missing two front toes, she would follow a different route coming and going. If she arrived on a logging road, she exited by way of a cattle track; if through a canyon, by a high pass. She avoided other wolves, although from loneliness she sometimes would howl behind the ranchers' barns. She would not go close to the message stations of other wolves, but instead would squat wistfully to make her mark at a safe distance, so that he could not catch her by the ordinary technique of setting a trap at a scent post or manufacturing a bogus station with the urine of a foreign wolf. Some outlaws, he says, entirely give up trying to communicate with other wolves and use only their own scenting stations. Once, indeed, she did step in one of his traps, but the hole carved into her foot by the two toes that she was missing happened to fit across the pan and saved her. She jumped for her life.

She traveled continually, having been hunted with hounds often after a meal, and there was no predicting where she would go. Over the years, hundreds of traps had simply been left blind for her in paths across the mountainsides she ranged, which gradually had lost their human smell and any surface scars to show the ground had been worked on. But some of them had become boneyards for other animals that had been caught instead, and the rest she avoided by her spartan custom of stepping mostly on the rocks and stones, or else on ground too hard to dig in without leaving a permanent sign. On the road, if there was any indication that a rider had dismounted or that a man had left his truck, even the day before, she immediately veered off, not waiting to discover what he might have been up to. Without the fellowship of a pack, with nowhere safe enough for her to go to relax except among the actual cattle herds, killing was her life and her relations with her pursuers her only intimacy, so when at last Marfa did catch her—when he had almost given up—it was in a trap that he had left blind some weeks before next to a corral she liked to hang about. She pulled the stake out of the ground and painfully dragged the trap as far as she could, but all the ranch hands turned out to chase her down. Only then was it revealed that notorious "Margaret," so security-ridden that she squatted meekly to piss like a bitch, all along had been a male.

When this methodical search had palled, Marfa dashed off behind his light little slipping lion hounds—skinny so their feet hold up and so they can twist through the canyon cracks and into any boulder pile (for which he has a "climbing dog")—to run down one of the infrequent lions left. He sight-trailed for the pack over the alkali ground, where the scent, as dry as smoke, had blown away. Where there were grass and sticks again they'd pick it up. Salt blocks, windmills and fencing are what makes ranching here. Durango is also the starving country where wetbacks come from, and any deer whose prints show up is tracked relentlessly. There are human outlaws in the Sierra Madre as well, and Marfa, lean from his regimen of two meals shoveled in twelve hours apart, living very nearly on a level with a lion, with the two expressions that his face falls into—boyish and bleak—went about with his rifle handy and his bedroll and mule and dogs.

Another noteworthy wolf he caught because his dogs showed him its single small inabstinence. It liked to go up on top of a mesa to a water tank with an earthen dam and wallow in that one soft place on a long-dead skunk lying in sweet-smelling grass. He captured a wolf called Wide Gait using a month-old turd which he had saved from its former ladylove, whose Spanish name was Nearly Black and whom he had trapped previously with an old turtle shell. "Dead as a hammer," he says.

Turds represent survival in the desert or the woods and are beloved by animals for that: a meal put to use, the gift of life. Of a woodsman, too, you'll hear it said, "He was the best deer-hunter that ever took a shit in the woods." Marfa showed me how to distinguish a ringtail's scats (small-bore, on top of a rock, containing scorpion

pincers and tails) from a raccoon's; a kit fox's fuzzy-toed, dainty prints
from a gray fox's; and trundled me about, pointing out abundant lion
scrapes in the sandy canyons we explored next to the Rio Grande.
Lions scratch with their forefeet for their feces and their hind feet for
urine, partly hiding the first but ballyhooing the latter. Their front
feet make a bigger, rounder print, so people sometimes think one
track is two.

This is country where one finds the arrows wetbacks put together
in the dry streambeds with stones—where once in the Christmas
Mountains Marfa found the skeleton of a "wet" who had gotten himself lost. He pointed out a mountain in Coahuila, a twelve-hour walk
up a canyon tributary to the Rio Grande, which has a cave so big a
plane could fly into its mouth, and cool high pine forests where a few
black bears are still holding out. He spoke about another sanctuary, in
Chihuahua, where until recently all the American cats could be
found—jaguarundis, ocelots, bobcats, lions and jaguars—though now
every such Shangri-la in Mexico is shrinking faster than a puddle on
hot city pavement. The last of the grizzly bears, he says, was blown up
with nitroglycerin wired to a honey-smeared log.

An ocelot leaves more scent than a bobcat and doesn't fight the
dogs as hard; a jaguarundi is lithest in the thickets and the toughest to
trail, he said. Lions and lobos are a force, a *frequency*, if you will: once
maybe the trombone, now the oboe in the orchestra. They are the
Headless Horseman who, once he is gone, exists only in fairy tales,
and although most of us can get along without hearing the oboe's
note or seeing the Headless Horseman ride, in Riley and Marfa I had
come close to locating the people who can't. Marfa, in particular, who
has hunted jaguars in the jungle in Campeche too, talks about retiring
to British Honduras, where in the wet woods he envisions the cats forever plentiful, leaving a trail for his dogs "as strong as a garbage
truck." In the desert in the early morning he lets the vultures be
his guide and trucks his dogs to where they are. Then, with the water
tinajas fifteen or twenty miles apart, he gets his lion.

RED WOLVES HOWL in a higher, less emotive pitch than gray wolves
and don't blend with each other quite as stylishly, though they do
employ more nuances and personality than a coyote family's gabble. A
coyote's howl sounds hysterical, amateurish by comparison, chopped

and frantic, almost like barnyard cackling, or, in an early description, "like a prolonged howl the animal lets out and then runs after and bites into small pieces." The only likely-looking wolves I actually saw during my several visits were two smashed dead on the highway, which I passed at high speed as I was leaving Texas. They were red, sizable and somber, at least from the perspective I had by then accumulated. They were probably mates, the second having lingered alongside the first, and now were angled affectionately rump to rump—the copulative position—in death.

Once, too, alone one night along Elm Bayou, I howled up a wolf a quarter of a mile away that sounded querulous and yowly, variable and female. We were beginning to converse, but I left it to answer another wolf howling a mile beyond. This wolf and I talked back and forth, until I started to wonder. The sound jerked and creaked too unsteadily for a wolf and yet was pitched too low to be a coyote, and wasn't barky enough for a feral dog—almost like a windmill. In fact, that's what it was; I'd left a real wolf for a windmill.

In these inquiries I had begun to glimpse the noble stretch of science when it grabs hold of a sea of data and persuades it to jell. In a still-primitive, ambiguously motivated backwater area of scholarship there was nevertheless a majesty to the picture as it emerged. Predators are smarter than herbivores, usually need to sleep more, and possess the invaluable ability to vomit, and when the findings on these biggest beasts are combined, one understands better the grizzly with its "attack distance" developed for a life on the plains, the black bear thriving by gourmand eating and a love of holes, the mountain lion avoiding competition and starvation by avoiding wolf country and its own kind, the wolf avoiding competition and starvation by a hierarchal social existence. Unluckily, the very means of population control that had enabled each of them to prosper while ruling the roost—the graphic social life, in some cases, and the slow, problematical birth rate of more solitary creatures such as bears or eagles—is now depleting them. These discoveries were being made, on the one hand, by scholars, many of whom might have been laughed out of the lab if they had been working in another branch of science, and on the other, by observers in the field whose woodsmanship was only a faint shadow of that of the centuries when the wilderness (and these animals) were real. But I'd met men who wouldn't have done badly in any era of woodsmanship.

7. WOLF KILL: PREDATOR AND PREY ENGAGE IN A CONVERSATION OF DEATH

BARRY LOPEZ

NO ONE KNOWS HOW WOLVES PICK OUT THE animal they will try to kill. Biologists suspect that acting on certain cues from the prey the wolves spot the older, weaker members of the herd and concentrate their killing there. They also kill "surplus young." This is orderly and contributes to the "balance of nature." However, it's not the rule; and since the old, the weak, and the very young are the ones least capable of eluding the wolf the suggestion is simply tautological.

In recent years at least three ideas have surfaced to suggest that what passes between wolves and their prey is more complex and less deterministic. Hans Kruuk, working with hyenas in Africa,

documented a surplus kill phenomenon. Hyenas, under certain conditions of extreme darkness, killed more animals than they could possibly eat. (Kruuk found the same true of foxes and black-headed gulls
in dense fog in England.) Kruuk believed surplus killing was the result
of a short circuit; the natural sequence of events (predator attacks,
prey flees, predator pursues) was upset because the animals couldn't
see each other clearly. The hyenas' "urge to kill" wasn't shut off, and
so they simply went on killing. Dave Mech, the American authority on
wolves, saw surplus killing by wolves in northern Minnesota in 1969;
he speculated that unusually deep snows prevented deer from escap-
ing, and this triggered killing by a resident pack far beyond its needs.

A second piece in the puzzle was suggested ten years ago by
William Pruitt, who discovered by accident that wolves signal their
prey—caribou in this case—if they are intent on attacking. In the
absence of such a signal, caribou browse at ease. Prey also signal
their predators; the antelope flashes his white rump, a deer suddenly
bolts. With both predator and prey signaling each other there is the
possibility of a conversation.

A third phenomenon suggests how little we know about predatory
behavior in general. Mech has shown that at least one wolf pack in
his Minnesota study concentrates its killing in a different area of its
territory each year, allowing the prey population elsewhere to recover.

Other phenomena, some worn and familiar, some recently discovered, take on new meaning. Wolves in hot pursuit of a deer bleeding
from its wounds will suddenly break off and let the animal go. Why?
One caribou in a small herd may leave off fleeing and present himself
to pursuing wolves in what appears to be an altruistic sacrifice. What is
happening?

Biologists deal easily with the physical aspects of death but are
loath to discuss it in a sociological context. This is odd, since the same
biologists agree that one of the most intriguing things about the wolf
is its social behavior. The behavior of the pack is comparable in its
complexity, cooperation, and exchange of information to a
Paleolithic hunting group. The scraps of information gathered by the
biologists who have actually seen wolves kill prey indicate that their
selection is neither arbitrary nor capricious. Indeed, the kill itself may
represent a response to something more complex than the simple
need to eat.

I think wolves kill the way Paleolithic hunters killed—by paying close attention to the movement of game herds and by selecting individual animals on the basis of various cues. The killing is by mutual agreement. This exchange between predator and prey might be called the conversation of death.

Wolves are the most elusive social animals in the Northern Hemisphere. They are rarely seen; major studies of wolves in the wild are complex, expensive, and can be counted on the fingers of both hands. All that is known about the wolf—its social organization, biology, ecology, behavior—has been learned in the past thirty-five years, with the perfection of aerial observation techniques and the development of the radio collar as an aid in tracking.

The wolf has long had a reputation as a wanton, innately evil creature, a sort of terrestrial shark. It runs down large ungulates, slashing at their hams, ripping their flanks, tearing at their heads until the animals weaken enough to be thrown to the ground; then it may rip open the abdominal cavity and begin eating before the animal is actually dead. Yet where the shark is a pea-brained loner the wolf has proved to be a sophisticated social animal with at least three systems of intra- and interpack communication: vocal, postural, and olfactory. He or she coordinates hunts, plans ambushes, peaceably shares food, plays with his or her young, courts a mate, and joins other wolves to howl in what one scientist calls "the jubilation of wolves." Following the publication of Aldo Leopold's classic *Game Management* and a pioneering study of wolves by the late Adolph Murie in 1944, it was accepted that the function of wolves in the scheme of things was to "cull" their prey, to keep it from overpopulating an area, overbrowsing it, and starving to death. But no one knew how they did it, or why.

Beginning in the winter of 1959, Dave Mech spent more than 400 hours over a period of three years in a tiny plane suspended over the 210 square miles of Isle Royale in Lake Superior, looking for wolves. During that time, when the snow conditions provided a contrasting background and the lack of deciduous growth allowed for increased visibility, Mech observed encounters between wolves and their major prey species, the moose.

Of the 160 moose Mech saw from the air on Isle Royale and judged to be within range of hunting wolves, twenty-nine were ignored, eleven discovered the wolves first and eluded them, and twenty-four refused to run and were left alone. Of the ninety-six that ran, forty-three got away immediately, thirty-four were surrounded but not harmed, twelve made successful defensive stands, and seven were attacked. Of these seven, six were killed, and one was wounded and abandoned.

Today, seventeen years later, Mech is more than ten years into a study of wolves in northern Minnesota, where the last wolf population in America outside Alaska is concentrated. He has watched them track, chase, and kill their primary prey species, the white-tailed deer. Mech knows the physics of how wolves kill and he knows something about why they kill, but he still does not know why one animal in a herd is killed and another goes free.

Postmortem examination of prey on Isle Royale and in other studies showed that wolves did select primarily the very young, the old, and the injured and diseased. However, the observation can be reserved: it can be said that these three groups "gave" themselves to the wolf, or that the animals fell victim because they were ill-equipped to escape.

Vulnerable prey animals apparently "announce" their condition to wolves by subtleties of stance, peculiarity of gait, rank breath, or more obvious signs of visible infection. Frequently wolves "test" a herd by making it run. The Nunamiut Eskimo, who live in the Brooks Range with wolves, have observed that hundreds of animals may be chased, many lackadaisically, before a burst of speed brings one down. The Nunamiut think a wolf can bring down any caribou it chooses, so if it's just tagging its prey they assume it's playing, testing, or perhaps waiting for a return signal from an individual caribou.

There is logic to the biologists' cull theory. The aged, diseased, and injured announce themselves and the wolf dispatches them. The young are cropped to control the size of the herds and perhaps to eliminate inferior or maladaptive combinations of genes at the outset. But the drive to make the facts conform to a theory of nature in the balance is based on at least one sweeping assumption: that wolves look for moose only to kill them. Testing prey might also be a deadly form of recreation.

Wolves will also attack an animal and then halt the chase for an hour to take a nap. One wolf may insist on attacking a certain individual while the rest of his pack will refuse. A pack on the hunt may investigate fresh moose tracks less than one minute old, pick up some subtle cue there and not pursue.

It has long been held that wolves employ hunting strategies. They are reputed to lie low in the grass, switching their tails from side to side like metronomes to attract curious but swift antelope close enough to jump them. They herd buffalo onto lake ice, where the huge animals lose their footing. On occasion wolves employ what seems to be a conscious strategy, sending one or two individuals out to herd prey into an ambush. They vary their tactics, adapting to the terrain and to the type of prey. They prefer to attack mountain sheep from above and to work a swamp in a line-abreast formation. They may split up to skirt both sides of an island in a frozen lake and then precipitously flush the game driven toward the island's tip. They use man-made roads to conserve energy and facilitate ambushes. All this is strategy, but it is not necessarily killing strategy.

Once begun, the wolf's chase of a prey animal may last only a few seconds, go on for miles, or carry on intermittently for days. However, the pathology of death is consistent. First, there is massive damage to the animal's hips, breaking its stride; then slashing, crushing and tearing, causing bleeding and inducing trauma; then harassment, tiring the animal; and, finally, disembowelment, causing death. With larger animals one wolf may grab the nose and hang on while the others undercut the animal and mob it to get it off its feet. Smaller animals, such as sheep, can be ridden down by a single wolf with a neck or head hold. Adult moose are often left to stiffen and weaken from their rump wounds and then killed. Once an animal is wounded and has taken its death stand, one or two wolves may harass it—make it exert itself, keep it bleeding—while the others rest or play. The pack may even depart, leaving one or two animals on a death watch. Yet some of the wounded survive. They have effectively announced their desire to live, as the others might have signaled their readiness to succumb.

The outcome of the hunt is usually settled in the first moment, the moment of eye contact between the animals. Mech writes, "The wolves and the deer remained absolutely still while staring at each other, 100 feet apart, for 1 to 2 minutes. . . . Suddenly the deer bolted, and instantly the wolves pursued."

The deer cannot stand at bay and fight off wolves as a caribou or moose can. It has no choice but to run. But with large ungulates, the outcome of the stare is less predictable. Immediately after a one-minute stare the moose may simply walk away, or the wolves may turn and run, or the wolves may charge and kill the animal in less than a minute. This hard stare is frequently used by wolves to communicate with each other and to take the measure of strangers. (Other animals, such as the gorilla, use a stare to communicate also.) What transpires in those moments of staring between predator and prey is probably a complex exchange of information regarding the appropriateness of a chase and a kill. This encounter is the conversation of death.

The conversation falters noticeably when wolves encounter domestic stock, animals that have had the language of death bred out of them. The domestic horse, a large animal as capable as a moose of cracking a wolf's ribs or splitting its head open with a kick, will almost always panic and run. Very frequently it will be killed. When a wolf wanders into a flock of sheep and sees them running into each other, flipping over on their backs like turtles and panicking, there is chaos. The wolf who has initiated a prescribed ritual has received nothing in return; he has met with ignorance in an animal with no countervailing ritual of its own. So he wounds and kills to excess.

When a wolf "asks" for an animal's life he is opening a formal conversation that can take any number of turns, including "no" and "yes," and can proceed either ritually or personally from there. It does not exclude play, play that can be lethal to the uninitiated; and it may encompass humor, although the encounter itself is not humorous. It may be compared to encounters between the war parties of Plains Indians, who had their own ritualized and idiosyncratic ways of fighting, dying, and laughing.

Paleolithic cultures in general tended to stress that there is nothing wrong with dying. This idea was rooted in a very different perception of ego: a person was simultaneously indispensable and dispensable (in an appropriate way) for the good of fellow beings. At a more primitive level, exactly the same principle may operate between wolves and their prey.

The moose's death is something that is mutually agreeable. The moose may be constrained to die because he is old or injured, but there is still the ritual and the choice. There is nobility in such a death. The wolf grows strong eating an animal that knows how to die with its whole heart; he wastes away on the flesh of animals that do not know either how to live or how to die. In just the same way Indians were reluctant to have anything to do with cattle. They would not eat them, raise them, or milk them, because there was no power in cattle.

When Robinson Jeffers wrote, "What but the wolf's tooth whittled so fine / the fleet limbs of the antelope," he was telling, I think, only half the story. Predator and prey grow stronger together by means of a series of tests, through all the years of their lives, tests that pit them against each other at both psychological and physiological levels, tests that weed both culturally and genetically.

Wolf and moose seem to be far better at interspecies communication than we are. There is no reason why they should be confined to the antiquated, almost Newtonian system of behavior that we have devised for them. We should not be afraid—but we are, and profoundly so—to extend to the wolf and the moose the physical and metaphysical variables we allow ourselves. It is not man but the universe that is subtle.

8. TROUBLE IN WOLF HEAVEN

THOMAS McNAMEE

SUPERIOR AND SKY BOTH SILVER: LAST week it was thirty-eight below, today it is as much above, and so we have this fog. Out in it somewhere is Isle Royale.

Come evening, a more propitious silver: full moon winking through a shredding scud. Don Brown and Stu Croll stretch out on the motel beds, shoes off and drinks in hand. The one dividend of not having been able to fly today is that tonight we get to watch Reagan on the tube wielding his ax. The President's budget speech doesn't mention the National Park Service specifically, but nobody in this room is predicting any special favors. When the camera settles for a moment on the newly installed Secretary of the Interior, James Watt, an ambiguous thin smile passes across Stu's face, and all he says is, "There he is." Don is impassive.

"Trouble in Wolf Heaven," by Thomas McNamee, originally appeared in Audubon, *January 1982. Copyright © 1982 by Thomas McNamee and reprinted by the author's permission.*

Donald R. Brown is superintendent of Isle Royale National Park, and Stuart L. Croll is what they call chief of interpretation and resource management—or chief ranger. After a long day's drive around the western end of Lake Superior from the park's winter headquarters at Houghton, Michigan, they are here in Grand Marais, Minnesota, waiting for the weather to get decent enough for a ski-plane to make it the forty or so miles to the island.

"What's the record for being stuck in Grand Marais?" asks Don. This is his first winter at this park, but he and Stu are old pals, from Grand Canyon and Olympic, and this is Stu's fifth winter here.

Puff and, aah, puff, goes Stu Croll's pipe: "Eight days."

Last night's moon was a canard. The island radios in: fog. Call to Ely, where the plane is: ceiling too low. Don Brown kicks at the slush. "Klister, if anything." His life has two prominent joys, working and skiing, and both are denied him today. We mess around in stores for a couple of hours, try to persuade ourselves that the overcast is lifting, and try a last-minute call. The fog is off the harbor at the island! Ceiling's up at Ely! And we're on.

Inland, north, across the Boundary Waters Canoe Area and on into the vastness of central Canada the black boreal forest stretches, white-veined with bogs and frozen lakes. In there is one of the two remaining American populations of the eastern timber wolf. We are flying east, to the other.

Shoreline ice gives way to open water. A fifty-mile-long archipelago materializes through the shifting mists. The old de Havilland Beaver's radial motor throttles back from a thunder to a roar, and we drop to the frozen bay. "Guck," grunts the pilot as we crunch through the slush and slither to a halt on the ice beneath.

A truck-sized, tank-tracked insect is grumbling down the hill to the harbor but cannot keep its footing in the rheumy snow. Don Glaser saunters out of the woods. "Welcome to Florida," he calls.

Glaser's plane, sitting on the ice, looks like an overambitious toy next to the Beaver. It needs a two-by-four propped under the skis to keep them from freezing into the slush when it gets cold again. To do this, you just pick up one whole side of the plane while somebody else slides the board under. An Aeronca Champ—fabric skin, aluminum bones—weighs seven hundred and fifty pounds. Glaser assures me that it flies.

Rolf Peterson moseys down pulling a toboggan, at the sight of which Stu Croll groans, muttering imprecations against the camp's infamous snowmobile. We will have to haul our gear the half-mile uphill to headquarters; and, if Stu's mechanical magic and grab bag of spare parts fail him, our water for the next eight days as well. It is nevertheless a cozy thought that you can still just drink Lake Superior.

Rolf says hello to us and bids good-bye to several of his scientific colleagues who are leaving the island. The Beaver, which Glaser, a noted wit, is out on the ice mooning, mounts into the sullen sky and is gone.

It is very quiet here.

ISLE ROYALE IS WILDERNESS, but it is not innocent of the hand of man. As early as 2000 B.C., people were mining the veins of pure copper that lay on the surface of the rock. They may have burned the forests to expose more of it, but by the time white miners arrived in 1840 there was no sign of previous disturbance. The island was almost entirely blanketed by a dense climax forest of white spruce and balsam fir, and the principal animal was the woodland caribou.

Because of its remoteness, the island had a limited complement of mammals. Besides the caribou, there were lynx, beavers, snowshoe hares, deer mice, one unique subspecies of red squirrel, and a few coyotes, foxes, martens, muskrats, and minks. But there were no moose—and no deer, no elk, no cougars, no raccoons, no skunks, no rabbits, no porcupines, no ground squirrels, no shrews. Once in a while an ice bridge might form to the mainland, and then wolves might visit, but there never were enough caribou to feed a permanent population. It was an easy sort of place for the caribou.

Meanwhile, back on the mainland of Minnesota and Ontario, things were getting tough for the caribou. Extensive logging and burning were replacing the caribou habitat of old conifers with paper birch and quaking aspen and little shrubs—the blue plate special of deer and moose, who were rapidly taking over the neighborhood.

Just after the turn of the century, some of the growing numbers of moose moved onto Isle Royale. Moose won't go very far out onto open ice, so, preposterous as it may seem, the fact is that they must have swum. It was a good twenty miles or better, but it is documented that the moose around Lake Superior do take the occasional lunatic swim—having no idea where they're headed and doomed to drown except for those lucky few who come aground at Isle Royale.

The new arrivals must have been delighted with the place. The copper prospectors of the nineteenth century had burned thousands of acres of the spruce-fir woods, in which the caribou's diet staple of reindeer moss had grown in abundance, and now in all those old burns there was moose salad galore. There had been some logging in the nineties, with the same effect. In addition, beavers, which had been all but wiped out by trappers in earlier years, were soon to stage a great renaissance, and that would mean new ponds with aquatic plants in the summertime and plenty of downed treetops all year round. Soon enough, in the meadows where old beaver ponds had drained, there would grow still more good things to eat. All this was bad news for the caribou, and by 1926 they had disappeared.

By 1930, when Adolph Murie began his studies on the island, there were somewhere between one and three thousand moose on these two hundred square miles. They had gobbled up virtually all the American yew. The pondweed and water lilies were gone from the beaver ponds, and the poplars, birches, mountain ash, and most of the shrubs were severely overbrowsed. The moose were eating up their newfound paradise. Within five years, all but about two hundred of them had starved to death.

The survivors got a lucky break in 1936, when a fire got started at a logging operation at Windigo and eventually burned over a quarter of the island: more moose salad, and, again, more and more moose. They were headed straight for another big die-off when in 1940 Isle Royale was made a national park and people started talking about introducing wolves. It took them until 1952 to get around to doing it, with four zoo-raised animals. These wolves, used to humans and not at all used to working for a living, made a nuisance of themselves, raiding campsites and scaring the daylights out of people. Eventually two of them were shot, one was trapped and deported, and the fourth, Big Jim by name, got away.

Nature, meanwhile, had beaten the Park Service to the punch. It was soon evident that Big Jim had company on Isle Royale. Right in the midst of all the uproar about whether to stock them, wolves had shown up on their own—probably trotting over on the ice bridge that had formed in February 1949. They liked it there just fine, and decided to stay.

"Potentially at least," writes Durward Allen in *Wolves of Minong*, "the wolves could build up, stabilize the moose herd, and bring some protection to the vegetation. It was the pattern of primitive times, now to be replayed in a world where such patterns are confused and obscured by the almost universal hunting of moose and the wiping out or heavy control of wolves."

Allen tried to no avail to get his employer, the U.S. Fish and Wildlife Service, to fund a study, "but after the election of 1952, there was no chance." Finally he left government service for the faculty of Purdue University, and in 1958 he began one of the most remarkable studies of predators and their prey ever carried out. It has been under way continuously ever since.

ROLF O. PETERSON came to Isle Royale in 1971 as Allen's graduate student, and since 1975 he has been director of the research program.

"Lots of changes here in the last ten years," he explains. "When I first arrived, we had maybe twelve hundred moose and about twenty wolves—one big pack roaming the whole island, plus a few loners and pairs. By last winter, the moose were down to about seven hundred, and we had *fifty* wolves, in five packs, each with its own territory. By the late sixties the browse in the old '36 burn had grown out of reach of the moose, and then in the early seventies we had a series of extremely hard winters. That meant more malnutrition and lower reproduction for the moose, and easy pickings for the wolves.

"A wolf pack keeps up very well with where moose are in their territory. They'll travel around and test every one they encounter, and if a particular moose looks a little funny they'll challenge him. If the moose is in good condition, he'll usually just stand his ground, and no wolf wants to mess with an angry moose. One good kick will shatter a skull. But if the moose is vulnerable—and the wolves can generally find out quickly—he'll run, and naturally the wolves will chase him. Of course, they can still kill only two or three out of every hundred moose they come up against.

"In the early seventies, though, it was so easy for them that they often weren't even finishing their kills. It was easier to kill another moose than dig out the frozen remains of an old carcass. It's not like that any more."

Rolf is sawing lustily at a moose femur—the marrow fat content is an indicator of an animal's nutritional state. "This kill, for example.

Two leg bones and a little bit of skull were all they left. Wolves are dying of malnutrition. They're trespassing on one another's territories, and we know that at least two trespassers have been killed by other wolves in the last year. Since last winter, the population has dropped from fifty to maybe thirty. Much of that was probably from starvation.

"Meanwhile, naturally, the moose population is stabilizing, because the wolves have killed off most of the weak ones. The calves born in the early seventies have been deficient all along, but very few moose between one and six years old ever have to worry about wolves. Now, though, they're starting to get old and being killed off. Because the moose population is down now, the browse is recovering somewhat, and we're getting better nutrition. Look at this: seventy percent fat content, I'd guess, which is darn good for February.

"Still, their long-term outlook is not bright, mainly because of the vegetation changes. We've got a white spruce invasion under way all over the island, and moose don't eat that. The whole place is gradually reverting to climax forest, which supports far fewer moose than all this young stuff they did so well on earlier in the century."

Don Glaser comes in and sees me scribbling notes. "You got anything in there about how handsome and virile the pilot is?"

"So how's she looking, Glacier?" asks Rolf.

"By golly, Rolf, I think we better get up there."

Rolf has been eager to get out in the Champ, having missed several days' flying in a row. "See, we finally froze up last night, and that'll give us a crust on the snow, which the wolves can run on and the moose can't. The moose would have been moving around yesterday in that slush, and now they'll be holed up under conifers unable to move much. With that full moon last night, the wolves will have been very active. Only thing is, it's hard to track them on a crust like this. But we'll see."

He and Glaser will see, but I won't: the Champ seats only two. I while away the afternoon in L. David Mech's *The Wolves of Isle Royale:*

February 15, 1960. At 2:10 P.M. the sixteen wolves were heading down Grace Creek. Suddenly, they pointed toward a cow two hundred yards to their left. Then they continued down the creek to where it wound closer to the moose. Heading inland over a knoll, the wolves surprised the cow twenty-five yards away.

The animal fled, but the wolves caught up almost immediately. One grabbed her right hind leg just above the hoof.
However, as the cow trotted through the spruces, she shook the
wolf loose. She then ran in a semicircle toward the creek, and
several times the wolves overtook her but failed to attack. Once
when she ran through a snowdrift, the wolves lost ground, but
they quickly caught up again.

As the moose started down a shallow valley, the wolves
attacked her rump. She soon shook them, however, and pro-
ceeded to the frozen creek bed, where the wolves attacked
again. One animal kept jumping at her nose and finally
grabbed it; others fastened onto her rump and flanks. The cow
fought hard and dragged the wolves about one hundred yards
downstream. Three or four times, she lifted the 'nose-wolf' off
the ground and swung it for several seconds before lowering
her head. This wolf maintained its grip for over a minute. The
moose continued fighting hard and finally shook the wolves
and ran back upstream, with the whole pack following.

The cow started into the woods and the wolves lunged
again. The moose kicked constantly and trampled two individuals into the snow. One of them crawled away but later seemed
unhurt. The moose then stood next to a small balsam along the
creek shore and continued to fight off the wolves, which soon
gave up temporarily and lay on the ice. At 2:35 P.M. they went
two hundred yards downstream and assembled. They returned
to the animal three times but found her belligerent, although
blood from her wounded rump covered several square yards of
snow. Nevertheless, there appeared to be no mortal wound.

From 2:50 to 3:25 P.M. the wolves lay on the nearby ice.
Meanwhile, at 3:20 the moose walked about ten yards and lay
down. At 3:25, the pack approached and she arose again.
Although appearing stiff, she charged the wolves effectively.
Many of them were eating the bloody snow where she had stood
first. At 3:40 the wolves lay down again, and at 3:50 so did the
moose. About a minute later, a wolf approached the moose and
she arose again. At 4:12 this occurred once more. Then the
wolves entered some spruces twenty-five yards south of the
moose and curled up. From 4:20 to 4:40 we were refueling, but
when we returned, the wolves were still there.

At five o'clock, they arose, tested the moose, and found her quite pugnacious. Ten minutes later, fourteen of the animals left and headed southward while two remained curled up within twenty-five yards of the wounded moose, which was also lying down.

From 5:35 to 6:05, the pack visited an old kill half a mile south of the creek; the animals then traveled back along a ridge until half a mile from the wounded cow. Meanwhile, the two 'guards' arose and stood near the moose. The pack headed almost directly toward them, and at 6:40 P.M., when we had to leave, the pack was within a quarter-mile and still heading toward the wounded moose.

The next morning at 10:50 A.M., the wolves were feeding on the carcass.

PETERSON, GLASER, CROLL, Brown, and I are the only people here. For the last six years, Isle Royale National Park has been closed up tight every winter, mainly for the sake of the wolves and the study. Not that there were ever many people interested in coming: the only way to get here is by chartered ski-plane—very expensive—and even then you'd want to be very sure your pilot knew his ice-reading. And the weather—believe me—is terrible.

Nevertheless, Don Brown is worried. Isle Royale is the only national park that closes in the winter, and there's been a lot of loose talk lately about easier access to the parks, elitist backpackers hogging the resource, let's build a tram to the bottom of Grand Canyon. . . .

"It's not as if people around here haven't got anywhere else to go skiing or winter camping," says Brown. "And there's nothing really special about the Isle Royale landscape. It's actually rather dull, don't you think? Even if you want total wilderness isolation, and wolves, you don't have to go far—Superior National Forest, in Minnesota, is open all year, and they've got plenty of wolves. They're hard to see, of course, because there are people around. The reason the study here has been so successful, of course, is that the wolves are *undisturbed*. We're very careful to help them get used to the study aircraft, and the pilot never goes too low, and he always throttles back when he's near them. And we never interfere with the wolves, *at all.* No trapping. No tranquilizing. No marking. No transmittering. The result is that they let us watch them, and Rolf's study goes on. Speak of the devil!"

Peterson comes through the cabin door, his pack heavy with moose bones: "Well, we visited a couple of old kills and picked up these femurs, and we found two new kills, with wolves feeding at both of them. They still ought to be there in the morning, Tom, if you want to risk your life with Glacier." So, if the weather holds, I am to see my first wolf.

"We've been talking about the winter closure," Brown tells Peterson. Rolf was the coauthor, with Don's predecessor, of the present policy, and just in the last few weeks Stu Croll has been codifying it into an official regulation to be circulated through the bureaucracy and published in the *Federal Register*—so the issue has been on everybody's mind lately.

Don Brown has been an instructor at the Park Service's training center at Grand Canyon, as well as director of the International Seminar on National Parks at the University of Michigan—a program designed to help other countries establish and maintain park systems of their own. He is of a naturally reflective, philosophical bent, and for him park policy flows from ethics. "Our primary task, as set forth by law, is to protect and preserve the parks for the enjoyment of future generations as well as people today," he says. "Recreation is obviously an important part of what goes on in the parks, but only to the extent that it doesn't degrade the resource. We've also been designated an international biosphere reserve by the United Nations, which gives us a further mandate for preservation. Isle Royale's single most precious resource is an endangered species, the eastern timber wolf, and the isolated and pristine habitat that it finds here. I don't believe we could have winter recreation and also continue to have the wolf."

Rolf Peterson explains: "In winter, the wolves do most of their traveling along the frozen lakeshores. Most of the moose also spend the winter near the water. If people were to come, they would have to use the same routes. The wolves here still show total avoidance of humans, even after thirty years of protection, and we obviously want to maintain that behavior."

"A lot of people," Don interjects, "are thinking that the increasing

number of problems with grizzlies in the West is a direct consequence
of the bears' growing familiarity with man—they're learning that
people aren't dangerous."

"It's very possible, too," continues Rolf, "that interference with the
wolves' travel could significantly reduce their nutrition at a very criti-
cal time. They breed in February, and one of the first effects of malnutrition is reduced fertility. And you have to remember that usually
only the alpha pair in each pack breeds. (Oh, the others would love
to, all right, and they try, but the alphas just won't permit it, and their
social structure is very strict.) So if we have, say, four packs on the
island, we only have about four breeding females."

Throughout this, there has been a faint background of huffing
and puffing and cussing from outside, and, finally, a triumphant
internal-combustion roar, and Stu has appeared, black-handed and
grinning, to proclaim his victory over the snowmobile. He joins us at
the kitchen table as Don resumes with one of Stu's favorite subjects:

"Obviously, the main thing that would draw people here in winter
would be the opportunity to see wolves."

"We have about fifteen thousand visitors a summer," says Stu,
"and of those maybe a dozen ever see a wolf. We close off the denning
areas altogether, and the wolves tend to travel in dense cover. In
winter, of course, there isn't much dense cover."

"So," continues Don, "the wolves would soon disappear from the
lakeshores, and then people would start trying to spot them from airplanes, and zooming in low for a nice look. Or they might find a kill
and stake it out until the wolves returned."

"Which," says Rolf, "as soon as they got wind of the people, no
wolves in their right minds would ever do. You see where all this leads.
The study would come to a dead stop. If you can't see the wolves, it's
kind of hard to study them."

"It would also cost us a fortune to open up in the winter," adds
Stu. "We'd have to maintain rangers, and probably a rescue chopper,
and the transportation costs would be ungodly."

"But how much pressure is there on you now?" I ask.

"Not that much," Stu concedes. "We get very few requests to come
here in the winter, and most of the people who make them are very
cooperative once we explain why the park is closed."

"Well, Don, do you anticipate there being more pressure in the
future?"

"We'll just have to see. Meanwhile, we've got something that's virtually unique in the lower forty-eight: a completely unmanipulated natural environment—a real wilderness. And I think that's worth preserving. Don't you?"

NEXT MORNING, Glaser and I take to the air. The island looks like something dreamt, black fingers of forest indistinct in the uneasy mists, and to the south the floe-pocked immensity of Superior under a leaden sky. The Champ crabs sidewise, scuffing the wind, and Glaser politely directs my attention to the air-sickness bag.

The landscape is wonderfully various, the forest types constantly changing: here, the familiar spruce-fir; there, long, ridge-following stretches of fire-spawned aspen and paper birch; to the southwest, climax stands of sugar maple and yellow birch; swamp forests of black spruce, white cedar, and fir; jack pine on the brushy, flame-scarred ridgetops; a relict stand of red oaks, veterans of warmer days; beaver meadows, scrublands, bogs. It seems somehow very empty. You can see straight down in, but for miles there is nothing there but snow. At last Glaser spots a moose. He opens the door and flies us in a descending corkscrew so I can lean out for a good clear look. Very windy, very scary; also fun.

We locate the first of yesterday's kills. It consists of a big brown patch of hair and scarlet streaks in the snow. An animal is feeding at it! We take a second pass, lower. It is only a fox. The wolves have gone.

At Angleworm Lake we skim the ice so Glaser can check the surface; then we double back and land to visit the kill here, this one from last week. It is an awesome sight. The dense mat of moose hair is a good eight by ten feet in extent, and several inches thick. A heap of half-digested rumen lies off to the side. The three legs (the fourth is already boiling in Rolf's bone pot, for the collection) are gnawed clean, right down to the hooves. There are a few blotches of blood here and there on the ice, and part of a skull. And this is all that remains of a creature that may have weighed a thousand pounds and stood six feet high at the shoulder. What little the wolves didn't eat, the foxes and the ravens have picked away.

Airborne again, we reconnoiter yesterday's second kill, but once again the wolves have finished it and gone. (Fifteen pounds at a sitting is a wolf's idea of a hearty meal, and he'll be back for more several

times a day—and then of course may have to fast for several days afterward.) For a couple of hours we scan the island, but there is no sign.
We spot one big cow moose running like mad through the woods,
which Glaser thinks may mean there are wolves in hot pursuit—but as
we circle back there are no wolves to be seen.

"Time for a poke"—another of Glaser's many special words, this
one signifying drink—"and, tonight, the sauna!" The summer rangers
have built quite a nifty one into an old falling-down shed, and this
must be our consolation for the wolfless day. We tie the plane down at
the dock. A raven coughs and rattles from a lakeside pine, and a pallid
dusk descends.

It rains all night, turning at morning into a thick and clotted
snowfall: there will be no traveling today, by foot, ski, or plane. The
woods are full of a filthy, choking stink, borne on the north wind from
the pulp mills of Thunder Bay.

The weather remains immitigably awful, and our paralysis settles
into routine—late sleeps, big meals, long talks, tall pokes, and saunas.
It snows a little, drizzles a little, clears a little but never enough. Rolf
hunches over his desk, writing funding proposals. Fully half his time,
he says, must be devoted to this.

Foxes dance in the fog at the door, ghost shapes, looking for
handouts after dinner. Even the deer mice abominate this weather:
three have taken refuge in the previously mouse-free kitchen.

"Should've brought my mousetrap," says Glaser. "Got a ball-
bearing mousetrap at home."

A laconic pause, and Rolf replies, "That right?"

"Yup. Big tomcat." Glaser is leafing idly through one of the
cabin's ancient dog-eared magazines. "Say, Rolf, here's one for me."

"What's that, Glacier?"

"Study abroad, it says."

Stu Croll has lugged about fifty pounds of paperwork with him
from the mainland, and it is now arrayed in shipshape stacks all
around his impeccable corner of the bunkroom: moose data here,
trail maintenance there, the latest draft of the winter-closure rule . . .
the objective correlatives of an orderly mind. "I don't think most
people appreciate how important a role science plays in the management of the national parks," he says. "We don't make a move without
consulting the researchers. A few years back, there was a proposal to
put in a new trail along the south shore of the island, but the wolf
study team said it might interfere with summer rendezvous sites—a

pack tends to come back to the same one year after year—so we dropped it flat.

"A national park is the ideal natural laboratory, of course, because every effort is made to minimize human influence on the ecosystem. And Isle Royale is the most ideal of all because it's an island. Except for the occasional great event like the immigration of the moose and the wolves, you've got a closed system, and there's no better place to study population dynamics. We've had some pretty dramatic findings, too—just look at this forty percent drop in the wolf population in the last year. Rolf's work has been showing how important vegetation succession is in governing populations all the way up the food chain.

"But this park's being an island also has its dangers. Island ecosystems are inherently unstable, mainly because of the low number of species. On the mainland you don't see the kind of wild swings you get here, because they're mitigated by the animals' ability to move on or spread out. So things can change here very rapidly. We've already seen the coyote completely wiped out by the coming of the wolf. With the vegetation changes we're having, unless we have a fire—which we would let burn naturally—we may see further reduction in the moose herd, and nobody really knows how many moose are necessary to keep the wolves going. I don't think there's anywhere else on earth where you can study this kind of thing this closely, and it's going to be really exciting to see what develops.

"We've also got studies under way on fire ecology, vascular plants, shoreline communities, atmospheric deposition, beavers, and echinococcus. That's the tapeworm that lives in the lungs of all the moose and is often the main factor in the weakening of the older ones. It's a neat system: the wolves eat the moose, and the echinococcus larvae become tapeworms inside the wolves, then lay more eggs which eventually reach the water and end up back in the moose.

"This is a wonderful place to work. I never wanted to do anything else but work for the National Park Service—and now here I am, in the midst of all this incredible beauty, constantly in contact with interesting people and new ideas. You just can't beat it."

THIS MISERABLE SNOW! It clumps through the rawhide thongs and piles up on top of the snowshoes, and Rolf's and my feet weigh about fifteen pounds apiece. The clammy drizzle mists our spectacles, and with the sweat of lifting our monstrous feet we fog them from the inside as well. A wipe of the bandanna reveals a little square of jungle surrounded by a high chain-link fence. This is a moose exclosure, to show what this place would look like if the moose weren't gobbling up the woods all the time. Luxuriant yew, fire cherry, and birch intertangle in a prodigious Gordian mess. Unlike the easy, open forest we've come through, with its stunted and widely spaced mountain-ash and chewed-on little firs, you couldn't walk three feet in here.

"It's food supply far more than predation that regulates the moose herd in the long run," Rolf is saying. "One problem I've got right now is that the margin of error with our moose census technique is still plus or minus about a hundred animals. So even though two years ago we showed about eight hundred moose, and last year seven hundred, and this year six hundred, those differences aren't statistically meaningful. And we can't really say for sure that the moose aren't still declining—though I believe they're not. We've been working for years on better methods of moose-counting, and we're now ready to work up a good model for predator-prey dynamics. That'll clarify a lot of things.

"The beaver data will be important too. We've had a seventy-five percent decline in the last six years, so the wolves are becoming tremendously more dependent on moose alone. Beaver used to be a big part of their summer diet. The beaver's main food is aspen, which is also declining, and wolves have undoubtedly played a role in the beaver decline. Of course, beavers do bounce back pretty fast, but with trends as they are, I can't say there's no possibility that the wolves could disappear entirely.

"Wait a second. What's that?" He has stopped short, sniffing the air. Now he points: a yellow patch on the snow at the base of a stump. "Fox scent post," he says. "Worst-smelling pee in the world."I cannot help thinking that this is a specifically lupine point of view. Wildlife biologists don't seem to like to talk about the degree to which they identify with their subjects, but most evenings after dinner we get evidence that's hard to gainsay.

Rolf Peterson and Don Glaser stand in the shrouded moonlight, tilt their heads to the sky, and from a grumble in their guts there rise long, chilling howls. They pause, and again, at an eerily wavering interval, their voices call to the wolves. All this week, the wolves have never answered. But there is clearly an exhilaration just in the attempt to communicate, and in the fact that sometimes the wolves do answer—whatever their answer may be saying.

Wilderness is dreamland. Only when the sickening chemical stench of the paper mills of Canada hangs in the mist do I half-wake and remember how ugly is the world Isle Royale has been spared membership in. And getting uglier, year by year, parking lot by parking lot. Why is it, I wonder, that ordinary dirt farmers' houses a hundred years ago looked so nice, had such a dignity and sense of proportion, and now even the rich live in ungainly sheetrock boxes? Has the price of our power—of our medical genius, our knowledge—*had* to be this desecration?

As natural beauty has withered in this generation, so has the cult of nature blossomed. Some may say this merely reflects the insistence of all elites on valuing what is rare. The cultists themselves, the preservationists, maintain that they are mounting a last defense against the death of beauty, against cultural if not biological suicide. With this view, of course, there comes an evangelical imperative.

In his book *Mountains Without Handrails*—the definitive statement of what the whole national park idea is about—Joseph Sax writes that the preservationist is a secular prophet who says, "Follow me and I will show you how to become the sort of person you really want to be. Put aside for a while the plastic alligators of the amusement park, and I will show you that nature, taken on its own terms, has something to say that you will be glad to hear."

The parallel to religion is apt. The modern nature-lover goes to the wilderness in search of a kind of religious awe, and he also must work under the same handicap as other true believers, namely, that those who are not of the cult seem determined not to understand. Tell them to get off their trail bikes and just sit still and listen till the nothing all around them slowly becomes a world? Suggest that the spiritual essence which has drained from their churches is turning up here among the silent trees? Good luck.

Nevertheless, the attuned can feel that spirit pulsing in the very air. And as is usual with enlightenment, the unattuned are many. We are all too familiar by now with the ferociously sacrilegious utilitarianism of the landlord of the cult's holy places, James Watt. And the number of those who seem, like him, never to have stood silent in the wilderness and felt nameless glory surge into their hearts is legion. It may well be that America's alienation from nature has reached the point where those who just don't care are in the majority; and the democratic consequence may be inevitable. Although the preservationists do offer great gifts to those who will join them, they remain, in the popular press and in the public mind, a Special Interest Group. That their special interest is the preservation, for all, of what is beautiful and healthful and culturally indispensable gives them only moral superiority—and you'll recall how *that* quality has fared in the history of civilization.

The imperative, therefore, is not to conquer the unenlightened but to convince them—of such incontrovertible and religion-free truths as the value of species diversity, for example. The only alternative, after all, is despair. And nature-lovers can take considerable comfort in having for ministers of their gospel the likes of Stu Croll, Don Brown, and Rolf Peterson.

IT IS THE EVE of our departure from Isle Royale. It has finally started to get cold, and for five minutes late this afternoon there was an azure rent in the overcast. A solid crust has formed on the snow, and I can stroll snowshoeless through the forest. Stu and Don head out across the frozen bay—parka-blue dots in a vastness of white. By the time we meet on the trail back to the cabin, it is almost dark, but a vivid glitter can be discerned in Don Brown's eyes. Something has happened.

Just as they were starting out, it seems, a wolf had come onto the ice. It had sniffed at the dock and trotted partway across the bay, and had turned as if perhaps it sensed the human presence. It was the first wild wolf Don Brown had ever seen; his voice is quiet, intense, reverential. The wolf had turned, and seemed to be looking at them. Then it had trotted on across the ice and vanished into the woods.

9. THE SUBARCTIC WOLF

RICHARD NELSON

I had hiked far up onto one of Indian Mountain's ridges, and I sat down on the hard snow to look over the valley below. Caribou were scattered everywhere, pawing through the drifts for feed. Suddenly a herd of several hundred began to run, first coming together and then curving toward a spur of my ridge, like a flock of birds turning in unison. I looked behind them and saw what had caused the panic—a pair of wolves coming on at full speed.

But they were no match for the caribou, who easily outdistanced them and left no stragglers. The wolves read them quickly and veered away, knowing they had no chance for a kill. Before the herd passed me, their mouths agape from the heat of their climb, the two wolves had found an old carcass and

---

were gnawing at it. I watched for a long time through binoculars as they pulled off bits of carrion, interrupting themselves
for bouts of wrestling on the packed snow. Finally they sprawled
beside one another, and while they slept I walked quietly away.
[Huslia journal, April 1977]

T H E WOLF (*CANIS LUPUS*) IS THE MASTER PREDATOR
among animals of the north, possessing intelligence
and strength, keen senses, and above all the ability to hunt coopera-
tively. Like the humans that they watch from afar, wolves multiply
their muscle and mind by cooperating in pursuit of prey, then share
the spoils. Indeed, for the Koyukon, the similarity between wolves and
humans is no coincidence—in the Distant Time, a wolf-person lived
among people and hunted with them. When they parted ways, they
agreed that wolves would sometimes make kills for people or drive
game to them, as a repayment for favors given when wolves were still
human.

A strong sense of communality, a kind of shared identity, has held
since that primordial time. Koyukon hunters still find wolf kills, left
clean and unspoiled for them, and it is their right to take what is
found. When hunters leave cached game behind they might place
some fat apart from the rest of the meat, and if wolves happen along
they are expected to take this rather than disturb what people want
for themselves. One elder told me that he does not care for killing
wolves, although he has done so a number of times. "They're too
smart," he said, "too much like people."

This remarkable and elegant animal is also given great spiritual
power in the Koyukon world, exceeded only by that of the wolverine
and the bear. It is less malevolent, less threatening, but extremely dangerous nonetheless as a spiritual being. Elaborate rules govern
people's behavior toward wolves, and severe punishment may come to
those who fail to show them proper veneration.

The wolf (*teekkona* in Koyukon) looks like an outsized sled dog,
weighing from about 75 to more than 150 pounds at adulthood, with
a uniform gray, brown, or black coat. Some wolves have dark markings
on their faces, a trait acquired in the Distant Time, when Raven
tricked a wolf-person by throwing caribou innards in his face.
Although wolves look and act like dogs, Koyukon people do not

consider the two animals relatives because they get along poorly. When dogs encounter a trapped wolf (or wolverine) they will refuse to attack it; in fact, they even keep away from wolf hides. The whole business of wolf blood in Alaskan sled dogs is vastly overplayed, incidentally. Very few successful matings occur, and on the rare occasions when they do the offspring are usually too intractable and untrustworthy to function as anything but curiosities. Koyukon people seem little inclined to involve themselves with this peculiar fantasy of outsiders.

Wolves are fairly common in Koyukon country, although their overall population varies and their movements strongly affect local numbers. It would be unusual to make a long trip without seeing at least one wolf track, however. Although wolves generally avoid settlements, they are seen or heard fairly often around the village of Hughes, apparently because the river valley is so constricted there. This proximity can be upsetting, but not because Koyukon people share the outsiders' fear of wolf attacks—they fear signs. When wolves behave strangely it can foretell misfortune. Once some wolves howled in a strange way across the river from Hughes, and someone died fairly soon afterward. Another time wolves came right into the village, and one of them was later killed when they fought among themselves nearby. This was a bad sign, and again someone died in the village a short time later.

According to the Koyukon, wolves tend to follow the same circuits around an area during winter, passing a given spot every ten days or so. They wander farther afield in February and March because it is their mating season. Often a male and female will pair up and go off by themselves, moving away from the pack until mating is over. The pups are born in a shallow den during May, and for most of the summer the pack remains nearby. These dens are used year after year, and Koyukon people know where many of them are situated.

Wolves prey on a wide range of animals, from voles to moose and caribou. One animal they apparently leave alone is man—they are too smart for that, one old-timer told me. When they kill an animal they often eat only the best parts immediately, then leave it for a while. But people say the pack will return to it again and again, even over the full stretch of winter. This makes them susceptible to Koyukon trappers, who can predict where they will most likely appear.

Kill sites are less important in hunting wolves, which people can do very effectively now that they pursue them with the fast and tireless snow machine. Even at this, wolves are often too quick and clever to be caught. A small, lean female is fastest, the hunters agree, and most likely to elude its pursuer. If a man comes near a free or trapped wolf he should never shoot while it faces toward him, because the shot will miss. One man who tried this told me that his first bullet did not fire and his second missed. Then, having seen that the taboo was correct, he waited until the animal looked away and killed it with one shot. After a rifle has shot a wolf, it should be placed in the front left corner of the house and left there for four days (Clark 1970:85).

Wolf traps and snares are set in a variety of ways, either baited or placed near carrion. Fresh kills are especially good places to catch wolves, because they will probably return fairly soon. Traps must be well set and perfectly concealed if they are to catch this wary creature. But something more is needed, because only certain people have luck for the wolf, and those who do not are rarely successful. Luck is easily lost even by those who have it. For example, a wolf should never be allowed to escape with a trap on its paw, though this sometimes cannot be avoided (this is true for wolverine and lynx as well). After this happens, the offended species may remain aloof from the trapper for years.

If someone kills a wolf that has another person's trap on its foot, the animal belongs to whoever owns the trap. In return, the trap owner should make a small payment to the one who killed it. "If he didn't, that animal would work against him. It would bring him bad luck." This also applies to the wolverine and the uncommon coyote (*Canis latrans*). I was told of one man who blatantly violated this rule, and his loss of several children over the following years was attributed to his severe breach of taboo.

Women are completely forbidden to hunt, trap, or skin wolves, a taboo that originates in a story of the Distant Time:

There was a girl who met up with a wolf, back in Distant Time, when wolves were human. The wolf wanted her for his wife, even though he had two wolf wives already. When he took her home his two wives smelled her and knew she was human. After a while she had a child—a boy—and the wolf decided to kill his two other wives. He did that, but afterward the spirits of those two wolf wives killed his human wife and ate up her insides. Since then, women are never supposed to kill wolves, and they should not work with wolf hides until the animal has been dead for a while. They must follow these rules until they are too old to have children.

IF A WOMAN should catch a wolf (or wolverine, lynx, otter) in one of her traps, a man must skin it for her. Also, while the animal is being skinned, children should stay outside the house (Clark 1970:85), though I am not sure this is followed today. I once saw a small boy try to play with a wolf hide, pulling it over him and growling like a wolf, but his parents immediately said, "*Hutlaance!*" ("It's tabooed") and made him stop.

Wolf pelts are extremely valuable today, for both commercial sale and local use. Koyukon women sew parkas, traditional boots, and mittens from this beautiful fur, but these can be worn only by men. Its most important use is for men's and women's parka ruffs—the long fur protects the wearer's face from chill winds and the hairs shed frost easily. The entire hide is used, even the head skin (for mittens) and the legs (for boots and mittens).

Wolf meat and organs are not used nowadays, but in the past the meat was eaten. The late Chief Henry told me he had eaten it, and Sullivan (1942:105) writes that the Nulato Koyukon used it in times of scarcity. I also heard of a man who eats a tiny piece of mesentery fat from each wolf he catches. Presumably there is a supernatural reason, although the person who told me about it was not certain.

After skinning a wolf, people used to sever all its leg joints, but nowadays they cut only the "knee" and "elbow" joints, either partially or completely. If they neglect this their children will become arthritic or crippled. Some people also cut the animal's brisket open and remove or expose its viscera, to avoid seeming to abandon the carcass without "using" it. Afterward the remains are placed somewhere out in the country along a trail, never burned like those of a wolverine. A man who burned a wolf carcass told me he had poor luck catching any more that year.

It is also important to put a piece of dried fish in the wolf's mouth, and to take a chunk of prized body fat from a moose or caribou, rub it on the snow, and "give it to the wolf" by burning it. While doing this a man should say, "You can go home to your father now." This ritual originated in the Distant Time, when Raven sent the wolf's son out to hunt for him. In exchange, the wolf asked that his son be given the best part of whatever he caught. And so people continue to give him special bits of food today.

On rare occasions someone comes across a dead wolf out in the wildland. When such an animal is found it is a locus of spiritual danger and must be left alone (one elder said it should be burned, but others said nothing at all should be done with it). A man told me he found a dead wolf years ago, freshly killed by another wolf, and the person with him wanted to take its hide for sale. But doing so would have caused grave danger, so he talked his companion out of the idea. Even touching such an animal may cause bad luck, illness, or some crippling malady, as people know from the tragic experience of a few who have ignored the elders' warnings. The death of this wild and powerful being without human intercession should be left completely within the omniscient domain of nature.

When we were about fifteen miles from Hughes, we saw a skinned wolf carcass alongside the trail. It was lying on pieces of wood and cardboard that kept it off the snow, probably so it wouldn't rot directly on the ground when the thaw comes. Its legs were all askew, their joints severed except for the tendons. The brisket was cut out so that we could see the animal's insides. And pushed between its teeth was a piece of dried fish.

A powerful spirit had been appeased. Yet those frozen, sightless eyes could still see; those severed, disfigured ears could hear. And so we left it to the stillness of the remote muskeg where it lay, hurrying away to the nether edge of its power.
[Huslia journal, April 1977]

10. THE IMPORTANCE OF PREDATORS

DAVID RAINS WALLACE

WHEN COTTON MATHER SAID THAT "WHAT is not useful is vicious," he made a definitive statement of one American attitude toward nature. It is a philosophical attitude as well as an economic one. For Mather and his fellow Puritans, wild nature was fallen, an abode of Satan. It could only be redeemed by domesticating it, by making it over into an approximation of the Garden of Eden, where man would rule harmoniously over peaceful and subservient animals, where, as Isaiah had prophesied, the lion would lie down with the lamb.

The Puritans found a distinctly unsubservient lion when they arrived in Massachusetts. (They thought the native puma was the same as the African lion until its lack of a mane eventually convinced them otherwise.) And the lion was only one species. The New England wilderness supported a diversity and abundance of predators, in numbers and kinds that seem a little fantastic to us today. Imagine, for example, a Massachusetts where a one-penny bounty was paid on timber wolves, as was the case in 1630, or where serious consideration was given to *fencing* Cape Cod to keep wolves out, as in 1717. One seventeenth-century author went so far as to say that wolves were "the greatest inconvenience the Countrey hath, both for matter of dammage to private men in particular, and the whole Countrey in general." Nothing was more opposite to the Puritan ideal of redemption through domestication than the predator. Not only was it a threat to livestock, but its very way of life—noisily or silently pursuing prey, untidily dismembering and devouring it—was a challenge to the entire spectrum of Puritan values: decorum, neatness, frankness, gravity. The predator was a kind of compendium of all that was undesirable in man as well as nature. Yet for us there are moral ambiguities in the Puritans' view. If the wolves who killed and ate sheep and deer were evil, what did that make the men who killed and ate sheep and deer? If killing was evil, what did that make the men who killed wolves? The Puritans' view of man and nature did not admit to such ambiguities, but in a world of dwindling wolves and growing violence and cruelty, we increasingly are troubled by them. We suspect that we have not understood the predator and the living world of which it is a part.

The Puritan attitude toward predators has been the prevalent one during most of America's history, and the rise of the United States saw a sharp decline of native carnivores. Still common in Massachusetts in 1700, wolves were extinct there a century later and disappeared from New England by the mid-nineteenth century. The wolves of the South and West didn't last much longer, though costly government extermination campaigns were required to remove the big, wide-ranging buffalo wolves from the High Plains. Mountain lions, grizzly bears, and other large predators succumbed to less systematic persecution in most of the country at roughly the same time as wolves. Smaller species such as the marten, otter, mink, and bobcat also declined or disappeared in many areas, either through direct persecution or as a result of the poisoning and trapping of wolves.

Until the 1930s, predators were not even welcome in national parks, wildlife refuges, or other nature preserves, which were conceived as retreats for "useful" animals such as ducks, deer, or songbirds. Government hunters killed so many mountain lions in

Yellowstone Park that the species has never recovered there, and Yosemite proved no refuge for the California grizzly bear, even though the park was established in 1867, about sixty years before the grizzly's extermination in that state. Predator control in parks and refuges was justified in some cases because populations of prey animals had been so decimated by overhunting by humans. But in most cases, as with the Yellowstone lions and Yosemite grizzlies, predator control simply was a general policy premised on the idea that predators were useless and vicious, an idea that many early twentieth-century scientists and conservationists, notably Theodore Roosevelt and William Hornaday (a founder of the Bronx Zoo and the National Wildlife Federation), found acceptable. (Roosevelt did urge the government not to kill *too* many lions in Glacier National Park, thus perhaps saving that population.)

There is another American attitude toward predators, historically less prevalent than the Puritans' but probably just as old, although its early expression was so sporadic that its origin is difficult to place. It is exemplified in the writings of William Bartram, a Colonial naturalist and artist, who explored the Carolinas, Georgia, and Florida in the 1770s. Bartram spent years camping near wolves, bears, lions, and alligators (18 feet was not an unusual length for alligators then), and never showed any particular dislike for them except on the rare occasions when they directly threatened him. He did, however, express considerable regret at witnessing the wanton killing of a bear cub and a wolf pup, and once he appeared thankful for the apparent forbearance of a wolf that had robbed him of some fish while he was asleep: "How much easier and more eligible might it have been for him to have leaped upon my breast in the dead of night and torn my throat . . . than to have made protracted and circular approaches, and then after, by chance, espying the fish over my head, with the greatest caution and silence to rear up and take them off the snags one by one . . . ?"

Bartram was a farmer, like most people in the American colonies, but he was also two other things that set him apart from the Puritans. First, he was a Quaker and thus inclined to take a less militant approach to the redemption of the American wilds. Second, he was an enthusiastic woodsman and hunter, and thus prone to certain ideas that the Puritans did not entertain. (Puritans viewed hunting and woodcraft much as they viewed taverns and dancing.) An imaginative hunter such as Bartram was likely to discern a certain similarity between the wolf, the lion, and himself. Because hunting was useful and good for him, it might be so for wolves and lions. Indeed, it might be so in some general way that links the lives of domesticated men and wild animals.

It is difficult to point to a seminal literary source for Bartram's tolerant attitude toward predators in the same way that one can point to the Bible for the Puritans' attitude. (The Bible was written by goat- and sheepherding people who lived in a land of leopards and wolves as well as milk and honey. Like many Middle Eastern and African pastoralists, the biblical tribes seem to have been neither enthusiastic nor adept as hunters.) Perhaps Bartram's attitude is simply a residue of the hunting-and-gathering way of life from which all human cultures have emerged in the past 15,000 years—a residue that was overshadowed by the new agricultural life, but never fully obliterated. As hunting was handed down as a sideline or sport, a set of attitudes went with it that often were at odds with agricultural ones. Bartram probably learned something of his attitude toward predators from the Creek Indians, who combined farming and hunting in an apparently harmonious way, allowing packs of red wolves (*Canis niger,* now an endangered species) to live right alongside their horse and cattle herds.

Bartram also was influenced by the so-called natural philosophers, who had been increasing in numbers and influence since the Renaissance. They saw nature not as an abode of evil but as a smoothly functioning mechanism created by a rational, beneficent deity. If predators were part of such a world, reasoned the philosophers, there must be a good reason for them. John Bruckner, a French author, proposed one in 1768 in his *Philosophical Survey of the Animal Creation:* "The effects of the carnivorous race are exactly the same as that of the pruning hook, with respect to shrubs which are too luxuriant in their growth, or of the hoe to plants that grow too close together. By the diminution of their number, the others grow to perfection."

Equating predators with hoes and pruning hooks would have outraged the Puritans, and seems overly anthropomorphic today, but Bruckner's statement is significant because it contains the germs of evolution and ecology, the scientific disciplines by which the modern world understands nature. The idea of the predator as a check on the "too luxuriant" numbers of its prey is an ecological idea, and the idea of the prey "growing to perfection" by a predator's "pruning" is an evolutionary one. Both ideas have been central to the development of biological science. Far from seeing predation as a flaw in, and threat to, the living world, Bruckner's scientific descendants have seen it as one of the creative foundations of life, a maintainer of ecological stability and promoter of beneficial natural selection.

It's not difficult to see why this benign view of predators took much longer to catch on than the Puritans' intolerant one. It's one thing for a leisured gentleman (as many early scientists were) to discern the benefits of predation on fossil horses or African zebras, quite another for a farmer to discern them in a wolf's killing of weak or sickly livestock. But the benign view did assert itself, as ideas often do, just when its opponent seemed to have won—when the Puritan ethic had killed off the big predators and was going to work on the small ones.

Quite suddenly, in the 1920s, the wolves and lions did not seem so threatening any more, or the deer and sheep so harmless. In Pennsylvania and the upper Midwest, where the last wolves and lions had been killed one or two decades before, exploding deer herds ate the woods bare and attacked crops, then starved to death in winter snow. On western range, semidesert conditions were spreading as sagebrush and mesquite replaced grassland eaten bare by sheep. The classic display of "too luxuriant" deer and livestock was Arizona's Kaibab Plateau, from which more than 6,000 wolves, lions, coyotes, and bobcats (as well as golden eagles and other raptors) were eliminated by government hunters in the first two decades of this century. Under pressure from livestock and from a deer herd that had increased from 4,000 to 100,000, "the whole country looked as though a swarm of locusts had swept through it . . . torn, gray, stripped, and dying." Government scientists such as the Forest Service's Aldo Leopold, who had promoted predator control in the Southwest while happily blasting any wolf that strayed into his sights, began to have second thoughts. The Puritan view of nature seemed turned upside-down. It no longer was the ravening jaws of the wolf that threatened the stability and safety of the world but the jaws of the lamb and the fawn. In its sudden absence, the predator began to seem a lost element of balance.

Such thoughts were not shared by the United States Congress, which in 1931 passed the "Eradication and Control of Predatory and

Other Wild Animals Act" under which our present system of federal predator control is administered. With traps and cyanide before World War II, and with Compound 1080 afterward, a vigorous campaign has been waged against predators. Its tacit goal, if one listened to livestock-industry spokesmen, was eradication from virtually all grazing lands outside national parks of any wild animal that might threaten a lamb. The campaign had almost succeeded in eradicating at least two species, the black-footed ferret and red wolf, when it ran afoul of the burgeoning environmental movement in the late 1960s. Two presidential commissions and one executive order later, the use of 1080 was largely discontinued, and the idea that predators that *weren't* killing livestock might be tolerated outside parks gained some official standing.

America is currently in a cold war with predators. Although the nation is no longer officially committed to their total destruction, predators must still contend with federal trapping and poison programs, with a fur industry that has killed more coyotes and bobcats in recent years than have predator-control programs themselves, and with the pollution and habitat destruction from which all wildlife suffers. The big predators of the lower forty-eight states, the wolf, grizzly, and lion, enjoy some official protection in areas where they've gotten rare enough to seem threatened. Whether that protection will suffice in the face of the unofficial persecution they still undergo is an open question. The West is still wild as far as predators go: many ranchers shoot first and ask questions later. The livestock industry recently has succeeded in forcing the Environmental Protection Agency to permit a return to the use of Compound 1080, citing a population explosion of coyotes (in fact, federal studies do not show a substantial increase in numbers of coyotes).

Meanwhile, the question of predators' usefulness or lack thereof has acquired some recent complications that seem a little ironic. On the one hand, scientific studies have cast some doubt on the ecological importance of the predator's "pruning" role. For example, Paul L. Errington's studies of mink and muskrats in Iowa marshes showed that numbers of muskrats are influenced much more by social and environmental factors than by mink predation. Errington found that a nucleus of healthy muskrats with access to food and shelter was virtually immune to mink attack (he even found a fat muskrat and a mink occupying different rooms in the same lodge), and that mink were dependent for prey on surplus muskrats that wandered outside this "zone of safety." In effect, muskrats regulated their own numbers as strong individuals excluded weak ones from food and shelter. One also might say that muskrats controlled *mink* numbers, rather than vice-versa, since mink could not prosper unless enough healthy, safe muskrats were breeding to produce a surplus.

Such studies cast new light on the extreme deer overpopulation near the turn of the century, suggesting that other factors than a lack of predators were at work. Deer found an unprecedentedly large supply of browse in the logged and burned forests of the early twentieth century, and they are more tolerant of crowding than muskrats, so their populations might have exploded even if predators had been present, although the explosions wouldn't have been so disastrous. The most recent theories suggest that predators *can* contribute to a reduction in prey populations, but usually only after a population has begun to decline on its own and many are weak from disease, starvation, or other stress.

The classic enemy of the predator, the American farming population, has undergone a drastic decline of its own in the past half-century, under pressure from an industrial economy that views land not as a potential Eden but as raw material. In a sense, the "usefulness" of the farmer is in doubt. The effects of this on the human-predator relationship are difficult to predict, since nothing like it has happened before. Adaptable predators such as the coyote and raven have benefited from depopulation of marginal farming districts, reoccupying them or, in the coyote's case, moving in for the first time. In prime areas such as the Midwest, however, industrial farming is becoming so efficient that virtually no wildlife is left on which predators can live. Should the industrial economy ever conclude that predators are bad for business, furthermore, its arsenal against them would be infinitely more formidable than the family farmer's. If certain trends continue, both farmer and predator may find themselves "useless" in a landscape of machines and robots that has no similarity to wilderness *or* Eden.

Such a prospect leads one to wonder if the predator–farmer conflict is such a necessary one. If both are threatened by a robot world, they must have something in common. How, after all, did the Puritans prevail in New England? Although they disapproved of hunting, they did not hesitate to practice it. One might say they prevailed by being better predators than the native ones. The conventional notion of the predator as some largish bird or mammal that steals chickens is a biological caricature. Chickens are predators too, as anybody who has seen them go after a snake will agree.

Predation is much more central to life than Cotton Mather, or even John Bruckner, could have imagined. It lies at the root of evolution. Animals very likely never would have evolved beyond a rudimentary, algae-grazing protozoan if some hadn't begun preying on others. The complex food chains that make up modern ecosystems never would have come about. Whether or not plant-eaters *need* to be "pruned" by predators, they *will* be pruned. If we killed every hawk and owl in the world, for example, evolution would start filling their abandoned niches with other species. Birds that now prey on small rodents and songbirds for a part of their diet—jays, crows, ravens, shrikes—would start to do it more. Most predators are, of necessity, quick learners.

Every time we exterminate a predator, we are in a sense creating a new predator. When we exterminated the wolf in New England, we created the New England coyote. We could control the wolf fairly easily because its highly developed social structure put a ceiling on its population growth. It's not so easy to control the coyote, which is more anarchic in its breeding habits. Scientists have estimated that 75 percent of a given coyote population would have to be killed every year for fifty years to exterminate that population. Even then, other coyotes probably would come in from elsewhere. They like to travel.

Predation is a larger phenomenon than our notions of usefulness. At least, it is larger than our *quantitative* notions of usefulness. The biggest, fastest computer won't tell us if predators are costing us more by eating livestock than they are saving us by eating rodents. The dynamics of predation are too complex and variable for the bottom line. As Paul Errington said: "Nature's way is any way that works." Our notion of usefulness usually has been quantitative, concerned with getting enough to live well on. If we value life on this planet, however, and we choose not to turn our eyes away from it—as the Puritans turned their eyes toward the heavens and the industrial economy turns its eyes toward outer space—we need a large notion. It is not only the quantity of things that sustains us here but the *quality* of them.

Indeed, it is the quality that mainly sustains us. We need not simply food but *good* food. When we speak of preserving wildness in the world, we are speaking of preserving quality. Isn't it presumptuous to say that we must preserve wildness in a world that is now, and is likely to remain, largely ice cap, ocean, desert, muskeg, and tropical bush? Wildness has its negative as well as its positive side: a mountain stripped bare by logging, grazing, and erosion is not less wild than it was before its "development," it merely is less good, of lowered quality. Wildness is a fundamental condition of the biosphere, which we can "preserve" only in a qualitative sense. We have no choice about wildness, but we *can* choose between the wildness of the Norway rat and the pariah dog and that of the rabbit and the coyote.

Quality is a standard by which predators have readily discernible uses. They do improve the health and vigor of prey by weeding out sickness and weakness. Perhaps more important from a human viewpoint, they are beautiful, both in themselves and as part of the landscape. An Ohio pasture is more beautiful, more alive and interesting, with a fox on it, as an Alaskan mountain is more so with a wolf on it. Even a garden is more beautiful with a cat in it—an unredeemed predator if there ever was one. I get much more enjoyment from watching coyotes in the hills around this valley than from watching deer. The coyotes simply *do* more. They play with bones, hide them from each other, peer curiously into the river, chase deer for the fun of it. There is something almost deliberately comical about a coyote doodling along through the digger pines and blue oaks with its tongue hanging out and its eyes almost closed. It seems to smile, happy with its raffish life.

Of course, qualitative values tend to be more debatable than quantitative ones. That coyotes kill ground squirrels is still a more convincing argument for their existence than their beauty is. To many people, sheep ranchers included, coyotes are not beautiful. They aren't always beautiful even to me. It's interesting how much wider a range of emotion a real animal in the wild can evoke than a filmed or caged one. Coyotes tend to look kind of cute in films—bright-eyed and bushy-tailed, as the saying goes. Along the craggy, shaggy old Eel River, they can look pretty rapacious, like highly resourceful killers, which of course they are. But then, there's a beauty in rapacity and resourcefulness too, in a gnawed deer rib cage on a sun-baked gravel bar.

A good, long look at any hunting predator can make you glad

there aren't too many of them at the same time it makes you marvel at their strength and grace. Fortunately, the biosphere decrees that predators always must be rare in relation to prey. There always are more plant-eaters than there are meat-eaters because plants are the basic form of food. The prey controls the predator because it is closer to the source of life. A predator capable of exterminating its prey soon would be an extinct predator. It's not easy for a coyote to catch a gopher or jack rabbit. I've seen them try; I haven't seen them succeed. (I watched one coyote in British Columbia that seemed to be having trouble enough catching a butterfly.) There has to be a lot of prey around so that the hard-working predator occasionally can hit the jackpot. One of the reasons the coyote is common is its willingness to take a wide variety of prey. Less adaptable species such as the mountain lion, which preys mostly on deer, can be ghostly in their rarity. I've lived four years among one of the densest lion populations in California, and I haven't seen one.

If there is one quality I value most in the mountain lion, in fact, it is rarity. Lions may be useful in pruning deer populations, promoting deer eugenics, and adorning the landscape, but none of these things excites me quite as much as the thought, every time I go into the hills, that *this* might be the time I finally run across one. Cotton Mather would have found this frivolous, but I don't think it is. Our inquiring primate minds need the novelty and stimulation of rarity. We need to feel that there is more to the world than we know.

11. SPIRIT OF THE HILLS

DAN O'BRIEN

SIMMONS WAS GETTING MORE pressure. More calls about the "wolf" in the Black Hills. He'd said it a thousand times, "Can't be a wolf, hasn't been a wolf in the forest for decades, closest ones are in Canada, and they're gray wolves." He said it as nicely as he could. He told the three ranchers who called him directly; he told the state senators who called on the special state telephone; and he told his boss when he called from Denver, "Damn near impossible, longest shot in the world." And besides, he was doing all he could. He already had the only real wolf trapper left in the United States out looking for answers. What more could he do?

There was nothing more that Mel Simmons could do, but it still bothered him. There was something special about a wolf, or just the thought of a wolf. Scared the pee out of people. Could be, he thought, being scared of wolves was genetic. People have been scared of wolves since the ice age, but they are not just scared that wolves will do damage or even that they'll kill people. People are scared because somewhere, way back in their Pleistocene consciousness, they remember or sense that, when the ice descended from the north and man was forced to learn to prey on the large mammals of the snow cap, man at this latitude was rivaled for dominance by the wolf. The truth of the matter, as Mel Simmons saw it, was that people panicked when they heard the word "wolf," because they are not truly convinced that the struggle for dominance is over. In man's primordial mind he is still not certain that his brains have beaten the wolf's brawn, that he is truly the most ruthless predator ever to roam the earth. People, Simmons thought, must still be afraid that the wolf is in the running. Why else make them the villain they are not? Vicious killers they are not. Ghoulish eaters of human flesh they are not. They're just animals making a living the same way they've made a living for millions of years. Besides all that, there were no wolves in his state, certainly not in his forest. Simmons said it once more, this time to himself.

But, as certain as the nonexistence of wolves in his state was the definite existence of politics. Who did these people think they were to put pressure on him to catch a wolf that didn't exist? They'd have to pass a law creating a wolf before he could catch it. But Simmons knew politics. A person didn't get a job like his by being ignorant of the workings of government. He knew that if this wolf notion continued, he'd be called upon for answers to some pretty silly questions. He might even have to make a trip to Medicine Springs to lend the whole thing a bit of officialism, make it look good. With a little luck, old Egan would clear it up in a week or so. In the meantime, Simmons dug out a bibliography of wolf literature and had his secretary see what the state library had that was current.

"CAN YOU SAY definitely that that is a wolf's tooth?" Bailey said to Egan.

Egan took the dog's head in his hands and held it up to the light. He looked at the tooth from every possible angle, stared at it a long time. "No," Egan said, "I can't say for sure."

"How about the hair?" Stockton said.

"I'm asking the questions," Bailey said. "How about the hair, Egan?" Again Egan looked closely. He rolled the strands between his fingers.

"Can't say for sure," he said.

"That's wolf hair," said Stockton.

"Shut up," Bailey said, turning on Stockton. "Just keep quiet."

"Could this be a wolf's tooth and this wolf's hair?" Bailey said.

"Yes," Egan said.

"Okay." Bailey was trying to be thorough. "Is it possible that the story that old Joe told Jerry is true?"

"Forty years ago it would have been," Egan said. "Wolves killed domestic dogs every chance they got."

"So you're saying that it's possible that there really is a wolf?" Stockton said.

Bailey waved him quiet. "There's been too damn much jumping to conclusions already," he said. "Joe could have had that stuff since he was a boy."

"It's a fresh skull," Egan said.

"Joe doesn't lie," Stockton said.

"You can't tell, Jerry." Bailey looked back at Egan. He picked up the skull. "Could a wolf, or anything else, do that?" He pointed to the tooth jammed through the skull behind the eye socket of the dog. "That was a hell of a big dog," he added and hefted the skull.

Egan looked at the skull again. "A big wolf could have done that," Egan said. He took the skull from Bailey. "A damn big wolf," he said.

An hour later the three men were bouncing down a dirt path that led to Joe Standing Elk's sheep camp. Neither Stockton nor Bailey were sure that they could find it, but they knew about where to look. It was hot, and Bailey noticed that Egan looked uncomfortable. He turned on the air conditioner, which blew dust at first. When the cold air came, Bailey sat even farther back in his seat and let the coolness hit him square in the face. Outside, tiny mirages, the first of the year, wiggled in the draws and tested their elasticity on the sides of the hills.

Joe's tent was right on the edge of the Hills. The pine trees rolled up behind the camp to the ridge that marked the beginning of the mountains and the end of the prairie. It was a neat camp. The tent was an old military-style hexagonal with a single ridge pole and three-foot side walls roped out to rails that Joe had lashed to dwarf pine trees. The stove wood was stacked beside the tent flap which was tied shut, and on the rocks around the camp and hung from the closest trees were tools and equipment. A bucksaw, wash pan and towel, lead rope and hobbles, an ax, even small lengths of rope were coiled and

hung in the trees safe from pack rats. Fifty feet from the tent the old
Indian had built a shade house. It was entirely pine and all freshly cut.
It had not been warm enough to need it yet, but apparently Joe was
getting ready for hot days they all knew were coming. The uprights of
the shade house were four trees. He had cut the tops off and used the
thick pine branches to lay across the rails he'd lashed to the trees. It
was twenty feet square and shut out all direct sunlight from above. In
the center of the shadow created by the roof of pine boughs was
an old kitchen chair. Joe had evidently established his summer
resting place.

The three men stood in the middle of Joe's camp. Egan felt
uncomfortable at being in another man's camp with the other man
gone. Stockton was fascinated and moved from place to place looking
closely at Joe's possessions, picking them up occasionally and rotating
them in his hands. Bailey showed no emotion. He simply scanned the
horizon for some sign of where the old Indian could be.

They had been in camp for only a half-hour when Bailey called to
them that he saw Joe. By this time Egan had found a comfortable
place to sit, on a rock, at the edge and above the camp. He had seen
the old Indian five minutes before, letting his horse pick his own way
home through the sage and yucca, but there had been no reason to
call to the others. Led by two sheep dogs, old Joe was coming; there
was nothing that could, or should, be done to hurry him. When Bailey
called back to them, Stockton was untying the canvas strings that held
the tent flap shut. There were three strings, and Stockton had unfas-
tened them all. Hearing that Joe was coming, he hurriedly began to
tie the strings back together. He was looking over his shoulder in the
wrong direction as he tied and managed to tie the bottom string on
the left to the top string on the right. Egan watched him from his
rock. When Stockton noticed what he'd done, he quickly began untying them again. But instead of calmly untying the knot, he jerked at it
until it was tight, then began to struggle with it. Joe was still several
minutes away, but now Stockton panicked. He looked over his shoulder again, then turned and stared for an instant. When he turned
back to the tent flaps, he had evidently given up on untying the knot.
With jerking movements and an air of finality he tied the bottom
string on the right to the top string on the left. His hands flew away
from the knot like a calf roper shooting for a ten-second time. As
Stockton walked away, Egan looked at the strings tied in an X across

Joe Standing Elk's doorway and shook his head. Then he climbed down off his rock to meet the Indian whose dogs had begun barking and circling Bailey.

Joe Standing Elk was indeed the old kind of Indian, like the Indians Egan had known in his youth. Joe was full-blood, Egan guessed, or very close. The color of his skin was much darker than the average Indian, and his hair, except for a touch of white at the temples, was very black and straight. He rode a short stocky horse that was as woolly as one of his sheep—it had not yet begun to lose its winter coat. His bridle was woven leather. Egan guessed that Joe had made it himself, and over the saddle was thrown a wool blanket. The saddle was invisible except for the wooden stirrups that hung below the red woven border of the blanket. Joe spoke softly to the dogs from his horse, and they both scurried to their place beside the tent and curled up, laying their heads on their tails but watching the strangers with solid black eyes.

Joe dismounted, tied his horse, and loosened the cinch before he turned to the men. He nodded Bailey a hello while Stockton jabbered. Once on the ground he looked older, the deep-cut lines in the face showing years, but giving no hint of how many.

Bailey and Stockton began to quiz him. It started out orderly, with Bailey asking the questions in an official, precise way. But Stockton insisted on interrupting the questions. "You said you saw it," Stockton said.

"Yes."

"Now hold on," Bailey said. "Let me get some background."

"Phoo on background. The man says he saw a wolf."

"It's easy to make mistakes. I just want to be sure."

"It killed his dog," Stockton said, and turned to the two curled beside the tent.

"Jerry." Stockton turned to look at Bailey. "Shut up, okay? Just for a minute?"

Joe was looking away from the two men, toward his tent. "Now, Joe, I know you told Jerry you saw a wolf, and I'm not saying you didn't. I just want you to describe what you saw to Mr. Egan here." Bailey pointed to Egan, who had been standing thirty feet away.

"Christ, Junior, he's an Indian. You think he doesn't know a wolf when he sees one?"

"Shut up, Jerry."

"You have no reason or right to tell me to shut up."

Bailey's face began to turn red. "I'm the goddamned sheriff of this county, and I'm trying to get to the bottom of this deal, and you're only making it worse." Bailey and Stockton were nose to nose now. Bailey's face was red, and Stockton was obviously shaken. "Now," Bailey said, "if you don't mind, I'm going to ask a few questions of Mr. Standing Elk."

His voice had calmed, but when he turned, Joe had moved away. Joe Standing Elk and Bill Egan stood under the shade house, the kitchen chair between them, looking directly into each other's faces. The old men talked. They nodded and held their hands up to subtly express themselves. Outside the shade house the sun had begun to get hot. Bailey and Stockton began to sweat but didn't join the two under the pine boughs.

When they finished talking, they nodded to each other, and Egan came toward the other men. Without a word they followed him as he passed and got into Bailey's car. On the way back to town Stockton asked Egan what Joe had said. Egan was facing front, sitting beside Bailey, who was driving.

"He said a lot of things," Egan said, and went on before Stockton had a chance to push him. "He said there is evil in the Hills and more coming every day. He's afraid there won't be enough good men to fight it."

"Is that all? Just superstition?"

"No," Egan said. "He said he wanted me to catch the wolf. And he wanted to know who had been in his tent."

12. WOLVES

JOHN HAINES

THERE WERE WOLVES IN THE COUNTRY, BUT

they too were more like shadows—a track now and then in the thin fall snow, a distant voice, a shape in the moonlight. There were not many of them in those years, the caribou having long since left that part of the country. Once they had been common, and I was told that Canyon Creek two miles west of the homestead had in early days been called Wolf Canyon because of the numbers of wolves that were sighted there. My old neighbor, Billy Melvin, swore to me that one night a large pack of wolves had gone down Banner Creek in deep snow, so many of them that the trail they left behind was firm enough to drive a team and sled over.

In mid-October of one year I killed a big moose on Cabin Creek, and left the four quarters cached upon a few poles and concealed under a heap of spruce brush. It was hard-freezing weather, and I had no fear of the meat spoiling. A few days later my wife and I and one of our dogs returned from home with a block and tackle to hang up the

"Wolves" is reprinted from The Stars, The Snow, The Fire *by John Haines. Copyright © 1989 by John Haines. Reprinted by permission of Graywolf Press.*

quarters. An inch of snow had fallen in the meantime, and everything that moved on foot left its mark to be seen.

Within three miles of the cache I found a large, fresh wolf track in our trail. It was joined by another, and then another. Three wolves were going before us, heading toward Cabin Creek. We walked on more quickly as we saw that their tracks remained steady in our trail. I began to worry that they would find our cache—in my imagination I saw our winter's meat exposed by the wolves, fouled and half-eaten. Leaving the dog with my wife, I hurried on ahead as fast as I could with my pack and rifle, going nearly at a run over the frozen moss.

When I reached our small cabin on the hill overlooking the creek, I stopped and carefully surveyed the brushy flat where I had killed the moose. No sign of the wolves. I went on down into the creek bottom to the meat cache. Sure enough, the wolves had found it, and their tracks were all around in the fresh snow. One of them had climbed on the brushpile and pulled away a few of the boughs. But whether they had been spooked by our coming behind them or had found the cache unnatural and therefore dangerous, they did not touch the meat. All three of them had left the cache and gone up the creek toward Shamrock divide. That afternoon and the next morning we dragged the heavy quarters to the hill behind the cabin, and hung them high from a rack between two spruce trees. Neither wolf nor lynx nor anything else bothered the meat that winter.

And once on a cool and overcast September afternoon when we had gone to the river to check the salmon net, we heard what might have been a short cry, and saw a brownish wolf loping upriver on the dry sandbars.

There was no ravenous wolf pack in full tongue chasing the dogsled homeward, nor a ring of bright and famished eyes waiting beyond the bivouac fire to be kept at bay by a blazing brand flung now and then into the darkness; nor from the darkness yelps and whimpers and the smell of singed fur—or so a story went that I read once many years ago.

But listen. One winter night I was awakened by something—a board in the housewall cracking in the frost. I got out of bed, went to the door and looked out the window to the cleared slope beyond the yard. Deep snow and bright moonlight lay on the hillside. I saw four dark shapes there, moving slowly uphill toward the timber. My field glasses were hanging from a nail close to the door; I quickly reached for them and put them up to my eyes. In that bright light I saw the wolves clearly—three of them grey and white, and one nearly black in the lead.

They did not stay long in the open; the timber was close, and they were soon absorbed in its shadows. But one of them paused for a moment and looked down toward the cabin, arrested by the rattling of a chain as one of our dogs came out of his shelter to look. Though it stood half in the shadow of the birches, I could see clearly the intent wolf face, its eyes and small ears, and the grey coat of fur standing thickly in the mottled moonlight. And then it too was gone. I opened the door and stood briefly in the cold on the open porch. But there was not a sound in that moonlit stillness.

The next morning when it was light I walked up the hill and found their tracks in the snow. They had come up from the river, crossed the road not far from our cabin, and gone up through the woods toward Banner Creek. The snow was loose and dry, and the wolves had plowed through it, each one leaving a shallow trough behind him. It was only in the hard snow by the roadside that I found a pair of firm, clear prints, and knew without question that they had indeed been wolves and not the phantoms of sleep.

Once before on a bright spring afternoon one of our dogs woofed and pointed its muzzle toward the river. Down there on the glittering, windswept expanse of snow we saw five wolves traveling downriver. I thought at first they might be a family of coyotes, but when I looked with the glasses I saw that they were too large and heavy-bodied. At the sound made by our dog, three of them halted and looked up toward the house. It was a long rifle shot even with a scope, four hundred yards or better, and steeply downhill into that sunny glare; I was only briefly tempted to try it. The wolves went on, trotting swiftly over the hard snowcrust, and were soon out of sight around the bluffs. Our four dogs barked and howled, but no answer came from the river.

Something like an answer came one night toward spring a few years later. We were awakened by a sound coming faintly through the walls of the cabin, like a distant singing. We got out of bed, and since it was a mild, clear night we went outdoors and stood in the snow to listen.

Far across the Tanana, a mile or more to the south of us, a group of wolves was singing. I call it singing, not howling, for that is what it was like. We could distinguish three, perhaps four voices—wavering,

ascending in pitch, each one following on the other, until they all
broke off in a confused chorus. Their voices sank into distant echoes
on the frozen river, and began again. A light and uncertain wind was
blowing out there, and the sound grew and faded as the air brought it
toward us or carried it away southward. It might have come across a
thousand years of ice and wind-packed snow, traveling as the light of
stars from a source no longer there.

The singing was brief, a few short minutes. Chilled by the night
air, we turned to go back indoors. Night, a breezy darkness, claimed
the icebound river, and the only sound was the distant throb of a
diesel rig on the road toward Fairbanks.

13. TRAILS IN THE SNOW

TOM WALKER

I

ON A TUNDRA CARPET OF AUTUMN GOLD WITH JUST a hint of pink dawn on the high peaks of the Brooks Range we shot a heavy-antlered moose. A fine morning: antlers to keep and winter's supper.

The three of us made short work of the butchering and one-and-a-half-mile pack to camp. Dusk found the meat pole bending under the weight of quarters and boned meat draped in cheese cloth. A cold, light breeze discouraged the few black flies that feebly buzzed the meat, but not the gray jays that even in the fading light pecked at the bloody cloth.

Darkness came, the breeze remained constant. It was joy to be in camp, moose meat hanging on the pole. We roasted tenderloin speared on willow sticks over the spruce fire that sparked and popped in front of our drawtight tents, pitched on the old campsite above the lake. The fire, though hot, could not keep the chill at bay.

"Trails in the Snow" is taken from Shadows on the Tundra: Alaskan Tales of Predator, Prey, and Man *by Tom Walker. Copyright © 1990 by Tom Walker. Reprinted by permission of Stackpole Books.*

It felt colder than the twenty degrees registered on the pocket thermometer.

The roast meat, surfaces burned and blackened, the insides pink and moist, tasted spicy and sharp, strong with the flavor of woodsmoke. We gorged and drank from a pail of throat-numbing creekwater, the ice jangling when a cup dipped in. Later, satiated, alone in deep thought, I sat staring into the flame and coals. The wind faded but the cold came alive. A spruce round chucked into the coals sent a storm of sparks upward into the ink of the new-moon sky. The ragged peaks to the north, lost earlier in the blackness, loomed now against a growing green backlight. In minutes the light grew into distinct bands: three immense waves flashing south, ghosting the ground in fevered light.

Horizon to horizon the sky writhed with descending patterns so intense it seemed that I could reach out and touch them. At times the aurora masked the outlines of Orion and the Great Bear, the light fading here, then there, only to brighten with a rush and snap elsewhere.

How long the wolf had been howling before I heard it, I couldn't say. Old sourdoughs speak of *hearing* the aurora. Perhaps in this time and place the cry seemed part of the moment and was missed. Only when the second wolf, then a third, began to howl, did the hair on my neck prickle and chills flutter on my spine. I came wide-eyed to my feet, staring north over the tall aspens, straining to see shapes coursing the muskeg. From out over the tundra and lake the wind blew through the willows, bringing the howling sharp and clear. Four, five, perhaps six wolves moaning in the night. I dropped wood on the fire and stood tense, watching, listening, the wind-tears streaming on my cheeks. Still louder came the howling, long, deep notes sung in unison. Now, for sure, closer.

All at once they stopped, leaving the night, the mother of fear and mystery, to the snap of fire in wood and sky. I waited. Silence. I looked up. The aurora had gone, the stars again blazed crisp.

Later, shivering in my sleeping bag, I tried to sleep, but despite the protests of my aching muscles, I lay awake listening to every twig and wind sound, my eyes wide to the stars and cosmic light.

A few mornings later I sat on the rocky knoll behind camp, glassing the flats beyond the lake. Its riffled water sparkled in the first light. Just as the light slanted full onto the tundra, two flashes of white streaked from the timber. A white wolf and a gray ran full out into the daylight as if pursuing something. Near the lake they slowed to a walk and came softly through the reeds to the strand, stopping side by side to drink.

I shall never forget that image. The shimmering water, the dancing reeds, and the two wolves, tails and fur curling in the wind, all bathed in amber dawn light. So indelible the image, I can still see the white wolf raise its head to scent the air, water dripping silver from its muzzle. I can see the wolves turning to nuzzle each other with tongue-lolling, laughing jaws. Then they turn away from the lake to dart back across the tundra and into the timber.

Moments like these forever charged that place with a special excitement. East of a fork of the Koyukuk River, on the southern edge of the Brooks Range, that valley, which I found quite by accident, came to be known to us as the Wolf Fork. For there, in that remote place, on an unnamed tributary, I stumbled on a wolf denning valley—a place where wolves bred, whelped, reared their young, and taught them to hunt.

To the north and east of the Wolf Fork rise the high peaks, and to the south and west the foothills of the mountains Bob Marshall called the Range of Blue Light. North and west on the ridgelines Dall sheep roam. In the spruce stands and willow thickets live moose, some bulls with outsized antlers spanning seventy inches or more. Although shy and seldom seen, grizzlies wander both alpland and forest, their tracks the only usual sign of their passing. (Sometimes late at night, sounds outside the tent hold imaginary menace. Shadows turn into bears.) Ptarmigan, spruce grouse, and snowshoe hares live here, as well as the grayling and char that fin the clear waters.

People also live seasonally in that seventy-five-square-mile valley. Just below where the Wolf Fork storms through a narrow gorge, two partners and their summer hands slave after the gold that collects in quantity on the shallow bedrock. Except to kill an annual moose, and shoot bears that wander into camp, the men grub the gravel too compulsively to pay much attention to their wild neighbors.

The Wolf Fork was remote and seldom-visited until an army of men came to build a span of oil pipeline on the very western edge of the valley. The event would change forever not only the valley but Alaska as well. The army of boomers and stiffs, by accident and design, changed the ways of wildlife, offering food sources too tempting to resist. Shy grizzlies grew bold, and losing all fear of humans, they menaced pipeline crews, remote villages, and mining camps. The iron and steel tornado passed, but the bears stayed, boldly entering any camp or habitation, seeking the easy pickings that sealed their doom.

And the miners dealt with them. On the Wolf Fork, as elsewhere, grizzlies that came into camp were erased with the crack of gunfire. One summer the miners shot eight grizzlies, bears turned dangerous by their proximity to man. The bears were buried in deep holes dug by D-8 Cats. Two years later, there were no bold bears to shoot.

Across all the valley and beyond ran the wolf pack. On almost any night there you could hear the wolves singing. Sometimes we'd see them, pups and adults alike, coursing the tundra or ghosting through the woods. Just for the chance to watch, I searched for the den. My hunt brought close contact, but the den remained an elusive prize.

The first time I saw a wolf there, Vic Zarnock and I were waiting on the edge of a gravel strip for the plane that would take us back to Fairbanks. We'd been hunting sheep in the mountains for a week, and Vic had killed an eleven-year-old, loose-toothed ram. I was dozing, leaning against my pack of gear and meat, when Vic pointed and said: "Look." There, not forty yards away, stood a vole-red wolf. It held our gaze a moment, then turned and paced down the gravel bar. Vic jumped up to rummage through his backpack for his instant camera. Finding it, he hurried off through the brush parallel to the wolf. A moment later he emerged from his crashing "stalk" and with a loud metallic *click* startled the wolf into a lope. Vic trotted back, a satisfied smile on his face. "Got him," he said, flipping the camera back into his pack. I could not speak.

By the following autumn, additional sightings had confirmed that many wolves lived in the valley. One day that second fall I got more than the usual fleeting glimpse. I'd climbed a bluff behind the miners' camp to glass the remains of a moose the men had killed for winter's meat. The gutpile was hidden behind a line of willows, but circling ravens and darting magpies gave it away. In the afternoon, returning to the lookout from a hike, I glassed again and this time spotted three wolves approaching the kill.

The wolves were in vigorous action, running in and out toward the remains. They'd dart in, then leap away, all acting in concert. In graceful high leaps and bursts of speed they seemed to taunt something. Then they came together and stood still. Moments passed with

little movement until one wolf leapt into the brush; the others stood
quiet, watching. All at once the two erupted into action, charging into
the brush at a full run. At equal speed all three wolves rushed back
into the open with a grizzly in full pursuit. One wolf limped and fell
behind, but just as the bear seemed close enough to pounce, the
other wolves darted in long enough to allow the injured wolf time
to get away. The chase went for many yards before a second bear
came running from the brush. The fractured pace allowed the second
grizzly to catch the first, but instead of joining forces to attack, both
bears stopped to watch the wolves sprint out of sight.

In the running fight, the wolves never really closed with the
grizzlies, but only came near. A grizzly may be quick, but no bear can
match a wolf.

The grizzlies stomped around for a while, bluff charging in the
wolves' direction but soon beelined back to the kill.

Several times I saw and heard the Wolf Fork pack, usually at a dis-
tance but sometimes at close quarters. Once, hiking with John
Thuma, I came face to face with a white wolf. We stopped to stare.
The wolf stared back a moment before slipping away into the willows.

No matter how often one sees wolves—it is never *often*—the
response is invariably the same: surprise mixed with confusion, then
adrenalin-rush. First: "Oh, a dog." Then: "No, you idiot, that's no *dog*,
that's a . . . " The excitement is intense.

That was the way of most close contact. A brief look, then nothing. One of the miners, though, had a slightly more interesting experience. On that same trail, near the same spot, he too came on a wolf
that moved quickly into the brush. He walked on. Looking back, the
miner was startled to see the wolf following. If he hurried, the wolf
hurried. If he slowed, the wolf slowed. A strong man more accustomed to the roar of diesel engines than the silent glide of a wolf, he
later admitted to fear. ("I didn't know what the damn thing was going
to do.") The situation twisted wildly out of control when, turning a
bend in the trail, the miner saw a grizzly walking toward him. ("*Good
lord.*") Into the brush and up a spruce he climbed. The snapping
branches startled both wolf and bear. Fifteen feet up he looked back
to see the two animals staring at him. What he felt when the grizzly
suddenly bounded toward him, he didn't say, but he climbed until
there was no more tree to climb.

The wolf went the opposite way when it saw the bear charge. The grizzly evidently never saw the wolf. He muttered and paced below the tree until near dark, then wandered off, allowing the miner to descend. The miner said the walk back in the dark aged him ten years.

One morning I saw six wolves. Don Schumaker and I had stayed in camp late that day, waiting for the windy rain to slacken. About nine o'clock the weather started to improve. While Don wrapped a swollen ankle, I climbed the lookout knoll by camp. Almost at once howling began, seeming to come, as it often does, from near, then far, then near again. Time and again I looked out over the bluffs, tundra, and river flats, yet I couldn't locate the wolves.

Long after their song began, I spotted the wolves a half-mile away to the south in a spare black-spruce thicket that sloped down to the river. Two adults with three nearly grown pups pointed muzzles skyward: five sounding like twice the number. For twenty minutes they howled, then stopped. The largest wolf, a gray, walked away from the pack and sat watching to the east. All the wolves seemed to listen for a while, but in time the other adult joined in a rough-and-tumble with the pups, tossing and wrestling on the lichen and moss.

Minutes later the gray adult jumped up and trotted east, head low, tail wagging briskly. The others stopped to watch. A huge black wolf came rushing toward them through the scrub brush. The gray and the black met, the gray fawning. The pups were soon on the pair, two crawling forward to rub against the black's neck and chest. The other adult did not approach. The five pressed tightly together, jostling and nudging with tails waving. The big wolf leaped from the mêlée and ran off uphill, leading the entire pack from sight.

I have never witnessed the wolves make an actual kill, though once through the spotting scope I saw four wolves chasing a cow moose. I imagine that the cow escaped, for she seemed to be pulling away from her pursuers as they went from view.

Once I stumbled on an hours-old moose kill. The bull's hams were rent and bloody, and great chunks had been torn from the viscera. Not at all a clean kill: the moose had bled to death. I backtracked a quarter-mile and lost the trail where the moose had come splashing from the river. Bloodstains painted the sand and rocks. Wolf tracks blended with splayed moose prints. On an incline where the bull had stumbled, I found large stains and tufts of hair.

I bent over the moose and traced the lacerations in the hide and muscle, putting my hands into the wounds. I rubbed the dry blood away to feel the jagged edges of ribs bitten through. It seemed impossible that teeth could shear half-inch moose hide, tendon, and bone. I groped into the chest, passed where the great lungs once had been and cut loose the remains of the heart. Big slices were missing from the lower half, only the tops of the atriums were left. The heart was dry.

I have not been back to the Wolf Fork in six years. From what I hear, there's no reason. The new park, Gates of the Arctic, forced the hunters east into the wolves' denning valley. The country changed. The moose went fast, the wolves soon after. I'm sure some animals remain but it wouldn't be the same. I choose to remember it as it was: big racks moving through the timber and ethereal howls rising under auroral curtains.

14. A CHORUS OF WOLVES

JAN DeBLIEU

SHORTLY AFTER FOUR O'CLOCK ON the morning of October 2, Chris Lucash and George Paleudis rumbled past the caretaker trailer at Pole Road in a telemetry truck. It was the day after the day they had awaited all summer; not just two but now eight wolves were free to wander the swamps of the Alligator River. Despite misgivings, Phillips and his staff had fitted the wolves at Point Peter, Pole Road, and Phantom Road with capture collars two days before. Just in case, they had also put conventional radio collars on two of the males. Then, on October 1, they had opened the door to all three pens.

The preceding weeks had been full of uncertainty as the engineers at 3M rushed to build six more functioning capture collars by Parker's deadline, the end of September. No one was sure how long the collars would continue to work, since their batteries were operating at peak capacity. But the final barrier to the wolves' proba-tional freedom had been removed. From this point on, every mile-stone in the project would be measured from autumn 1987.

Lucash and Paleudis were too numbed by exhaustion to feel the elation they had expected. Paleudis was a wiry man, small but strong, energetic, and a bit brash. He had graduated from college in June and immediately gone to work as a wolf caretaker. On this morning both he and Lucash were exceptionally cranky. They had worked until eight o'clock the previous night, and then they had been too keyed up to sleep. Easing their way around ruts and potholes in a truck with a broken muffler had done nothing to sooth their weariness or improve their moods. As Paleudis pulled up to the intersection of Pole and Phantom roads and turned off the engine, Lucash motioned to the telemetry receiver. "Help yourself," he said. Paleudis made a face, slipped on the headphones, and began rotating the large antenna on top of the truck.

At 1:00 A.M., when Phillips had last checked the wolves' location, all the animals had been in their pens. The signals from the wolves in the Phantom Road pen, a half mile to the west, should have been easily audible. Paleudis could hear nothing. He checked the fre-quency settings and antenna connections. Nothing. "Something's weird," he said. "They're not there."

He pulled off the headphones and handed them to Lucash, who was more experienced as a tracker. Lucash tuned the frequency dial to the setting for the Phantom Road male and spun the antenna slowly in a circle. To the northeast he heard a faint high-pitched pulse. "They've moved," he said, surprised.

If the Phantom Road wolves had begun to explore, perhaps the wolves in the Pole Road pen had, too. Intrigued, the men turned the truck east, retracing their way. The signal for the Phantom Road male grew stronger; although Lucash could not tell for sure, it seemed to be coming straight from the north. Paleudis eased toward the care-taker trailer until Lucash motioned him to stop. The Pole Road pen was directly north, but the signal for 211, the Pole Road male, was strong from the east, from the road in front of the truck. "I don't believe it," Lucash said. The Phantom Road pair had run the Pole Road wolves off their home turf.

Both men sat for a minute in surprised silence. In captivity the frisky Pole Road male had seemed much more dominant than the Phantom Road male. But with the opening of the pen doors all rules of behavior had been redrawn. "Look down the road," Lucash said. "I bet the Pole Road wolves are sitting in the middle of it. I bet we see 'em." In reply Paleudis started the truck and eased slowly ahead. The vehicle lurched and bumped along, its headlights flashing into the trees. Paleudis had driven only a few yards when a pair of topaz eyes appeared. It was the Pole Road male, running right at them.

"Chris," Paleudis said, "I don't feel very good."

The wolf was clearly not frightened of the headlights or the unmuffled roar of the truck. Behind him the trackers could see the fainter glint of the female's eyes. She seemed to want to follow her mate, but she was hanging back, unsure. If Lucash and Paleudis had been hunters gunning for wolves, they would have had two easy marks. Fifteen feet from them, the male turned and trotted off toward a broken-down Ram Charger, parked fifty feet away. The female followed.

Paleudis turned off the engine and sat, silent, incredulous, and very, very tired. If the wolves had retained a shred of the species' natural wildness, he thought, they would have bolted into the underbrush at the first sign of humans. As the animals neared the Ram Charger they reversed direction and trotted back toward Lucash and Paleudis. Twenty yards from them the male suddenly slowed, then turned and ran back up the middle of the road.

It was the last thing the young biologists had expected; they had not the faintest idea what to do. The animals continued to trot between the two vehicles, cautious but more curious than afraid. Lucash muttered cynically that they looked like pet dogs. Finally the male, wandering toward them, moved into some grass at the side of the road. The female refused to turn aside. She walked up to the left bumper of the truck, sniffed it, crossed the road, and came alongside the door on the passenger side.

Lucash was ready. He flung open the door and leapt out, screaming and clapping his hands. The female, caught off guard, skittered sideways into the cane grass on the shoulder of the road. It was too dark to see her, but Lucash could tell by the rustling stems that she was crouched within ten feet of him. He started toward her, kicking hard into the grass, and heard the soft sound of stalks being crushed as the female lay down. She reminded him of a dog that had been beaten until its spirit had shattered beyond repair.

OVER THE NEXT two weeks, reports of wolf sightings poured into the refuge office:

On October 3 Phillips and some trackers saw the male from Phantom Road running down the middle of a road. He ran clumsily and refused to duck into the bushes, although the trackers followed him for a hundred yards with the horn blaring. "It was pathetic," Phillips said. "We could have run him over."

A man walking along a dirt road saw a wolf briefly and reported that the animal disappeared into the brush very much like a deer.

On a road deep in the refuge, a man in a truck noticed a wolf running forty yards in front of him. He followed it for a mile, until the wolf collapsed on the roadside, exhausted. It lay there panting while he pulled up next to it.

A couple driving on the highway south of Manns Harbor saw a wolf in the middle of the pavement "acting like a lost German shepherd." They stopped, but it refused to move until they honked their horn.

A hunter was walking down a path when a wolf swam across a canal, climbed the bank, and strolled up to him. The regular hunting season did not open until the middle of October, but the refuge held a brief season for muzzle loaders earlier in the month. The man assumed the animal coming toward him was a pet German shepherd, since it had a large collar and seemed so friendly. When he noticed the darts in the collar, he realized he was eye to eye with a wolf. He shouldered his gun and began to yell. The wolf cringed and walked away sideways, its tail between its legs.

As far as Phillips could tell, the sightings included every one of the six wolves just released. The animals did not seem to understand that trucks and cars could harm them. More discouraging, a few of them were not at all frightened of direct contact with people. Maybe they could be trained to be warier. Lucash, Paleudis, and Phillips started carrying rifles loaded with cracker shells so they could haze any wolves that refused to move off the roads. The male at Point Peter had taken to lingering along the shoulders of the main highway. Unless he could be taught to keep off the pavement, it was only a matter of time until he was hit.

And it was only a matter of time until hunters from Manns Harbor began to encounter wolves. When the regular season opened October 13, Taylor had the roads through the preserve posted with small pink signs. RED WOLVES ROAM FREE ON ALLIGATOR RIVER NATIONAL WILDLIFE REFUGE, they read. PLEASE REPORT SIGHTINGS. Below was a warning that anyone caught harming a wolf could be fined $100,000 and sentenced to a year in jail.

Phillips grew noticeably tense. It seemed to him that the wolves had started moving off the roads more quickly when they were approached by cars. The frequent sightings continued, and it was conceivable that the hunters from Manns Harbor would make good their promise to put out traps or deer carcasses laced with strychnine. Still, he was gratified by the number of calls he received from local residents who had seen the wolves. Most of the callers sounded concerned and excited to have spotted such rare animals. Toward the end of the first week of hunting he had begun to relax a little. For the time being, the delicate balance of tolerance between the wolf and the human population of the Dare County peninsula appeared to be holding.

BUT THE LARGEST problems still lay ahead. In the excitement of the latest release, the trackers had not had much time to monitor the activities of the wolves at South Lake. On October 15 the male was spotted by a motorist just north of Highway 64, the major road west from Manns Harbor. To reach the highway he had walked seven miles around the lake. When he encountered a canal a few yards north of the road, he stopped. For several days he lounged on the canal bank, picking at a dead fish and ignoring the trackers, who fired at him with cracker shells to try to drive him back into the woods. On October 18 he began moving slowly east along the canal toward Manns Harbor. Four miles separated him from the houses on the outskirts of town.

Phillips, though concerned, had another, more immediate crisis at hand. The female from the Phantom Road pen had left her doting male behind and taken to wandering. By October 19 she had meandered south for fifteen miles. Early that morning she crossed the refuge boundary and ventured onto private farmland.

The terrain was no different, except a bit drier. No livestock ranged there that she could kill. But she was off federal property. Phillips and John Taylor decided she would have to be captured and returned to Phantom Road. Parker, who happened to be in town, concurred.

Early that afternoon, Parker, Taylor, Phillips, and two refuge staff members set out with nets, catch poles, telemetry sets, and, in case the capture collar did not work, two air rifles loaded with tranquilizer darts. Lucash and Paleudis had taken a rare day off to go fishing. Before driving south, Taylor posted another staff member, a Manns Harbor resident named Jim Beasley, in a truck along Highway 64. No one really expected any trouble from the South Lake male. But if he began to move toward town, Beasley was to radio for help.

Shortly after seven o'clock Lucash and Paleudis stopped by the refuge office to make a phone call. The two-way radio was on, and they could hear Beasley calling Taylor and Phillips, who were apparently out of range. Lucash grabbed the mike. "What's going on, Jim?"

"We got, uh, a situation here. He's at the post office."

In the previous three hours, the South Lake male had walked to the fringe of Manns Harbor along a ridge north of the highway. Beasley could do nothing but call for help and follow. By seven-thirty the wolf was walking between houses, sniffing at flower gardens.

It was just before dark. Lucash keyed the mike and called loudly for Phillips. The radio in the office was more powerful than the one in Beasley's truck, and there was a chance the capture party would hear it. No reply. Lucash reached behind Phillips's desk and grabbed one of the triggering transmitters used to fire the darts in the 3M collars. He called into the mike a last time. To his surprise Phillips answered, his voice urgent and broken by static. The group had given up trying to catch the female and had started back. They were a little less than an hour from Manns Harbor.

Jim Beasley was a friendly, talkative man who, like most Manns Harbor residents, was well known to his neighbors. As he sat in the parking lot of the post office holding a small telemetry antenna, he could not help but attract attention. By the time Lucash and Paleudis arrived, three local men had stopped to see what Beasley was up to. One claimed to have seen a wolf on private property. The men leaned against their pickups, muttering among themselves. Lucash started to set up the triggering transmitter, but changed his mind. Neither he nor Paleudis believed the capture collar would work, and there was no sense trying to fire the darts in front of an audience.

By then the wolf was circling through a pecan orchard across the road. Beasley drove slowly out of the parking lot, turned into the driveway of a house next to the orchard, and let Paleudis out. Paleudis carried a hand telemetry set—a small receiver, a set of headphones through which he could hear the beeping radio signal, and a two-foot-high antenna that looked like a chopped-off television antenna. He inched his way around the side of the house, holding the antenna in front of himself like a divining rod. The signal grew stronger. In the weak light of dusk he could see the wolf running back and forth along a fence on the edge of the orchard. He wished he had carried the trig-gering transmitter; the wolf was only fifty yards away. Suddenly the animal ducked through a gate and disappeared into a trailer park. Paleudis groaned.

He walked back to the post office to find that the capture party had arrived. Phillips was talking tersely to Beasley. Taylor, though calm, was clearly worried. The Fish and Wildlife Service had no legal right to set foot on private property without permission, even to catch a wolf, and Taylor did not want anyone to get hurt. Parker wandered nervously from man to man, asking each what he thought. No one had any clear plan. Ideas tumbled out to be picked up, turned over, dropped, and picked up again. All agreed that they needed to stay poised and quiet; they needed to catch the wolf with little ado.

The easiest thing would be to try firing the darts in the 3M collar. Parker and Lucash crossed the road on foot and made their way to the fence on the edge of the trailer park. Lucash propped the trigger-ing transmitter on a post and dialed the code to open communication with the computer in the collar. "Oh my Lord, I hope this works," Parker prayed. "I just wish it would work, if only this one time." The computer was supposed to respond with a long beep, signaling its readiness to fire the darts. But the transmitter remained silent. They would have to try darting the wolf with air rifles.

Paleudis and Beasley, meanwhile, had followed the wolf into the trailer park. Walking along with the headphones on, Paleudis sud-denly picked up a strong, pulsing signal from an open pasture. If they could corner the wolf in the pasture they might get several clear shots at him.

Now the men split into two teams, each with a radio tracker, a marksman, and two other people to run interference. Parker and Taylor carried the guns. Both were skilled marksmen, but both were also nervous. If they hit the wolf in the head or the belly, the tranquil-izer in the dart would probably kill him.

The teams moved quickly through the pasture, toward a small

pond where the wolf had stopped to rest. The wolf, sensing trouble, began to pace. The radio signal that betrayed his location glided back and forth, a restless ghost. Parker, sneaking through some tall grass, thought he saw movement in front of him. Squinting hard, he made out a dark profile within fifty feet, a reasonable shot. He brought the gun to his shoulder and fired. The wolf, untouched, skittered to the west.

Taylor, Parker, and most of the other men ran back to the trucks, hoping to catch up with the wolf and drive him farther west, away from town. Beasley and Paleudis, left behind, looked at each other, bewildered. With both dart guns now hundreds of yards away, there was nothing for them to do. "I just hope the wolf doesn't come back this way, because we're not going to be able to do anything but sit and watch him come," Paleudis grumbled. He paused to listen to the signal. "I just hope . . . Hey, I think he is; I think he's moving back here. Hey, you guys, he's coming this way, fast."

In a sudden burst the wolf dashed for cover, running far around Paleudis, darting into the pecan grove. Beasley had called for help on a two-way radio he carried, and Lucash and Phillips pulled up just as the wolf bounded into some brush next to a house. They were forty feet from him, with no gun. Phillips reached for the triggering transmitter and dialed several commands to the computer in the 3M collar. No response. He got out of the truck cautiously and skirted the house with a large salmon net, thinking the wolf might see the net and freeze. As Parker and Taylor drove up, the wolf exploded from the brush and turned toward an open sand quarry. Paleudis sprinted after him, with Parker and Beasley at his heels.

The quarry was east of the pecan orchard and farther off the main road. Slowing down, Paleudis could see lights from several trailers on its edge. Parker and Beasley caught up, breathing heavily. The signal moved toward the trailers, and half a dozen dogs began to bark.

The night had taken on a surreal quality. What had been a small knot in Paleudis's stomach solidified into a dull ache of dread. The three men walked quietly toward the trailers, catching glimpses of the wolf as it paused to sniff at a bush or a tree. As Parker neared a trailer, the back door flung open with a loud bang. "Who's out there?" a man's voice called gruffly.

"It's just some of us from the Fish and Wildlife Service," Parker drawled in his most friendly tone. "We heard there might be a wolf roaming around back here, and we just wanted to check."

The man peered out into the darkness, grunted once, and said he had a brother who worked for Fish and Wildlife. He admonished Parker to be careful—didn't he know he could get shot, sneaking around like that?—before ducking back inside. Paleudis sighed in relief.

A dirt road ran from the quarry to the main highway. As the men moved away from the trailers, Parker saw the wolf standing in the middle of the road, looking back at them. He drew up his gun and fired. The wolf bolted, crossed the highway, and disappeared into a thickly settled section of Manns Harbor.

HAROLD BUTLER WAS settling down to watch television about ten o'clock when his teenage son glanced out the window and saw a strange profile in the front yard. "Daddy," the boy said, "there's a red wolf outside."

"No there's not," Butler said, even as he got up to look. But there it was, standing in the driveway sixty feet from his doublewide trailer. "Huh," he said, opening the front door and stepping out. The wolf looked at him and walked slowly away, toward the road. With a flashlight, Butler could see the wide collar with the two darts sticking up. It was a red wolf, all right. His three hunting dogs were barking loudly, and over the racket Butler could hear voices and a truck. Hesitant, he started down the drive. A gunshot sent him scrambling behind a bush for cover.

The capture party, in disarray, had begun cruising the roads through town, trying to stay on public right-of-ways instead of running through yards. Occasionally, Parker ventured down driveways or back alleys, getting off another several shots. Once he thought he had hit the wolf in the base of the tail; the animal seemed to slow down a little, but still eluded them. All the group could do was ride through town and wait for a stroke of luck. And luck had appeared, momentarily, when the wolf paused in Butler's yard.

As Butler recalled the incident later, the men from the Fish and Wildlife Service tried to downplay the seriousness of having a wolf loose in the neighborhood. "They kept telling me things like, this animal's almost like a pet and we know where it is all the time. They gave me the impression it had been hit with a tranquilizer and it'd be down any minute. Then they started coming through my yard with their . . ." —he stopped to grope for a word—"their detectors and stuff."

For the moment, though, Butler had no choice but to go back inside, grumbling about what he might do if the wolf threatened one of his children. The capture party checked his yard and left. But an hour later Butler glanced out his window and saw the wolf sniffing his daughter's bicycle, which was parked ten feet from the trailer. Angrily he grabbed a revolver and burst out the front door, firing in the air as he stepped off the porch. As the wolf fled he went back inside and called the sheriff.

Phillips, Lucash, and Paleudis were riding together when they heard the shot. "That's it," Phillips groaned, "that's it. We're looking for a body."

Taylor was the first back to Butler's trailer. He and his wife were on the front steps, waiting for the sheriff. "What happened?" Taylor asked as calmly as possible. "Did you hit the wolf?"

"No I didn't hit the wolf," Butler retorted. "I didn't try. But I damn sure might if he gets near my property again."

A few minutes later two deputies arrived. Parker and Taylor, embarrassed and worried, apologized for the commotion. The deputies' presence, they knew, would draw even more attention. But with the officers standing by, they could stalk the wolf aggressively, even on private property. They regrouped and hatched another plan. The wolf was holed up in a yard next to Butler's. Parker and Taylor, each accompanied by a tracker, would try to box the animal in, until he could be darted. Everyone else was to stay on the road. Tired and discouraged, the group had little faith that the plan would work, but they had no other ideas.

Parker and Taylor moved toward the wolf carefully, shining flashlights on bushes, fences, outbuildings, cars. If the animal had been hit by a dart, he showed little sign of it now. The signal drifted through a side yard as if he were sizing up the advancing men, looking for a way out. As the biologists closed in, he burst forward, slipping neatly across the road, running toward Pamlico Sound.

Paleudis, standing near a patrol car, saw the wolf move into a grassy yard. "He's here," Paleudis hollered, "you guys, he's over here." The shouts brought Parker running.

Near a grove of trees the wolf paused to look back at his pursuers. As he turned, Parker was on him. The dart gun fired a final time; the wolf flinched, fled through the trees, and collapsed near the water.

"I'm amazed someone didn't get hurt."

"My goodness, yes. There was a lot of potential for trouble."

"But it was our worst-case scenario, and we got him, we got him."

No one had much gumption for work the next day. The South Lake male had regained consciousness and was curled up in a kennel with a bowl of dog food. The day before his release he had weighed seventy-two pounds, but in four weeks he had dropped to sixty-one pounds. Parker and Phillips came to work prepared for a flood of phone calls, but received only a few, mostly from reporters. No one pressed them about why the capture collar had not worked; with the wolf in custody it did not seem to matter.

The mood of the wolf crew was grim, and there was still the problem of the Phantom Road female, loose on private property to the south. Phillips had hoped she might wander back north, but she had settled into thick forest and not moved even a quarter of a mile. There was nothing to do but try to corral her too.

Around noon the following day another capture party assembled near a dry woodland twenty-five miles south of Manns Harbor. The group included the people who had worked to catch the South Lake male, plus a couple of extra refuge staff members and me. The wolf was holed up in an old cypress grove that had been logged forty years before. In the decades since, gum, oak, and bay had pushed up past the cypress knees and the stumps that had been left to rot. Looking into the woods, I could see skeins of cat brier and stands of a thorny plant known as devil's walking stick. I wondered how an animal could make its way through such vegetation without getting badly cut.

Farm roads edged the grove on the west and south. From the strength of the radio signal, it seemed likely that the female was resting only a hundred yards from where the roads crossed. "This is good; this could be real easy," Phillips said when all the members of the party had arrived. The rest of us looked dubiously at the wall of undergrowth that awaited our attack.

"Here's what I thought we'd do," Phillips continued crisply, dropping to a crouch and picking up a stick to draw in the dust of the roadbed. He made an X to mark the intersection. "We'll send several people in this way," he pulled the stick along one road, "and some more from this other road. They'll form a semicircle behind the wolf and try to drive her out so we can get a shot at her." It sounded like a reasonable plan, although any number of things could go wrong.

I pulled on a jacket to protect against briers and picked up a hand radio. Lucash and I were to work our way in from the west. Before we set out, Phillips issued a final warning over the radio. "Be careful to watch for holes where the cedar stumps have rotted away. They can be deep and treacherous." He did not have to remind us to watch also for poisonous snakes.

Bay and oak swayed high above us, and the air smelled richly of humus. We thrashed our way into the woods, jogging in short bursts to break through bushes and vines. Fragments of sunlight brightened the orange pine straw that was scattered thickly across the uneven ground. I jumped onto a log and followed it through brush as far as I could, then hopped off and chose another, feeling clumsy and slow. Fifty yards in I was directionless; if not for the distant breaking light that showed where the road had been cleared, I would not have known west from south.

I pushed through the undergrowth for what seemed a long time. Lucash, wearing a telemetry set, was only fifteen yards behind me, but I kept losing track of him through the branches and vines. A bush crackled in front of me, and I saw Beasley waving his arms to get my attention. With two other people beyond him, the semicircle was in place.

"She's fifty yards that way," Lucash called, slipping off the head-phones and waving one arm. "Go to your right, slow."

If the wolf decided to run between us, there would be no way to stop her. We turned and began working our way toward the road, drawing the circle closed. I moved in front of Lucash slightly, stepped off a log, and fell through humus almost to my waist. By the time I had extracted myself neither Lucash nor Beasley was in sight. I started forward hesitantly, but stopped when Lucash appeared through some vines. He waved to me to backtrack around him.

"She's right . . . Dammit, the signal keeps fading. She's right in here." His voice trailed off as he stepped down from a small rise toward a tight ball of myrtle. I ventured closer, brushing away branches. The slivers of sunlight had begun to play tricks on my eyes. In that one small patch of roots and limbs were dozens of places where a cinnamon-colored wolf could hide. I combed carefully through some bushes, wondering what I should do if my hand fell on wolf hide.

"Here she is. I see her." Lucash was half diving under branches and downed logs. "Move around slow—real slow—and help me block her off."

The Phantom Road female had flattened herself into a hollow formed by the exposed roots of a large oak. Her body was pressed into a bank of dirt directly beneath the trunk. I moved slowly into position beside Lucash and peeled off my jacket, holding it in front of me, hoping to block her only avenue of escape. She had tasted freedom, and she could still bolt. Instead she buried her face in the roots and turned her back to us. "Steady, girl," Lucash said edgily.

But she had no intention of moving. As we waited for the nets and catch poles and, finally, the kennel—the trappings of a life she had supposedly left behind—the wolf began to shake, and a deep sadness descended over me. She was beautiful, with her short, tawny fur and her alert, elegant ears. Her instincts had served her well; without the trickery of telemetry we never would have found her.

The men arrived with the kennel. Lucash and Phillips pulled the wolf from beneath the tree, staying clear of her jaws. They dumped her into the upturned kennel, snapped the door closed, and hauled her unceremoniously to a waiting truck.

THAT FALL AND WINTER of 1987–88 was one of the hardest periods the men and women who worked on the red wolf reintroduction would ever face. The recapture of the Phantom Road female stripped us of any naïveté. We had known all along that the wolves might wander, and that under law their movements would have to be restricted. What we did not anticipate was how quickly one would leave the refuge, and how cunningly wild she would behave when we arrived to bring her back.

I was not part of the full-time staff for the project, just an occasional helper. Within weeks after all the wolves were released, however, I had begun to wonder how much the reintroduction could accomplish. The cypress grove where the Phantom Road female had chosen to hide was dry, full of good cover, and right next to farm fields that attracted rabbits, rodents, and deer. In contrast, the land within the Alligator River refuge was some of the swampiest, most

inhospitable in the region. It was the kind of land the wolves themselves would probably avoid if given their pick of places to roam. Was
it fair to restrict them to such marginal habitat and expect them to
thrive?

Yet, Phillips reminded me, the wolves were being granted a
chance to live in a facsimile of freedom, which was more than they
had been granted in the East for a hundred years. By December they
were seldom spotted from the roads. And slowly they began to show
evidence of being able to kill prey larger than rabbits and raccoons.
The first clear sign came in mid-November when Phillips, sorting
through samples of wolf scat, found the remains of a hoof from a
young deer. The scat was from the Pole Road male.

Shortly after their release, the Pole Road wolves had reasserted
themselves and driven off the Phantom Road male and his wandering
mate. They took to traveling south of their old pen and swinging
north in a regular circuit, sticking to a well-defined home range. The
change in their behavior was nothing short of remarkable. They were
acting like wild wolves.

The toothless male at Point Peter and his mate seldom strayed far
from their pen. The wolves at South Lake were not so sedentary. After
his capture in Manns Harbor, the male was taken back to the South
Lake pen, locked in for ten days, and let go. Three weeks later, trackers found him within a mile of Manns Harbor, looking thin and worn.
They set out traps and caught him easily. A few days later they also
trapped the female at South Lake, although she had never shown any
inclination to seek out human settlement. Phillips replaced the two
collars on each of the wolves with the radio telemetry collars he had
favored using all along.

The South Lake wolves were taken to a marsh twenty miles south
of Manns Harbor—far enough, Phillips believed, to keep the male out
of trouble—and let go. In mid-December the female was found dead
on a nearby beach. An autopsy concluded that she had died from an
infection of unknown cause.

The Phantom Road male, abandoned by his wandering mate,
stayed in the vicinity of Pole Road for most of October. Trackers frequently found scat and long scrape marks on the roads where he and
the Pole Road wolves were vying for territory. On November 8, after
the Phantom Road male had not moved for several days, Lucash and
Phillips trapped him. He had been bitten in the neck several times
during a fight. Without medical treatment he likely would have died.

After her capture in the thick forest south of the refuge, the Phantom Road female was held for several days in her old pen and released. Again she wandered far south, but this time she proved even more wily. When a group of people tried to surround her in the woods, she ran neatly around them and disappeared. Although somewhat chagrined, Phillips was pleased by her wild behavior. He and Lucash set traps for her and caught her two days later.

The Phantom Road wolves were reunited in captivity in mid-December. It is impossible to say how they may have reacted to each other, but one thing seems clear: neither was happy to be caged while the Pole Road wolves were running free. Over the next two weeks, the Pole Road pair visited the Phantom Road pen frequently enough to wear a path around the outside.

The day after Christmas, Phillips, Lucash, a volunteer named Marcia Lyons, and I drove to Phantom Road to check on the doting male and his wandering mate. The female's foot had been cut when she was trapped, and the wound had not shown signs of healing. Phillips, concerned that it might need stitches, had arranged for her to be taken to be examined by Larry Cooper, the veterinarian. It was cool and rainy—pneumonia weather, someone called it—but the biologists had celebrated Christmas together, and we were all in good moods. We reached the pen about midmorning.

The wolves were in one of the small wooden houses, lying tightly together. Lucash popped the roof off, shoved the male to one side with the end of a catch pole, and slipped the noose around the neck of the female. He remarked that she seemed unusually listless. As we grabbed her shoulders and began to pull her out we all gasped. Her left front foot was gone, and the leg had been stripped of flesh. All that remained were blood-streaked bones and tendons, swinging free.

"Bring her up, get her in the kennel," Phillips barked. We had frozen, but his words brought us back; we lifted together and swung her as gently as possible into the cage. Phillips latched the door, turned the kennel on its side, and leaned on it, breathing as heavily as if his lungs were about to explode. My own chest felt as if it had been rammed by a timber: I wanted to cry but couldn't find my way past the shock of what I had seen.

Later, Lucash would discover a bowed section of fence where the female had leapt against it, probably as a gesture of threat against the Pole Road wolves. One link of the fence was lined with bits of fur and flesh, dried by the cool winter winds. The female's foot must have gotten caught in the link, and the Pole Road wolves had pulled the leg through and attacked it.

Just then, though, there was no ready explanation. Lucash and Phillips picked up the kennel, carried it to the truck, and slid it into the bed. As I stood by the tailgate the Phantom Road female looked out at me, her almond eyes glazed and without spark. It occurred to me that I had never before looked a wolf directly in the face.

"Honey," Phillips said, his voice raspy with emotion, "you're outta here."

THE PHANTOM ROAD female was euthanized by Larry Cooper that afternoon. Her value to the red wolf project had been in her wildness, and while she might have survived with three legs the biologists agreed that only the healthiest wolves should be part of the first reintroduction.

In the spring of 1988 the biologists released two more female wolves, a yearling and a two-year-old, to replace the South Lake and the Phantom Road females. They were chosen for release with the thought that younger animals might be less tolerant of people and cars. In mid-April, the Point Peter wolves began spending large amounts of time around the farm fields within the refuge, which were several miles north of their pen. For a week they marked the dirt roads in the area with large scat and deep, obvious scrapes. After that, the female kept to one small thicket, moving little if at all. It was classic breeding behavior. At exactly the same time, the Pole Road wolves stopped traveling through their territory and confined their movements to a dry hardwood grove, as if they were digging a den. No one had expected the wolves to breed the first season after their release, but Phillips, Lucash, and Paleudis grew cautiously excited.

In late April, the Point Peter female abruptly moved back to her old pen, as if she had lost her litter. Through mid-May the biologists watched the dirt roads carefully for the small round tracks of pups, but found none.

One morning Phillips was flying low over the refuge when he spotted the Pole Road wolves. The budget for the project had been increased, and he had started radio tracking from a plane several times a week. The wolves trotted briskly along a dirt road, paying little attention to a small clumsy animal that followed. From the air the pup looked young—too young, Phillips thought, to be away from the den—but it moved quickly, and the parents seemed to trust it would keep up. If any others had survived, they were out of sight.

Near the end of May, the toothless male at Point Peter was hit by a car and killed. Phillips decided to put out meat supplements for the Point Peter female, just in case she was caring for young. And indeed, one Saturday the female was seen moving slowly along the highway with a pup too small to travel through the brushy pocosin. Phillips blocked traffic in one lane, until the female could escort her pup safely across the road and into cover.

With the two births and the two new releases, the number of free-ranging wolves stood at nine. In mid-June, however, the male that had wandered into Manns Harbor the previous fall was hit by a car. A short time later, the Pole Road female returned alone to her old pen. She crawled inside, stuck her head halfway into one of the wooden houses, and died. When the biologists found her body, she weighed less than thirty pounds. An autopsy showed that she had contracted a uterine infection, probably after she had given birth.

She and her mate had been by far the most self-sufficient of the wolves in the wild, and the favorites of the wolf crew. No one had suspected she was sick. And, now the biologists could only assume that her single pup had starved.

"YOU'VE GOT TO WONDER," Chris Lucash said, "whether this project is ever going to go anywhere."

We were sitting in a tavern on a late June night lamenting the fate of the wolves. One of the young females, released at the South Lake site, had just been retrapped after she began making nightly trips into the small community of East Lake. She was being held in a new complex of pens. Her intended mate, the old Phantom Road male, had wandered from South Lake into the outskirts of Manns Harbor and had been recaptured without incident. Phillips leaned far back into a booth with a preoccupied look on his face. Paleudis stared dejectedly at the table.

"We talk to the locals," Locash continued, "and they tell us we're crazy to put wolves out there because of the chiggers and ticks and deer flies. Then hookworms start showing up in the scat. They've probably got heartworms too. There are hardly any foxes out there;

the locals say they can't survive. How the hell can we expect wolves to make it?"

"It isn't all that bad," Phillips interjected, "but I don't think this place is ever going to be anything more than a showcase."

I asked what he meant.

"There's no way we're going to have a viable population of wolves out there. We don't have the room. South Lake obviously isn't a good area for wolves, probably because there isn't enough prey. We've put four wolves there, and three of them have left. Based on what we've seen so far, these wolves depend on roads for travel. And on the south end there are more roadless areas.

"Now, maybe a pup that's born and raised in the wild will be able to move through the woods better. But for now we can only conclude that not as many wolves can be put on the refuge as we originally thought. We're going to have a heavily managed population, with animals being moved in and out for genetic diversity. We're probably going to have to supplement them, too, not just with food but with heartworm medicine, for example."

We were all silent for a few minutes. From the beginning we had known that the red wolf project was being watched by wildlife scientists nationally, and that a failure would not bode well for the release of predators elsewhere. What constituted failure, I wondered.

"If nothing else," Phillips said, "at least the public has learned a lot about the problems involved with saving endangered species. If this project goes belly up in five years, and people are asking why the federal government spent so much money on it, we'll at least be able to point to the educational value. I would argue that increasing public awareness is one of the most important things you can do to save endangered species."

As the biologists continued to talk, I thought about the original objectives of the project—the plans to use the capture collars, and to confine the animals strictly to the refuge. By spring the capture collars had all been replaced with conventional telemetry collars. I had never been comfortable with the concept of the capture collars; it was based, it seemed to me, on two contradictory promises. The devices were not supposed to change the animals, or inhibit their wildness, in any significant way; yet they were also supposed to keep the wolves under a constant thumb. One could not expect to have both.

When the wolves arrived in North Carolina in 1986, biologists had predicted that the refuge would hold thirty to thirty-five healthy, free-ranging adults and pups. The number had since been scaled down to between ten and fifteen. It occurred to me that Phillips was right; with so few wolves, the Alligator River project would be little more than the skeleton of a wild population. I had not expected the project to turn out like this. I had not anticipated that the species would be faced with so many demands to behave in a manner acceptable to human society. Neither had it occurred to me that wolves would be rotated in and out of the refuge like interchangeable parts.

During the time I had spent getting to know Phillips, I had heard him talk several times about conservation as a slow, incremental process. He was optimistic; he predicted that wolves would eventually live in North Carolina without an edict restricting them to public land, maybe even without radio collars. But I was growing impatient. In the bleakness of that night, I tended to doubt that the red wolf project would ever accomplish much more than it already had.

FOR THE REST of summer and into the fall the biologists concentrated on analyzing the telemetry data they had gathered since the release of the wolves. Much of their time was also spent caring for the animals in the new pens, built in a dry, piney grove known as Sandy Ridge. There was talk of making Alligator River a second major breeding center for red wolves. A number of animals had been brought to the refuge from Washington State on the understanding that they would not be released that year, if at all.

Parker had reduced the time he spent at Alligator River and was looking for other areas where the red wolf could be reintroduced. In the autumn of 1987, a pair of wolves had been flown from the Washington breeding center to South Carolina, where Parker hoped to start a new program on Bulls Island. He had decided that the best way to cultivate wild behavior in red wolves might be to free them at a very young age. The recovery team had agreed to let him experiment with releasing two-month-old pups on the island.

The wolves bred in their pen on Bulls Island that spring, and in July they were released with two pups. A few weeks later, the mother was killed by an alligator; but the father and pups adjusted easily to freedom and seemed to have little trouble learning to hunt. If all went well over the winter of 1988–89, Parker planned to move the Bulls

Island pups to the refuge in North Carolina. The father would be trapped, paired with a new mate, and freed to raise a second litter in the wild. In this way, Bulls Island would become a training ground for young wild wolves. Parker also hoped to release wolf families on barrier islands off the coasts of Florida and Mississippi.

One cool October afternoon I drove alone to a remote site near a series of clear-cuts on the south side of the Alligator River refuge. Phillips and Lucash had driven down earlier in the day with some volunteers and John Windley, a biological technician on the wolf crew.

That evening we were to hold a vigil for the Pole Road pup. Although we all had assumed the pup had starved after the death of its mother, in midsummer Phillips spotted it from the air, tagging along after its father. For weeks the biologists would find no sign of it, then someone would come across its prints or glimpse it from a plane. Recently Phillips and Parker had decided the pup was large enough to wear a radio collar, and plans had been made to trap it.

The thought of handling the pup intrigued everyone. Phillips needed only two helpers to set the trap lines and check them during the night, but more than a truckload of us asked to go along. Just before dark we assembled at the intersection of two dirt roads, a little less than a half mile from where Lucash and Phillips had positioned the first trap.

A half moon lit the hazy sky and illuminated the furrowed bark of two great pines beside the road. Their trunks, thick black shafts, rose straight and branchless for fifty feet. I took a seat in a truck with Phillips, Lucash, and Windley and settled in for the night. Each trap had been equipped with a radio transmitter that was designed to start beeping when the jaws sprang closed. Every fifteen minutes Phillips pulled on a set of headphones to listen for signals.

We were on edge, but pleasantly so, like children waiting in the dark for unknown treasure. We traded jokes, shared bag lunches, and slapped lazily at stray mosquitoes. Eight o'clock came, then nine. Windley remarked that the prime time for catching the pup had passed; the wolves were usually most active at dusk and dawn. "You going to stay out all night, Mike?" I asked.

"As long as it takes," he replied with a yawn. The Pole Road pup was not likely to be wary of traps, and he expected to catch it by morning.

A military jet passed low overhead, its tail lights flashing red and green. Its vibrations startled me. Normally the jet activity ended at dark. In the distance we could hear the low rasp of lasers being fired. "That pilot just spent more on one bombing run than the wolf project will see all year," Phillips said, disgusted.

We waited, mostly silent. It occurred to me that our quarry, being raised utterly wild, was one of only two such red wolves in the world. No human had ever touched it. The thought of it wearing a radio collar saddened me. But hunting season had just opened, and Phillips believed a collar might protect the pup somewhat from poachers. The refuge was not open wilderness, I reminded myself.

Without speaking, Lucash eased open the door of the truck and stepped outside. I caught the door before it closed and followed him. The night air, though damp, was cool and refreshing on my face. Across a canal I could see nappy spires of cedar rising into the silvered sky. Somewhere in the silent woods two wolves rested near each other, no doubt hoping to avoid whatever human mischief was afoot. I trotted a few steps to catch up with Lucash, who was strolling down the softly lit road. "Chris," I whispered, "does it ever bother you to think this refuge is nothing but a huge zoo?"

He turned to me and frowned, then smirked. "Why do you ask, you nosy writer?"

"Because it bothers me."

He resumed his ambling pace, kicking at a rock. "Yeah, it does. But not as much as it used to. I've gotten more philosophical since so many wolves died this summer. I figure it this way: At least some wolves are out, and they're learning to be wild. They're not wasting away in pens. They're building up tolerance to parasites and learning to catch what they eat. Maybe it is a big zoo, but at least it's preparing them for a wild existence, if that ever becomes possible."

Not long before, there had been hope of removing the red wolf from the endangered species list by 1995. I knew that no one, not even Warren Parker in his most optimistic mood, talked in those terms anymore. Besides the lack of good habitat, a recent study on the red wolf gene pool had drastically changed the thrust of the program. Until 1987, administrators in the Fish and Wildlife Service had assumed that the red wolf could be safely restored by building a cap-tive population and three separate wild populations from 250 animals. Now researchers feared that, with so few wolves, the diversity of the species would slowly melt away. According to the new analysis, the population would not be stable with fewer than 550 animals—330 in captivity and 220 in the wild.

The total population of red wolves was still less than 125. In the past year everyone—the biologists, the breeders, the field technicians, the highest service officials—had come to realize that the future of the species depended on its genetic recovery. And genetic recovery could not be accomplished without decades of careful breeding.

We had perhaps as long as half a century before the red wolf could be restored to a healthy condition. Meanwhile the species would have a chance to rebuild its wild skills, and its social and cultural heritage, at Alligator River. Just as important, it would once again become part of the natural and cultural landscape of North Carolina. Lucash's words had struck me and shaken the pessimism I had felt for months.

In fifty years human values could be reshaped; it had happened before. Enough space might still be found for the species to live almost as freely as it did before settlers waged their crusade to kill it. Who could say? The resurrection of the red wolf would not unfold as quickly as I might like, or in exactly the way I might hope. But unfold it would.

THE POLE ROAD PUP did not step into a trap that night, nor the next, nor the next. By the end of the week, Phillips conceded temporary defeat. All winter the wolf crew tried, off and on, to catch the pup. More than once the biologists found tracks where the pup had walked up to a trap, sniffed it, and fled. Its wily behavior pleased them, although it cost them many long nights of waiting.

That fall the Pole Road male began keeping loose company with the second of the young female wolves released in the spring of 1988. In late December, the male was discovered dead in the woods from a freak accident; he had been devouring a raccoon and had somehow strangled on the animal's kidney. To Phillips, his death was as disheartening as the loss of a friend.

Across the peninsula, near the farm fields on the east side of the refuge, the Point Peter pup grew up healthy and wild, but not as sly about traps as the pup from Pole Road. The wolf crew captured her without trouble, weighed her, fitted her with a radio collar, and released her immediately. Two months later they trapped the pup's mother, the Point Peter female. They planned to pair her with the old Phantom Road male and keep her in captivity until any pups she bore were old enough to be wormed and vaccinated against disease.

It was a mild January day when the biologists trapped the Point Peter female and drove her to Sandy Ridge. As soon as they released her from the kennel into a pen she ran to the fence and began to pace back and forth, gazing at the woods beyond. "She clearly wanted out. She absolutely refused to look in toward the center of the pen," Phillips said. "It was real sad. It made me feel like we were going backwards."

And this animal, I remembered, was the highest strung of the original eight wolves, the one believed to have the slimmest chance of adapting to freedom, along with her toothless mate. What would happen to her daughter, I asked Phillips. "Who knows?" he replied. "She may have a hard time for a while. I don't know for sure that wolves get lonely, but I can imagine they do, they're such social animals."

The Point Peter female was freed again in August 1989, along with her new mate and their four young pups. There were, suddenly, quite a number of animals for the biologists to track. Twelve wolves roamed the Alligator River—the family group, five new animals that had just been released, and the Pole Road pup, which finally stepped into a trap in late spring. She was petite but feisty, with the brindled black markings of her father. In the last days of summer, the biologists released another four wolves, all of them two years old and paired with potential mates.

Phillips, his mood buoyant, kept copious records on where the animals moved in relation to each other. Parker, too, seemed to have a renewed optimism. He talked of using the Alligator River refuge as a halfway station where captive-born wolves could begin to adapt to freedom. Eventually, he predicted, a much larger population of red wolves would be established on a large tract of land, possibly in the Great Smoky Mountains National Park. He also hinted that the day might soon come when the owners of the farms around the Alligator River refuge would agree to let wolves wander onto their property.

That fall of 1989, a sound that had been too long absent from North Carolina reverberated through the forests of the Alligator River, piercing the humid nights and sending chills through those of us lucky enough to hear. It was the sound of wolves, a quavering chorus that, with grand irony, reached its most frenetic pitch when-ever a military jet roared through the sky.

On cool nights we rode around in trucks just after dark, tracking the faint, pulsing signals from the collars of sixteen wolves. We still had our favorites, but there were too many, at this point, to keep track of easily. We rode in a pickup, Mike Phillips, John Windley, and I, to see what we could hear. A half moon rose, hidden off and on by scaly clouds. Phillips stepped outside the truck, cupped his hands to his mouth, threw back his head, and began to howl. A minute later we heard the response. The wails, coming from two directions, began low and ominous but quickly rose in pitch. They blended with a beautiful dissonance and built to an eerie crescendo. They filled the night, but carved out a hollow in my chest. I turned from them, aching.

There are only two things left to tell, for now. One night during that same period, I went out with Phillips to track the movements of the Point Peter female and her pups. Occasionally the biologists monitored some of the wolves all night to see where they moved and when. It was an uneventful evening, and we spent most of our time chatting and reading. At daybreak, though, Phillips suggested that I go with Mike Morse, one of the biologists on the project, to look for scrape marks the wolves had made during the night.

To reach Morse I had to pole a small skiff across a canal and walk through some grasses to the edge of a farm field. Morse had worked full-time as a volunteer for the project until a few months before, when Phillips had found the money to hire him. He was good-natured and gregarious, one of those people born with a natural efferves-cence. We were both groggy from lack of sleep, but he seemed better able to cope with the coming of daylight than I.

We climbed into an army range jeep, circa 1965, and bounced down a dirt road to an intersection near where the wolves had bedded down. Morse pulled up to a large pile of scat and stopped. "Oh yeah," he said with gusto, "oh yeah!" There was scat on both sides of the intersection, accompanied by long dark slashes in the dirt. Judging from the surrounding tracks, one side of the intersection had been claimed by the males from Bulls Island, the other side by the Point Peter female.

Morse crouched to examine a set of fresh prints in the damp dirt. "Look here," he said. "This is neat as hell." Beside the tracks were those of a smaller animal, one of the new Point Peter pups. They led to a pile of scat and two scrape marks, one very short, one two feet long. One made by a novice, one by a pro. I caught Morse's eye and smiled widely.

Hope is born of small things. The promise of life for red wolves grows both from their long evolution as a species and the wild behaviors that have emerged from captivity intact, if not unscarred. To me, the scrape mark made by that five-month-old pup symbolized the beauty and tenacity of the natural world. We have not yet crippled it, not completely. With luck, we never will.

One afternoon I wandered over to the North Carolina Aquarium on Roanoke Island, which is next door to the Dare County Airport. I had been to the aquarium many times before. Once, in November 1986, I had listened as Warren Parker explained to a gathering of reporters there how red wolves would be prepared for release. On this particular day I entered the aquarium with some trepidation, for I was going to see a new exhibit on red wolves.

I found the exhibit in a free-standing octagonal glass case. Inside were the bodies of two red wolves I had known, stuffed and lifelike. One, the female from South Lake that had died of an unknown infection, was standing on an arched log with a rabbit in her mouth. The other, the Phantom Road female, was crouched on her stomach below the log, her head raised, her severed left front leg hidden by a pile of leaves. Both wolves were looking into the distance as if they had been alerted by some noise.

I walked to the front of the case, where I could study the Phantom Road female's bright glass eyes. The last time I had seen her, her gaze had been dulled by pain and shock. She had been granted life when Sue Behrns plucked her from her dead mother's womb. She had been brought to her death by the wild impulses that Warren Parker and Mike Phillips and all the rest of us wanted so badly to save.

It was a weekend, and the aquarium was crowded with parents and young children. A couple with a baby in a stroller walked up to the red wolf exhibit and paused. "They look smaller than I thought," the man said.

"Yeah," said the woman, "but they're pretty. I wonder why they call them red wolves. They're more tan." The baby whimpered in sleep.

I looked back at the Phantom Road female's topaz eyes. The taxi-
dermist had done a good job; it almost seemed that there was still a
spark of life in them, and in the body itself, poised to whirl and run.
The couple moved on. "Thank you," I whispered to the wolves, turning to leave. "Thank you."

15. A TALE OF TWO WOLVES

DAVID E. BROWN

My hatred for wolves goes clear back to my early boyhood days in Texas, and has been strengthened by countless experiences with them throughout my lifetime. Never once have I known a wolf to do anything to change my opinion of him; and although I would very much regret the passing of bear and lions from these Southwestern mountains, I would shed no tears whatever over the death of the last lobo.

> —Dub Evans
> *Slash Ranch Hounds,* 1951

A WINTER NIGHT IN 1965 COMES READILY TO MIND. IT was then that another wildlife manager and I heard a wolf howl from the northeast corner of the Papago Indian Reservation. Not only was the animal's eerie cry to remain etched in our minds, and make one of the hundred such camps extraordinary, we sensed that we would never hear its like again—not in Arizona anyway.

"A Tale of Two Wolves," by David E. Brown, originally appeared in the January/February 1992 issue of Game Journal. *Copyright © 1992 by David E. Brown and reprinted by the author's permission.*

For we were not the only ones who heard the howling. Local ranchmen heard it too, and had found other evidence of a wolf's presence. The next day, predator control agents arrived with traps and "getters." Although no wolf carcass was ever found, the howls and reports abruptly ceased. Some thought one of the cyanide-loaded getters had gotten him, or since this was not wolf country, that the animal had moved on. Whatever its fate, the animal was never heard from again.

While I heard no more wolves in the succeeding years, I was to hear plenty about wolves. In 1976 the Mexican wolf was declared an "endangered species" by the U.S. Fish and Wildlife Service—by then a largely academic classification as the *lobo* had been extirpated within the boundaries of the United States. The last Mexican wolf reported from Texas and New Mexico had been killed in 1970. No wolf had been born in the wild in Arizona since 1944. The last Mexican wolf "holdouts" in Mexico were being eliminated in Durango and Chihuahua by an American trapper named Roy McBride. The only reports of a *lobo* in the U.S. were vague accounts of a wanderer from Mexico taking up residency in the upper Arivaipa Canyon area in Arizona's Sulphur Springs Valley—"rumors" that were soon replaced by stories of a "wolf" quietly taken by a private trapper for a reputed bounty of $500 put up by local stockmen.

Like most Arizonans I forgot about wolves.

Then, one day while browsing through the Arizona Game and Fish Department's library, I came upon four reports commissioned by the U.S. Fish and Wildlife Service on the history and status of the Mexican wolf. These accounts, prepared by Dan Gish for Arizona, Gary Nunley for New Mexico, James Scudday for Texas, and Roy T. McBride for Mexico, read like a fascinating novel. They documented a 50-year campaign against the wolf in the Southwest, a war that was won only with the aid and total commitment of the U.S. government. Getting rid of the wolf was not the result of accidental overkill brought about by overzealous ranchers, but the successful conclusion of a well-considered strategy. Published as *The Wolf in the Southwest,* these accounts made a fitting obituary for the region's most hated and respected predator.

But not everyone accepted the wolf's final demise. In 1977 the U.S. Fish and Wildlife Service contracted with Roy McBride to supply the agency with some of the last wild-trapped *lobos* for breeding stock.

Several wolves were captured, and captive breeding programs were instituted at the Arizona-Sonora Desert Museum and the St. Louis Zoo. A "Mexican Wolf Recovery Plan" was drafted, and eventually approved. The hope was that somehow, sometime, somewhere a *refugium* for the Mexican wolf would be found within the animal's historical range in the United States.

But such a hope has yet to materialize. Reintroducing an endangered predator is infinitely more difficult than preserving one. Now, more than ten years after the initiation of the captive-breeding program, no wolves have yet been released. Despite the Mexican wolf being a federally endangered species, and mandated by Congress to be a U.S. Fish and Wildlife responsibility, the agency has decided that it must have the state's permission prior to reintroducing the wolf to any area from which the same agency had previously eliminated the animal.

For obvious political reasons, none of the three states having potential release sites suggested a wolf reintroduction site. Nor are they likely to. The Texas legislature has even passed a law outlawing the reintroduction of wolves, and the only release site seriously considered in New Mexico—the arid, but ungrazed White Sands Missile Range—was withdrawn from consideration on the grounds that such a release would attract too much attention. No one has even proposed a release site in Arizona.

It thus appears that the restoration of a wild population of wolves to the Southwest is far in the future, if ever. The potential political opprobrium from a wolf reintroduction is just too great. Neither the U.S. Fish and Wildlife Service nor a federal land management agency is likely to endorse a specific reintroduction program, much less a state game and fish commission. The hatred of the stockmen for wolves is too intense, and their political outrage is too vociferous, for such a proposal to be sanctioned in the halls of Southwest state legislatures—the same legislatures that allow stockmen to remove any animal that poses a threat to livestock on private or public land. With no Southwest National Park or other suitable *lobo* habitat available that is livestock-free, I have resigned myself to hearing wolf howls only in my memory.

But something keeps nagging at me. How is it that such ancient countries as Greece, Italy, and Spain have wolves while America's Baby States do not? Why is it that the wolf has persisted through so many waves of Mediterranean civilization into modern times? What is the status of wolves in these countries now? Are there any lessons to be learned that might be applicable to the Southwest?

I decided to go and take a look. In the spring of 1987 I went to Italy's Apennine Mountains and Abruzzi National Park; in the spring of 1989 I visited the Cantabrian Mountains and other Spanish *sierras*. Thanks to Franco Zunino, Italy's foremost brown bear biologist, and Tony Clevenger, who was studying bears in the Cantabrians, I got to meet wildlife biologists, university professors, public officials, villagers, farmers, shepherds, brown bears, and wolves.

What I saw was both familiar and surprising. Except for the presence of beech forest and other, more subtle floral differences, southern Europe's mountains had a Southwest flavor. Many of the oaks and other plants had a "familiar look" and several times I was hard pressed not to imagine that I was not in California, Chihuahua, or New Mexico. The European red deer is the same species as our elk, as is their brown bear and our grizzly. So are the wolves. And, while the farmers and shepherds expressed tolerance for bears, they detested the wolf with the same intensity as did their Southwest counterparts. The animals' unsavory dining habits and propensity to kill for fun are guaranteed to rile those whose life is spent in animal husbandry.

But centuries of battle with canine adversaries have resulted in a number of stock-raising techniques being practiced in Europe that are not seen in the Southwest. Although the attitude toward wolves in rural Italy and Spain is similar to that of Western stockmen, the procedures to deal with them are different. While Italian and Spanish wolves continue to be trapped, poisoned, burned-out, and shot as were their Southwest brethren, their domestic prey is looked after more judiciously.

I saw no cattle in the backcountry that were not attended by a cowherd. All of the cows come home to the barn at night, and no one would think of leaving cows and calves on the open range. Nor are cattle allowed to graze in the woods or in rough, brushy country. Guard dogs, some with spiked collars to give them an advantage in a fight against wolves, accompany every herd of cattle, sheep, or goats.

Sheep are folded every night and guarded by shepherds as well as dogs. Large, unwieldy flocks must be rare—at least I did not see any. Surprisingly, much of both countries' rangeland looked better than comparable areas in Arizona and New Mexico despite having been used and abused for several hundred rather than 100 years. Livestock numbers and seasonal grazing patterns appear to have attained some sort of equilibrium with the capacity of the land to support them. And, as in rural America, the young people are moving to the cities; almost every village has fewer people now than 20 years ago. Some have been abandoned entirely.

As for *why* the wolf was able to survive in these countries and not in the Southwest, I now have no doubt: There was never a federal agency dedicated to the extermination of the wolf in Italy and Spain. Divided into principalities, autonomous regions, and provincial governments, these nations have never had a coordinated predator control program that, year after year, continued to field wolf trappers throughout the length and breadth of the country. With only local control efforts, the wolves could recoup their losses; areas cleared of wolves were soon repopulated by offspring of others raised in some other province.

Moreover, attitudes in the European countryside toward wolves appear to be changing. As villages shrink and vanish, new national parks and *cotas* are created and old ones expand. Livestock depredations on such lands are supposed to be compensated by governments which have a policy of maintaining some wolves as representatives of the nations' wildlife heritage. Should present trends continue, the hatred of wolves in the villages will gradually turn to acceptance, and may eventually even become appreciation.

Within Italy's Abruzzi National Park is the village of Civitella Alfedena with its large enclosure containing a dozen or so wolves for tourists to observe and photograph. Next to the enclosure is a two-story building devoted to exhibits on the wolf. Wolf traps, wolf posters, and all sorts of paraphernalia dealing with wolf lore are here for public display. (My favorite was a 19th-century poster of a pack of wolves attacking a snowbound train in the Alps, the passengers fighting off the animals from the roofs of the railroad cars.) The message is that Europe's most maligned animal need not remain man's enemy, and that if certain precautions are followed when grazing livestock and a modicum of tolerance is practiced, Italians will have wolves around for some time to come.

The educational display was effective. In a few minutes I learned more about the wolf in Europe than in 20 years of reading. By the large numbers of school children present, I strongly suspect that most Italians know more about wolves than the average American.

As for the future of the wolf in these countries, much depends on the effects of the Common Market. Should Italy's and Spain's agricultural and pastoral "efficiency" begin to rival Germany's and Switzerland's the wolf will be in serious trouble. If, however, these countries continue to expand their parks and wildlife areas (Italy now has two designated wilderness areas), and educate their public on the value of predators, the wolf's future should be secure. It would be a shame for these countries to lose the wolf now after he has withstood man's assault for centuries.

To return the wolf to the American Southwest will also involve a change in attitude, not so much by the wolf's old enemies who are in the wane, but by wildlife enthusiasts who have sought to maintain peace with the livestock industry. A new generation of conservationists needs to understand that the wolf and the grizzly are as much a part of their heritage as are elk, bighorn sheep, and mountain lions. Of what purpose are New Mexico's and Arizona's multitude of national forests, stellar collection of national parks, and great legacy of wilderness areas without the wolf and the grizzly? There is no reason why the citizens of Italy and Spain should enjoy more diverse fauna than the people of the American Southwest.

16. THE WAY WOLVES ARE

RICK BASS

IN 1892, FRANCIS PARKMAN WROTE ELOQUENTLY about how even then America's big predators (other than man) were disappearing: ". . . Those discordant serenaders, the wolves that howled at evening about the traveller's camp-fire, have succumbed to arsenic and hushed their savage music. . . . The mountain lion shrinks from the face of man, and even grim 'Old Ephraim,' the grizzly bear, seeks the seclusion of his dens and caverns."

Because we could not take time to manage our livestock effectively, wolf depredation upon free-ranging sheep and cattle was a significant hardship on ranchers before and during the turn of the century. Rather than trying to change management practices and strike a balance between the land and themselves, ranchers instead eradicated wolves completely, with the government's aid. The last known wolf pack to den in Montana was in the 1930s. They were gone for sixty years, but now they're coming back. Biologists believe Montana's large deer herds are what's "luring" them back.

Public support is largely in favor of the wolves' return—two-thirds of the general population and up to ninety percent of visitors to national parks, want wolves back in the United States. A balance must be struck this time, however, and that balance should be based on a human understanding of wolves: their biology, sociology, and history. In the century before—and in all of our centuries before that one— we have rarely taken the time to pay attention to the wolf itself. Myths and misconceptions have surrounded the animal over the ages.

Wolves eat about nine pounds of meat a day. A typical pack of six wolves in Montana will kill a deer or elk about once a week. They like to hunt at night and sleep in the day. Usually, only one pair from each pack mates, once a year—the alpha male (the dominant male in the pack) and the alpha female. They have a long courtship that some- times begins in the late fall and intensifies in January, and the pair then breeds in late January or early February. Gestation is sixty-three days—the same as for dogs. The pups, usually numbering six, are born in April. The pack spends the summer taking care of the pups. "Aunts" and "Uncles" babysit the young wolves whenever the alpha female leaves the den. By the fall the pups have grown so much that they're indistinguishable from the adults. They're ready to learn to hunt.

Wolves are loyal to both their pack and their mate; sometimes they mate for life. Stanley Young, a biologist in the Southwest, tells of trapping a male Mexican wol., the wolf's mate returned to the capture spot for sixteen nights in a row, until she too was caught. John Murray, a writer in Alaska, tells the story of a pregnant alpha female in Denali National Park who strayed too far from her den. She had to stop on her way back and give birth out on the tundra, in a small depression out of the wind. It was twenty-four hours before she could move the pups, so the rest of the pack brought her snowshoe hares and stood guard to protect her and the newborn pups from any prowling grizzlies.

Wolves are full of passion and mystery. Mythology tells us that pricking oneself with a sharpened wolf's breastbone can stave off death. Native Americans say that wolves' howls are the cries of lost spirits trying to make it back to earth.

For sure, they're making it back to Montana. It's estimated that Montana may now have between forty and sixty wolves. Some of those wolves may even make it down to Yellowstone, where wolves have been absent for almost seventy years. One famous Russian proverb says that "the wolf is kept fed by his feet." A wolf in Scandinavia, pursued by dogs and hunters, traveled 125 miles in twenty-four hours. Young "disperser" wolves often leave their pack when they are unable to gain an alpha ranking and go off on their own, looking for new territories. It is conceivable that wolves could return to Yellowstone in this manner.* The park has an overabundance of deer and elk—one of the highest concentrations in the world—and it is thought that the wolf would provide a good selective pressure on the burgeoning herds.

Wolves are *loaded* with passion. Two years ago a wolf pack in Alaska hunted down and killed three grizzly bears because the grizzlies had wandered too close to their den while they had pups in the den: a show of disrespect on the grizzlies' part. Normally grizzlies dominate wolves—they run them off of a wolf-killed carcass and claim the spoils, draping themselves across the kill—and grizzlies will even eat wolves, when they can catch and kill them.

This time it wasn't about food. It was about territorial defense, and anger. Seven wolves went out the next day and killed those three grizzlies in what biologists can only explain as an unprecedented display of revenge.

Wolves will also fight to keep their territories free of other canids—coyotes, dogs, and even other wolf packs. They scent-mark the boundaries of their territories with urine, making circuits every few days to keep the boundaries well established. Sometimes prey species such as deer and elk learn that adjacent wolf packs do not like to "test" each other's borders, and so the deer or elk hang out along the "no-man's land" between the two territories—often a geographical feature such as a high wooded ridge or a river bottom.

There are romantic histories in the West of lonely wolves taking up a friendship with someone's pet dog—especially around the time when the wolves were being killed off—but more frequently wolves hate dogs.

Again, there seems to be at times—especially in August—an

---

*In August 1992, a lone wolf was filmed in Yellowstone.

excess of passion. Steve Fritts and Bill Paul studied the interaction of wolves and dogs in Minnesota, and wrote:

> Several breeds of dogs were killed, ranging in size from a minia-ture poodle to a Norwegian elkhound. Based on our investiga-tions and interviews with dog owners, we believe that small- to medium-size dogs, which may be particularly excitable and vocal, are more likely to provoke attack by wolves.
>   . . . While preying on dogs, wolves displayed a lack of fear of humans and buildings that is otherwise unknown except when they are diseased, disabled, or preying on deer. In several inci-dents investigated, wolves evidently focused their attention on dogs so intently that they were almost oblivious to buildings and humans. . . . In one case, a wolf attacked a dog near the doorstep and wouldn't retreat until beaten with a shovel.

The tendency at this point of discovery of the way wolves are is to counter such a "bad" image with a "good" one—to tell about the male wolf in Montana last year who, after the female was shot, raised their six pups by himself. But this judgment, this notion of good and bad, is what led to the imbalance and misunderstanding between wolves and humans in the first place. *It's just the way they are.* We need to make up our minds this time as to whether or not we can live with it.

THE ROMANTIC MIND might note that sixty-plus years—the wolves' absence—is how long it would take for ninety-nine percent of the old-time Indian-killers, buffalo-killers, and wolf-killers to die off: as if the wolves could not bring themselves to return to a country where such wanton killers still ruled.

There is no other word for our behavior, back then.

The easiest way to kill wolves then (and now) was with poison, and it was used from Mexico up through Texas and all the way across the West and up into the Arctic. Joseph Taylor wrote in his 1891 book, *Twenty Years on the Trap Line,* that "poisoned wolves and foxes in their dying fits often slobber upon the grass, which becoming sun dried holds its poisonous properties a long time, often causing the death months or even years after of the pony, antelope, buffalo, or animals feeding upon it. The Indians losing their stock in this way feel like making reprisals, and often did."

Bully for them. Stanley Young tells in his book, *The Last of the Loners,* how buffalo hunters and wolf trappers in Kansas in the 1870s had paved a road with wolf bones. The torturing and maiming of wolves is listed in stunning detail in Barry Lopez's book, *Of Wolves and Men;* setting live wolves on fire is the method that gets to me the most.

The torture seems to have been a cultural phenomenon that, with the exception of poisoning, may have vanished. Poisoning continues with vigor in both Canada and Mexico, and is one reason the Mexican wolf—there may be only a dozen left in the wild—has been unable to repopulate the southwestern United States.

In the 1860s, three "wolf-getters" took more than three thousand wolves, coyotes, and foxes with poison in a single year. The entire kill netted them $2500. Songbirds—larks—were killed for bait and laced with strychnine and then scattered like candy along known wolf runways.

It becomes an unwritten rule of the range for ranchers to carry poison in their saddlebags and never pass up a carcass of any kind without injecting it with strychnine.

"They would kill a buffalo and cut the meat in small pieces," William E. Webb wrote in 1872, "which were scattered in all directions, a half mile or so from camp, and so bait the wolves for about two days. . . . Meanwhile all hands were preparing meat in pieces about 2" square . . . putting a quantity of strychnine in the center. One morning after putting out the poison they picked up sixty-four wolves, and none of them over a mile and a half from camp."

Sixty-four wolves, in a morning? (The pack sizes were larger then, out on the plains, to bring down buffalo from the great herds— that size of wolfpack won't ever be seen again, unless the buffalo herds return.)

I picture a mile-wide circle of dying wolves, the prairie *writhing* with them in the moonlight as they flopped and back-flipped in their slow deaths. . . .

THE PRIMARY PREY of wolves in northwestern Montana is white-tailed deer. Wolves are such social animals that they will rarely kill or eat anything that they have not seen other pack members—their family—kill and eat.

Occasionally, however, a wolf, or wolves, will kill livestock. They're nowhere near as big a predator of sheep and cows as are coyotes, and if ranchers would stop and think about it, they might realize that wolves are one of the easiest biological ways to suppress coyote populations. And the ranchers' argument about how wolves pose a financial burden on them doesn't hold water anymore: a private organization, the Defenders of Wildlife, has been reimbursing ranchers 100 percent for each confirmed wolf predation of ranchers' livestock for the last few years, and continues to do so. (Defenders does not reimburse for coyote depredations.)

The ranchers say they're responding to the economics of the situation, but what they're really responding to is history, and a deep, old cultural tradition of wolf-hating. It's going to be real hard to change. Despite the complete reimbursement by Defenders of Wildlife, and despite the fact that the wolf is (theoretically) protected under the Endangered Species Act, some ranchers in Montana are still shooting wolves. At least five have been shot in the last two years. Sometimes the ranchers call the authorities (the U.S. Fish and Wildlife Service or Animal Damage Control) to come and get the wolf after they've killed one, despite the fact that there's a $100,000 fine and jail sentence of one year for killing a wolf. (No charges have ever been pressed.)

This is not to say that all ranchers these days are wolf-killers. For every wolf-hating rancher, there does appear to be one who's willing to try and let things sort themselves out—to give the wolves a chance.

What the wolf-hating ranchers are remembering are the old trap-crippled renegades who took to preying on the huge herds of cattle moving across the federal lands after the buffalo had all been killed off.

Wolf watchers in Montana these days tend to give the wolves names like "Puppy" and "Pappa Wolf," but back during the wolves' first incarnation in this country they had names like "The Black Devil" and "Bigfoot, the Terror of Lane County."

"Old Lefty of Burns Hole," in Colorado, was trapped by the left foot in 1913. Lefty succeeded, writes Stanley Young, "in twisting off the better part of his left foot from the trap . . . and then making its escape. As a result of its missing front foot, the stub of which completely healed in time, it had adopted a very peculiar gait. It never put the stub of its left foot to the ground. . . . In eight years, Old Lefty was credited with the killing of 384 head of livestock."

The Syca Wolf of southern Oregon was an old male with greatly worn teeth, and was credited with the killing of many horses and cattle. Three Toes of Harding County (South Dakota) had $50,000 worth of killings attributed to him. The Queen Wolf—also called the Unaweep Wolf—wreaked significant havoc in the early 1920s, and had a malformed foot caused by a trap injury.

In reading a history of the "famous" wolves of the West, a picture emerges that does not grant the wolf total absolution from cow-killing, but one which has rarely been commented upon: the preponderance of injuries that seem to turn wolves toward easier prey.

The Ghost Wolf of the Judith Basin killed $35,000 worth of live-stock in Montana in the 1920s and early 1930s, and seemed to have turned pathologic, often just wounding livestock. The Ghost Wolf had been shot in the hind leg and knocked down, but escaped capture by hiding in a snowdrift where it couldn't be seen. Ranchers tried to run it down in their cars. Once, five Russian wolfhounds cornered and attacked it, battling for hours, but it got away when, writes Bert Lindler, "the wolf escaped up a steep mountainside, with the man, horse and dogs too tired to follow."

Sixty-five traps and poison baits were set out for the Ghost Wolf at one time, to no avail. Bert Lindler interviewed Ed Kolar, eighty years old, about his memories of the Ghost Wolf: "He [Kolar] remembers when the wolf killed a short yearling. 'The cow came home with the whole rear end torn out of her,' Kolar said. 'We had to kill her.' "

The Ghost Wolf was also called the White Wolf. Trappers stayed in the area for five and six months at a time, laying out poison balls and baits, killing everything but the White Wolf: Lindler writes:

On May 8, 1930, Earl Neill and Al E. Close tracked the Ghost Wolf from Close's ranch into Pig Eye Basin in the Little Belt Mountains. They were aided by a German shepherd and an Irish terrier they had trained that winter hunting coyotes.

The dogs jumped the Ghost Wolf, who fought them. They kept pushing the wolf toward Close, who was hiding behind a tree. When the wolf was forty yards away, Close stepped out.

"And do you know, I almost didn't shoot," Close said. "It was the hardest thing I think I did. There was a perfect shot, the grandest old devil. . . . I thought swiftly that these were the hills over which he had hunted. I knew that it was the cruel nature

of the wilderness—the fight for the survival of the fittest—that
made him the ferocious hunter that he was. . . .

". . . Luckily I came to my senses in time and let the bullet
fly fairly into the face of the old criminal."

SO FAR IN MONTANA, in their present reincarnation, there haven't
been any terrible devil-wolves. A pack of four wolves killed two steers
but ate only twenty pounds of the meat before turning away. Would
they have killed again? We can't say for sure; they were shot with tran-
quilizers from a helicopter (one escaped) and relocated to a more
northern part of the state, where two of them were then shot, while
the third one killed four lambs

Wolf recovery in Montana cannot succeed without the ranchers
helping in the new balance. It is a matter of understanding that
some livestock—but probably not much—is going to be lost, but that
it is going to be paid for by people who love the wolf, such as
Defenders of Wildlife.

Wolves *prefer* wild game; that's proven. Wolves' depredation on
livestock in extreme northern Minnesota—the only place in the lower
forty-eight where wolves aren't listed as endangered species (they're
given a "threatened" status in Minnesota)—affects less than 1 percent
of the ranches in that area.

Similarly, up in Canada, in Manitoba, livestock remains were
found in only 1 percent of all the scats collected in a national park,
despite the fact that the park is surrounded by farmland and cattle.

In Montana, coyotes sometimes kill between three and seven cows
per year out of an individual herd. Wolves have killed only 16 cows in
Montana over the last four years; this averages about one cow per year
out of every twenty thousand available.

Under the federal wolf recovery plan, a wolf is given two chances
these days. It is relocated to a new area, following livestock depredation (if it can be trapped or darted; otherwise it is killed). Then if
depredation occurs a second time, the wolf is killed or captured and
put in captivity.

As wolves begin to regain public notice in Montana, ranchers
sometimes attribute coyote-killed livestock to wolves. One rancher
reported losing a 250-pound calf to wolves this summer and called
federal authorities, who discovered that the calf had died from an

ulcerated rumen, not predation. The rancher agreed with that analysis and felt badly about having called the authorities out on Father's Day.

Steve Fritts, a federal biologist in Montana who studied wolf depredations on livestock in Minnesota, writes, "It seems that depredations at some farms may stop even though few or no wolves are removed; at other farms depredations continue despite wolves being captured regularly."

Healthy wolves prefer to live in the woods and hunt wild game, shunning contact with humans and their livestock. The Russians have a proverb concerning the wolves they would catch as pups and try to turn into pets: "You may feed the wolf as much as you like. He will always glance toward the forest." Wolf studies indicate that when winters are hard and the snows are deep, wolves prey even more regularly on wild animals rather than on that 1 percent of domestic livestock, because the deep snow favors the wolves during a chase; their huge snowshoe paws don't cause them to flounder and sink through the snow the way the hooved animals do: deer, elk and moose.

But all these wonderful statistics are only that: numbers. Wolves *will* kill cattle every now and then. (*Everything* will kill sheep, unless the sheep are watched constantly and carefully: coyotes, wild dogs, eagles, ravens, bears, even other sheep—they trample each other in a stunningly mindless fashion.) It is an unfair pressure to place upon the species to expect that all wolves will avoid all cattle all of the time.

The truth of the matter, however, is that wolves in the West will never be out of control again. The great buffalo herds are long gone, ancient ghosts, and with them the big wolf packs that followed them.

And I like to imagine, to *hope*, that a new culture is being formed: that as each year passes, a little education and tolerance is happening—the ranchers getting more used to the new balance that is trying to affirm itself between wilderness and farmland: a balance that does not always (1 percent of the time?) stop at an arbitrary fence line, a rusty barbed wire or buck-and-rail fence that will be gone anyway in thirty or forty years.

Barry Lopez writes of interviewing some old aerial hunters and trappers in Minnesota: "The aerial hunter, trapping on the ground one year, caught a large male black wolf in one of his traps. As he approached, the wolf lifted his trapped foot, extended it toward him, and whined softly. 'I would have let him go if I didn't need the money awful bad,' he said gently."

THE FACT THAT some humans will always be mystified, even terrified by wolves—the nearly unshakable depth of that knee-jerk reaction, the old culture—was made painfully clear to me one January, at a bar in Fairbanks, Alaska.

The winter-sadness that sometimes goes with that landscape in that season, was starting to set in, and at our table there were some hunters and nonhunters, some animal rights people, and some just plain environmentalists.

There was that long late-night winter-depressed aura hovering, which, coupled with the general rage environmentalists sometimes find themselves rousing to whenever they're together and talking— their life's battle becoming a common ground for discussion—stories of atrocity being traded. *Laments.* Breast-beating. None of it was making anyone feel better, but it all had to be said.

A friend who races sled dogs was sinking into the winter, trying to claw her way back up out of the winter's pull with her rage alone. She was talking about this guy she heard bragging in this same bar—some dentist from Anchorage, talking to his friend from Seattle about the "sport" of aerial hunting—chasing wolves across the tundra and through the willows in a small plane, and shooting at them from the plane—or sometimes running the wolves to near exhaustion and then getting out and throwing on the snowshoes and hobbling the last hundred yards to where the wolves are backed up against a small bluff, panting, and shooting them in that manner, shooting all of them.

But this dentist and his friend from Seattle were talking about a flight where they'd never landed the plane. According to their brags, my friend said, they'd just cruised along behind the wolves, with full flaps down and the throttle cut way back, aiming into a heavy wind, riding right on the pack's back—just a few feet above it, following it, and gaining on it, and sinking lower and lower, as the shooter leaned and labored out the window to get his gun into position.

My friend says the dentist was speaking with dumb awe, as he bragged: that that was the hopelessness, the utter life's despair hopelessness of it, that the dentist had been *right there,* so *close,* and yet had not been able to grip life's simple mystery, that what he was doing was wrong, that he was breaking up a social bond, that he was signing wolves' death warrant, the death warrant of our respect for our place on the earth, and for respect in all forms and fashions.

But the dentist was so *close* to understanding, my friend said. He had *almost* seen it, she said: just by the way he was talking, the awe in his voice, and his eyes—he had almost seen it.

"I was right there," the dentist was saying, speaking as if in a trance. "I tell you, Joe, it was like nothing I've ever seen or done— Joe, for a few seconds there, we were right in with them, following right behind them—and the big leader looked back, and for a minute, Joe, following along behind them like that, it was like *we* were one of the pack."

17. THE EAST FORK PACK

RICK McINTYRE

AN EXPERIENCE I ONCE SHARED WITH THE EAST Fork wolves aptly illustrates the joy of belonging to a pack. Late one evening I tried to find the pack, but my initial scan turned up only a few caribou. I was about to give up when a white object, about a mile across the tundra, caught my eye. Looking through my binoculars, I saw that it was a wolf. Its coloration—bright white fur—matched the markings of the East Fork alpha female. Hoping to watch her hunt, I set up my 45-power scope.

As I focused on her, I noticed a second wolf stretched out fifty feet away. Looking over the nearby area, I found a total of five wolves. Except for the white female, all the other pack members were light gray in color. Soon they all got up and trotted off to the east. I then saw that the largest of the gray wolves had a pronounced limp in his front left leg. He held his paw in the air and rarely put his full weight on it. This was my old friend, the alpha male. He and the white female were almost certainly the parents of the other wolves.

"The East Fork Pack" (1992) is taken from Rick McIntyre's A Society of Wolves *(in press), Voyageur Press, and is reprinted here by permission of the author.*

As the pack traveled, the limping male fell behind. At times he would rush forward on three legs and momentarily catch up. Later, after he had dropped several hundred yards behind, the other pack members halted and patiently waited for him to reach them.

The wolves frequently stopped to socialize. The white female invariably was the center of attention. The younger wolves repeatedly came up to her and touched noses or rolled on the ground under her. She, in turn, gave most of her attention to the limping male. The pack was in high spirits, like a group of kids on their way to play ball in a vacant lot.

Later in the evening, while the pack rested, all five wolves simultaneously sensed or saw something. Jumping up, they ran off in close formation, shoulder to shoulder, to the west. The excitement caused the old male to ignore the pain in his crippled foot; he now ran on all fours for the first time. One of the young wolves ran faster than the others; it broke away from the pack and sprinted ahead.

As I followed the action in the spotting scope, my field of vision was too narrow to see what the wolves were running toward. I guessed, from their intense reaction, that it must be a caribou, their main prey. I panned my scope as the pack raced across the tundra, expecting at any moment to see the caribou.

The lead wolf was now ten lengths ahead of the others. At that point, something new appeared in the margin of my scope. A moment later it was clear enough to recognize: the pack was chasing a grizzly bear! I was transfixed by the drama of the scene. The bear was just a few lengths ahead of the first wolf, who was now about seventy feet ahead of the pack. Surging forward, the lead wolf closed the gap to five feet. The grizzly then looked back over its shoulder.

As both animals ran, they momentarily locked eyes and communicated with each other in a way that no human could decipher. Whatever passed between them, it caused the wolf to end the chase. The bear continued on a short distance, stopped, glanced back, and then calmly began feeding on grass.

The wolf who had led the charge trotted back to its companions, and the pack immediately leaped into a session of exuberant play. They wagged tails, touched noses, playfully nipped one another, ran side by side, and rolled on the ground. The wolf who had played tag with the bear was the focus of the play. From a human perspective, it looked like a joyous congratulatory celebration. For fifteen minutes, the wolves gave uninhibited expression to their emotions. Several hundred yards away, the grizzly ate its dinner in quiet dignity.

That evening I watched the East Fork pack for about two hours. Since then, whenever I think about wolves and what it means to belong to a pack, I look back at that experience. The East Fork wolves taught me something that I could never have learned from books or research papers. They demonstrated the joy of companionship that wolves experience by belonging to a pack.

FOR ME, THE EAST FORK pack was symbolized by their limping alpha male. He was the toughest animal I've ever known. During the seven years that I knew him, his front left paw was so badly swollen that he could hardly use it. He had lost part of that foot, most likely to a steel trap set just outside the park boundary.

I often saw him chase caribou. Knowing that he couldn't catch anything by running on three legs, he used his bad foot and somehow sprinted at speeds close to that of much younger wolves. He endured what must have been an extremely painful ordeal and often got his prey. After a chase ended, he would lie on the tundra and lick his maimed foot, sometimes for an hour, before he could go on.

One summer, while on a solo hunt, he found a moose. Since the moose weighed five times more than he did, taking it on by himself would be foolhardy, but he did it anyway. Over the next thirty-six hours he attacked the moose at least fourteen separate times. The moose fought back by stomping and kicking him. His bad paw must have been hit, for it bled profusely.

Each attack weakened the moose. Near the end of the drawn-out battle, it waded out into a swift river channel. Jumping into the water, the wolf swam out to his opponent. As they fought, the moose held him underwater and nearly drowned him. He slipped away and came back for one last round. By then the moose's wounds had taken their toll. Weak from loss of blood, he couldn't fight back any longer and the wolf finished him off. After the moose died, other East Fork wolves came along and helped the alpha male eat the carcass.

The wolf paid a heavy price for his hard-fought victory. His injuries slowed him down considerably in the following weeks. Within a month he disappeared, and I never saw him again. The beta male, a wolf who was also a skilled hunter, took over the alpha position. This male, like nearly all the other East Fork wolves, was almost certainly fathered by the limping wolf.

The limping male was a superior wolf. Despite his disability, he became the pack's leader and one of its best hunters. He passed on his genetic line to the pack, and that line will likely dominate a large section of Denali for many generations to come.

Beyond that, he allowed me to watch him and his family for many years. Through those experiences I began to learn firsthand about wolves. I will never forget the limping alpha male.

18. THE HYPERBOLIC WOLF

PAUL SCHULLERY

I HAVE BEEN HOPING FOR WOLVES IN YELLOWSTONE FOR nearly twenty years now, and in that time I've seen the public's attitude toward wolves shift from ignorance, fear, and hate to something very near affection. Even in the states surrounding the park, where so much resistance to wolf restoration still exists, the latest survey suggests that a majority of the people are probably in favor of wolf restoration.

I take all this as evidence that Americans are gradually becoming more realistic about wolves and their effects on a landscape. We have not done this easily; one does not escape from one's culture quickly, and ours has been a violently anti-wolf culture for a long time. Nor have we done it completely. In the wolf debates of today, I see plenty of evidence we're still sorting out our beliefs, and still struggling with some painful departures from wolf reality.

The radical anti-wolf forces have probably earned the most

"The Hyperbolic Wolf," by Paul Schullery, originally appeared as a guest editorial in the Winter/Spring 1992 newsletter of The Wolf Fund. Copyright © 1992 by Paul Schullery and reprinted by the author's permission.

criticism. The most ardent wolf-haters have left themselves open for easy shots from any calm person. A man I knew who recently moved to Greater Yellowstone from wolf country tells me that "wolf hysteria" will only get worse when wolves are restored. He says some people will blame wolves for everything. The car won't start? Crops aren't good? The livestock industry continuing its long, regrettable decline? It's them damn wolves. From what I've seen of the wolf issue so far, that level of foolish hostility will continue.

A few people will continue to believe that a hundred or so wolves will be able to "decimate the livestock and wildlife" of an eighteen million-acre area, all scientific evidence to the contrary, and that wholesale destruction of Greater Yellowstone children, hauled from their very porches, will follow, all historical evidence to the contrary.

But then, the pro-wolf forces have some excesses to answer for too. Those of us who embrace the idea of the wolf, the spirit and the symbol, tend to get pretty hyperbolic about it. At our most glowingly affectionate, we have turned wolves into happy families, sort of middle-class American predators who love their children and are devoted spouses and only eat the occasional sick and injured animal "that would have died anyway" (what a great concept that is).

Worse, we have burdened the wolf with grand management responsibilities. There are still many people in Greater Yellowtone who (once again, a surprising amount of scientific evidence to the contrary) perceive Yellowstone National Park's elk as a problem in need of solving, people who believe that this elegantly complex natural setting is so sadly out of kilter that only the wolf can save it from some kind of vaguely defined doom. They believe Yellowstone, especially the Northern Range, is an elk farm without predators (the grizzly bears, black bears, coyotes, and cougars that currently kill anywhere from 25 to 40 percent of each year's elk calves, as well as many adult elk, apparently don't count). A hundred or so wolves are going to do something, something nearly mystical, to straighten out everything.

Some of this matters if we ever do get wolves back in the park. While the misconceptions of the wolf-haters may do little more than make them look foolish, the extreme ambitions and expectations of the wolf-lovers are likely to backfire on the wolves. When the first wolf wanders out onto private land and eats a sheep, or when the wolves get settled in and there are still thousands of elk out there eating park grasslands just as if it were something elk do naturally, the people who were converted by simplistic "Wolves are our friends" rhetoric are going to feel mightily betrayed.

We must be sure we don't ask too much of wolves. They will move into a complex, dynamic, and constantly changing system. They will encounter several other effective and well-established predator species, some far more numerous than they, and they will have access to half a dozen large mammal species, and many more small mammals and other animals to prey upon.

A hundred or so wolves (and fewer than that at first), moving into a system already occupied by thousands of predators and tens of thousands of prey animals, may end up disappointing everyone's greatest dreams and worst fears. It is probable that a lot of the time, the simple "background noise" of variation in this complex system will make it very difficult to tell what effects the wolves are having; this isn't some machine that is easily dismantled for our observation. It is certain that whatever effects wolves do have will change constantly; after fifty years we may not have yet seen them have the same effect two years in a row. After a hundred years, if we are still watching, we will still be learning how they fit here.

At my crankiest, I want to give the hyperbolists a good rhetorical shaking. Listen, people, wolves aren't going to cause the decline of Western civilization, any more than they're going to restore blissful symmetry to the cosmos. They will cause some fascinating changes, and once in a while they may cause some trouble. If we can muster the wisdom, we can find more than enough satisfaction in the changes to let us tolerate the trouble.

19. WOLVES

LINDA HASSELSTROM

I know your pirate face,
your eagle nose, scarred throat,
at any time of day,
any mood or season.
I know all of you
in the dark, your cough,
your mountain scent
in a sweating crowd.
Every inch of me
would know any inch of you.

Now I know your swollen grave
by smoking red sunset,
by ice-white moonlight,

by snow drifted into deer tracks
between the rocks.
I've seen an eagle spiral up
at sunset over your mound.

In the wolf hour
I've heard you howling on my scent,
tasted your touch,
seen your wolf soul.
You find me constant,
staring into the dark.

20. WOLF COUNTRY

JOHN A. MURRAY

The Pygathoreans used to marvel when they met with a city-bred man who had never seen a divine being.

—*Testimonia* of Apuleius

THE LAND TO THE WEST SIDE OF DENALI National Park is for the most part bereft of standing vegetation. From the ground it looks as if a flash flood recently swept through the country, washing the upright trees away and leaving only the coarse indestructible grasses, the bog mosses, the eternal rock lichens, the low stubborn alpine willows, and the hard-working blueberry bushes. As a consequence, the terrain freely reveals its secrets: megalithic boulders abandoned by dying glaciers on the sides of hills, clear tarns scattered wherever the ice surrendered its frost to the sun, and cold rivers whose banks at lower elevations would be thick with boreal owl forest. In the smooth contours of the land—the ancient watercourses and the finely sculpted uplands—I have always been reminded of the native Athapaskan wooden shaman masks, which just

as thoroughly reduce form to essentials. Ansel Adams passed this way
in 1947 and commented that the foothills of the Alaska Range
reminded him of Death Valley in southern California, where the lines
and surfaces of the desert mountains can also be easily seen and
appreciated. Some may think because of its starkness that the northern tundra is a bleak realm, but I have always found it to be a perfectly
hospitable place. When the evening sun has sunk a few degrees across
the broad summit of Denali, and the long rays of red-shifted light suddenly reveal the hidden green canyons and amphitheaters of the
summer highlands, the view is particularly magnificent. It is on this
land—which like all truly wild lands still retains its full complement of
pre-Columbian fauna—that the subarctic wolf (*Canis lupus
pambasileus*) lives.

IN 1988, MY FIRST YEAR in Denali National Park, I saw only one
wolf, and the sighting was for such a brief moment (literally the time
it takes to read this parenthetical aside) that I couldn't stop and relish
the view, much less obtain a photograph to share with friends. In my
mind's eye I will forever see the young black wolf running, as all dogs
do, on its clawed toes through the alpine willows near the Teklanika
River in earnest pursuit of some *thing*. I would guess that the wolf was
chasing a snowshoe hare (*Lepus americanus*)—their numbers were
abundant that season—but the prey could easily have been any one of
a dozen small animals that live as unwilling peasantry on the bountiful
estate of these Darwinian overlords. Or, for that matter, the wolf
could just as well have been playing—chasing its shadow or following
a butterfly or pursuing a packmate in a game of tag. I must confess
that the only statement I can make with confidence about wolves,
having observed them now for four summers in the park, is that I
know virtually absolutely nothing about them, and that the more
I watch this spirited clan in the field, the more I comprehend the
immensity of our ignorance. In each season I've spent in Denali, a
wolf has done at least one thing that those thick Faustian monographs
declare wolves cannot, will not, could not possibly do, such as attack
and kill a grizzly bear, or single-handedly bring down a robust bull
caribou, or strike out for the territories and next be reported 350 air
miles away. The word *wolf* to me does not so much refer to an animal

whose lifestyle has been basically agreed upon since Pliny as pose a
Socratic question worthy of the dialogues of Plato.

I had better luck in the 1989 season and was afforded an
extended view of a large wolf in early June. I was also able to preserve
the sighting on videotape. When I first saw this wolf standing across
the drainage near the top of Sable Pass, I thought it was a cow caribou
from the moonlight gray of the body and the open-country length of
the leg, but as soon as I put the binoculars on him I could see that it
was a mature male wolf. For the better part of the next hour this wolf
actively hunted parka squirrels (*Spermophilus parryi*), so named for the
handsome winter parkas the Athapaskans traditionally fashioned from
the soft fur coats. The wolf's hunting method was fairly straightfor-
ward: he would lope around on the tundra in a random pattern
and then stop and listen with those amazingly flexible wolf ears for
any rodent hearts racing in the grass. Twice in the time I watched,
the wolf captured and swiftly gulped down a squirrel. Once he
attempted to raid the ground nest of two long-tailed jaegers
(*Stercocarius longicaudas*), which pursued him for quite a distance—
diving with sharp beaks at his exposed flanks—before returning to
their nearly ransacked home.

The wolf, I realized, was a much more efficient hunter of small
game than the grizzly bear, its only real competitor in the New World.
I could also discern that the wolf, in terms of morphology, was
designed for a completely different mission than the bear. The wolf
was composed of a number of sharply formed, triangular shapes—
beginning with those pyramidal ears—all built around the flat plane
of the shoulder, on which the other wedges converged and pivoted
as on a point of leverage. The muscular legs were engineered for
marathon running and for short explosive bursts. By contrast, the
grizzly can be reduced to a number of intermeshing circles and
spheres—beginning with the round ears—and has the low center of
gravity and heavy body mass necessary to absorb weight and happily
sleep, like Falstaff, through the pitched battle that is winter in the
high latitudes. The hoofed animals that comprise the primary prey
base of the wolf are, not surprisingly, built from squarish components,
particularly the white mountain sheep (*Ovis dalli*), whose internal
frames—from boxlike hooves to blunt head—are based on the right
angles intrinsic to the geometry of balance and conducive to rapid

escape over rugged terrain. The aspect of the wolf that impressed me the most during this viewing was the economy of his form. Everything that was not imperative to his life has been removed. What remained was the ultimate survivor. All the daring specialists—dire wolves (*Canis dirus*), saber-toothed cats (*Smilodon fatalis*), and giant short-faced bears (*Arctodus simus*)—who had challenged him were gone, but the conservative generalist, impartial consumer of anything from mice to moose, had outwitted the innovators and ultimately prevailed in the competition to endure.

By and by, the wolf worked his way farther and farther from my position. Finally the wolf was just a gray dot on the green horizon, about to disappear from sight. It was at this moment that the wolf ran into a family of three grizzly bears—a blond sow and two nearly grown cubs—that were grazing on some new grass beside a lingering snowbank shaped like a mammoth tusk. The wolf stopped dead in his tracks when he saw the bears—about fifty feet away—and then altered his course by forty-five degrees to avoid any further contact. Interestingly, the bears completely ignored him. Just before the wolf vanished over the ridge, he stopped and raised his head back to howl at the bears, but the vagaries of the mountain winds prevented me from hearing a note. I returned to camp late that night, exhilarated, but I also yearned more than ever to hear the howl of a wolf. Every one in the far north I'd listened to—from frostbitten prospectors leaning over pool tables at the Healy Roadhouse to legendary mammalogists lecturing from podiums to crowded auditoriums—had insisted that the howl of a wolf is the ultimate essence of the North American wilderness, and that no person can consider his or her outdoor experiences on this continent to be complete without having heard this Wagnerian hymn to all that is forever defiant and indefatigable in nature.

Probably the most dramatic event involving wolves in that summer occurred on the morning of July 23, when a pack of twelve wolves attacked and killed two young grizzly bears on the west side of Sable Pass, not far from where I observed the big male wolf in early June. In fact, it is likely that this big male, the alpha male of the East Fork of the Toklat pack, led the assault. Although I was not present on Sable Pass that day, I was able to interview several eyewitnesses and later read the summary report compiled by the National Park Service. Reviewing these seven accounts, I was continually reminded of Akira

Kurosawa's well-known film *Rashomon,* in which four people involved in a violent crime subsequently relate contradictory versions of what transpired, based on perspective and self-interest. Although all seven men and women on Sable Pass that morning saw the identical wolf-bear incident, their descriptions of the event were often strikingly different in terms of narrative emphasis and important details. To put it another way, the wolf was just as slippery as the subatomic particles described in 1927 by physicist Werner Heisenberg, who stipulated the impossibility of any two observers simultaneously obtaining identical measurements on the same piece of the universe. The wolf, in short, is as problematic as a positron.

The story begins the day before, when a grizzly bear sow and her three yearling cubs were seen at the natal den site of the East Fork pack, which is located on a steep, south-facing embankment about a mile upstream from naturalist Adolph (Ade) Murie's historic wolf study cabin. Murie first studied wolves here in 1939—he even kept one as a pet—and noted in his book that the wolves were extremely sensitive with respect to their whelping den. Perhaps because of this bear intrusion, the East Fork wolves then organized themselves into a pack—large-scale pack hunting is more common in the winter—and appeared to follow the grizzlies' scent trail up the adjoining drainage to the top of Sable Pass. Once the bears were sighted, the wolves began a classic stalk. In what I found described in my old Marine Corps infantry tactics manual as a "single envelopment," the wolves divided into two groups—an exposed maneuver unit to provide a diversion and a hidden attack element to surprise and overwhelm. Once the former revealed themselves to the bears, the fiercely protective sow began a series of bluff charges aimed at driving her adversaries off. At the moment the sow was the farthest from her cubs, the concealed ambush element rushed in, separated the two most isolated cubs, and immediately killed them. The enraged mother bear lunged for the quick-footed wolves and attempted to defend the now lifeless carcasses of her cubs. Sensing an overwhelming advantage, the entire wolf pack encircled her and the last cub, their muzzles and paws red with blood, and began a series of coordinated group attacks. It did not take long for the sow, realizing the extreme danger of her situation, to break through the ranks and bolt for the horizon with her sole surviving cub. The wolves returned to the carcasses, tore the two dead grizzlies into smaller pieces, and carried the body parts back to their den to feed the puppies. The two surviving bears were not seen for several days. When they were finally spotted, it was reported that both bears appeared to be seriously injured.

About a week later, the less violent side of wolves was demonstrated when the poet John Morgan, a colleague at the university, and I spent a night on the East Fork near the base of Polychrome Mountain. John built a house for his family on a wooded hillside above the Tanana River, and has published two books of poems about the Alaskan wilderness. He and I always enjoy discussing our favorite poets, from Homer and Vergil to Theodore Roethke and Robert Lowell. I left camp at around five-thirty in the morning to check on some bears I'd observed the previous night at the top of Sable Pass. John decided to sleep in. Shortly after I departed, John heard something outside his tent and warily unzipped the flap, only to discover a large wolf standing on the gravel bar about ten feet away. Startled by John's presence, the wolf ran for several hundred feet, whereupon he stopped and looked back once before loping out of sight. Fred Dean, another professor at the university, told us later in the day that this wolf—the alpha male of the East Fork pack again—had been chasing a bull caribou up and down the river all morning. The wolf probably had come over to investigate during one of his breaks from the hunt (a large male wolf is strong enough to run a caribou to death over a period of one or two days). The important thing to remember from this incident, it seems to me, is that the wolf displayed both the curiosity and shyness that, more often than not, characterize wolf behavior. While it is true that wolves are capable of violence—as are humans— they pose no threat to people and are far more accepting of us than is commonly thought. This compatibility was further underscored in the winter of 1990 as wildlife researchers were surprised to find a large wolf pack quietly living in the suburbs of Anchorage, a city of a quarter-million. The scientists shouldn't have been surprised. Wolves have been companions of the human race since before the discovery of bronze.

One of the advantages of living in wolf country is that fellow scriveners from the Lower 48 arrive every summer on the same warm winds that bring the white-fronted geese, the Lapland longspurs, and the arctic warblers. In fact, Denali National Park has become to the nature essayists of our time what Paris was to the expatriate novelists of the twenties; sooner or later, virtually every member of the guild travels here for inspiration and camaraderie. In 1989 I had two such visitors: Dave Wallace, whose home is in northern California, and Dave Brown, who lives in southern Arizona. Both have written extensively about wolves. Dave Brown's book *The Wolf in the Southwest* comprehensively documents the extinction of the Mexican wolf. Dave Wallace wrote about wolves in *Life in the Balance,* his companion volume for the Audubon television series, and has also published an insightful essay entitled "The Importance of Predators." Unfortunately, neither of these naturalists saw a wolf during their stay in Denali. This is not all that unusual. Although there are more than 100 wolves on the northern range of the park, only about one visitor in ten sees a wolf, as compared with nine in ten who observe one of the 200 bears that occupy the same area. The major reason for the difference in figures is that wolves are nocturnal, even in the period from late April through early August when there is no darkness at this latitude. Most visitors are active during the day and retire after dinner. Almost all of my wolf sightings—and only a portion are related here— have been after ten at night and before eight in the morning, when the available light diminishes to the extent that the wolves—along with their close relatives the foxes and coyotes—are given a slight but significant advantage over their prey. Bears, primarily vegetarians, are active at any time of the day or night, although sows with cubs often sleep during the hours after midnight.

Dave Wallace and I hiked far up the Savage River—actually, the river is as gentle as a Rocky Mountain trout stream—one cloudless June day and saw much sign of wolves in the form of fresh tracks and scat piles. All of the scat piles contained the physical remnants of caribou, and although we saw several small herds of caribou, as well as grizzlies, and Dall sheep, the local wolves were nowhere to be seen. Dave continually amazed me on this hike with his detailed knowledge of natural history. Later, in early August, Dave Brown and I were similarly thwarted in our attempts to view wolves. Like Ansel Adams before him Brown saw many geographic parallels between the interior of Alaska and the American Southwest. Both regions suffer from water scarcity. Although, in the summer months, the tundra of Denali appears to be almost tropically fertile, the only reason the area is not a desert is that the ground is permanently frozen a few feet or yards beneath the surface. Both the mountains of southern Arizona and the mountains of central Alaska receive less than fourteen inches of precipitation annually. Dave Brown correctly observed that wolves survived in Alaska only because there is no livestock grazing, a practice that has devastated the public lands of the West by destroying watersheds, accelerating desertification, transplanting nonnative species, diminishing native ungulate populations, and setting up predator control programs that resulted in the loss of the wolf and grizzly. In Denali we could see that once livestock is removed from the equation, there is little conflict with respect to human culture and predators. We both agreed that as feed lots continue to supersede public lands grazing in terms of efficiency and profitability, and as more and more sheep and cattle allotments are retired and purchased by state game departments, there will be an increased likelihood that wolves and grizzlies will be returned to their ancestral ranges west of the Mississippi.

Nineteen ninety was to be the year of the wolf. Wherever I went in the park I saw wolves, and the sightings were as fine as they come. After several solo jaunts in April and May—the best time of the year to be alone in the high country—I made my first major safari in early June with Eric Heyne, who also teaches in the English Department at the University of Alaska. Eric is known for his fly-fishing skills and for his love of frontier literature. He once drove his Ford Bronco all the way to the Arctic Ocean on the Dalton Highway, which is not as easy as it sounds. Eric proved an excellent companion. Our opening day began auspiciously, as we observed a mated pair of grizzly bears cavorting on one of the lower ridges of Cathedral Mountain, so named by pioneer Charles Sheldon in 1906 for its resemblance to an immense medieval church. What better place, we concluded, for an outdoor June wedding than on a mountain named Cathedral? About an hour later, Eric and I encountered wildlife biologist Fred Dean in the alder hell below the Murie cabin. Just below his position a young bull caribou was standing in the middle of the river. Fred quickly briefed us on the situation. Several wolves had attacked the caribou shortly after six in the morning. To prolong his life, the caribou had backed into the river, where he had a slight defensive edge over the shorter-legged wolves. The animal had remained there—in mid-stream—for five hours. Using my binoculars, I could see that the wolves had torn the long tendons of the hind legs and had also begun to disembowel him. Fred theorized that the wolves had gone to their den to sleep for the day and would return at twilight to complete the job. There was, however, always the possibility that the hungry wolves would come back earlier, and so Eric and I decided to wait it out. For the next four hours, Eric, Fred, and I—soon joined by my friend and park naturalist Rick McIntyre and Japanese photographer Michio Hoshino—stood silent vigil in the rain above the river. Eventually the caribou pulled himself up on the riverbank below us and sought shelter in the vegetation. Needless to say, if we had been outside Denali, we would have taken action to euthanize the animal, but in a national park nature is allowed to proceed undisturbed. Eric and I departed at three that afternoon. It was just too dispiriting to watch helplessly as a fine, brave animal suffered. The next morning the caribou had vanished. There was no blood, no hide, no gut pile, no bones, no tracks. There was not even a raven. There was only the river, whispering some secret to itself.

Two weeks later I returned to the park for the summer solstice. There is no celebration of life on this planet—not the Carnival in Rio de Janeiro nor the Fiesta in Pamplona nor the Mardi Gras in New Orleans—quite as exuberant as early summer above the sixty-third parallel. Day after day, the bright polar sun circles endlessly in the sky, not ever fully setting but only dipping behind a peak now and then for a few hours of rest. As a result of the continual bath of light that suddenly pumps extravagant amounts of energy into the warm and revivified organism that is the subarctic, all nature grows and multiplies prodigiously. Everything gives birth—from mosquitoes to monkeyflowers to moose. Within the span of two lunar cycles, an almost wholly dead landscape is miraculously transformed into a fertile paradise. This profusion, of course, translates into newfound prosperity for the wolf. Like a rancher whose overwintered herds of cattle and sheep double in the calving and lambing season, the wolf finds itself—after a long season of want—in the clovered fields of abundance. Nature has timed the birth of the wolf pups to correspond perfectly with this time of plenty. Now the pack must hunt not only for one another—as they did all winter over the snows—but also for the hungry new life back at the den, and for the lactating mother who also relies on them for nourishment. The wolves know instinctively that their lives, individually and communally, are bound together in the next generation. An uncle or an older sister may not be the direct biological parents of the young, but nevertheless their genetic material is represented in the litter, and it is to their advantage to ensure

that the strongest pups survive and prosper. All the attention of the
pack now focuses upon the young: feeding them, protecting them,
playing with them, and eventually educating them. Although wildlife
biologists assert that affection in animals is only a self-rewarding
behavior that enhances survival, it is hard not to believe that tender-
ness is something more, a quality at one with the light that pours over
the land and gives it life, when you watch, through a powerful pair of
lens, a wolf pack leader lovingly nuzzle his young ones as the weary
mother looks proudly on.

It was on the night of the solstice—recalling for you that there are
no stars to this "night"—that I finally heard the howl of a wolf. The
experience marked a watershed in my life, with the thirty-six revo-
lutions around the sun that came before separated forever—by a
divide as real as the Alaska Range—from the years to follow. If you put
two guitars side by side and pluck the low "E" string on one guitar, the
low "E" string of the instrument beside it will vibrate. So too, I discovered, does the howl of the wolf resonate upon the heart. As might be
expected, the howling came as a complete surprise. I was crossing
Thorofare Pass at around one o'clock in the morning—with any
thoughts of *Canis lupus* about as far from my mind as the moons of
Neptune—when suddenly I spotted two wolves on the tundra about
thirty yards away. When I reached for the video camera the two wolves
lay down, and the big one, the wolf out in front, raised his dark
muzzle to the sky that was as gray as his fur and howled back over his
shoulder. This wolf, I noticed, had a distinctive pattern of markings
on his face. Taking my gaze off him to admire the nearly pure white
wolf a few yards behind, I noticed four other wolves, all in the prone
position of their leader. At that moment, the entire pack began to
howl, their voices lifting and falling as if seeking some familiar har-
mony. As the wolves sang with growing enthusiasm, they lifted themselves off the ground and began walking—dancing would be a better
way to describe this—around each other. I was stunned and transfixed, uplifted and overwhelmed. Most curious, at least to one who
knows as little about wolves as I do, was that the wolves did not stop
and go about their way, but sang on and on, like musicians improvis-
ing melodies on a major chord progression. In their capacity to make
me feel both happy and sad at the same time, these mournful, octave-
climbing runs reminded me most of the Delta blues—the three-
chorded laments of Robert Johnson, Mississippi Fred McDowell,

Muddy Waters, T-Bone Walker, and Howlin' Wolf. As the singing of the wolves persisted, and in fact became more vigorous, it occurred to me that the pack was trying to communicate something to me. Their song, I concluded, was not an invitation, but was, rather, a plea to be left alone. Reluctantly, I turned and continued on my journey west over Thorofare Pass. I looked back once, near the summit of the pass, but the reverie was over. The six phantoms had disappeared, melted back into the tundra like those sudden mountain fogs that begin to die even as they are born, and there was no trace of the wolves or their chorus, except for the goose bumps that would not go away.

I had just decided that the morning could get no better—that this would indeed be the finest day of my life—when I reached the far side of Thorofare Pass and there, spread out before me like a vision from Dante's *Paradise,* was the entire unobstructed mass of Denali (20,320 feet), the highest mountain north of the Andes. There was not a cloud for a hundred miles, and the summit of "the Great One" was just then catching the first red rays of the sun, which was rising— irony of the arctic—from due north. Four rolls of color slide film passed through the camera over the next three hours, as I photographed the spectacular peak from a variety of vantages around Glacier Gorge and McKinley Flats. Although I could not reach Wonder Lake, where Ansel Adams took his famous black-and-white picture from the blueberry ridge above the ranger station, I was able to plant the tripod at a number of other exceptional locations, including a linked chain of beaver ponds in a little valley near the headwaters of Moose Creek. Ade Murie discovered during his two-year study of wolves in the park that beaver comprise a vital source of food for wolves in the late winter when other resources are scarce. Apparently, the wolves become so hungry at this time that they dig right through the tops of beaver lodges. Around six o'clock in the morning I was joined by Rick McIntyre, who had served as park naturalist on the west end of Denali for fifteen summers. Rick expressed relief when I reported that I had not remained long with the wolves on Thorofare Pass. Researchers working for L. David Mech, a scientist studying wolves in the park, had determined that the alpha female of the Toklat pack had unexpectedly given birth on the pass while hunting in late May. Here she still remained, in a makeshift den, with her defenseless pups exposed to the dangerous elements and to other predators, such as grizzly bears and golden eagles. The wolf pack was no doubt trying to get to her and the pups with food—which they regurgitate—and were howling to try to turn me away and to warn her that an intruder was present. Rick wondered if we should proceed with our plans to explore the Toklat country that day, as I had had no sleep, but I insisted that we proceed. There is plenty of time to sleep during the long twenty-one-hour nights of the Alaskan winter. Little did I know that the day would only get better, and that it would be another fifteen hours before I retired to my favorite sleeping bag.

To fully come to terms with the wolf in Denali, I knew from the outset that it would be important to observe the species interacting with other large mammals. First, the hoofed prey animals—Yukon moose, Barren Grounds caribou, Dall sheep—provide the bulk of the wolf's energy requirements. Second, the wolf most fully lives—in a sense achieves its realization—as a free-ranging hunter of the big vertebrates. The parka squirrel hunt on Sable Pass and the caribou incident on the East Fork had duly impressed me, and I was grateful for having experienced them, but I remained anxious to personally view the wolf as an active, and aggressive, citizen of its community. Curiously, both interactions I am about to relate to you—which were completely different in kind—transpired on the same hillside above the main fork of the Toklat River and within a single twenty-four-hour period. That they both should occur in June, and around the solstice, is fitting, for it is during this period that predation is more intense in the park. In the first case, which happened about six hours after I viewed the wolves howling on Thorofare Pass, Rick McIntyre and I spotted something unusually white on a hill across the shallow glacial valley that connects the Plains of Murie with the Toklat River. With binoculars, this white form resolved itself into a grizzly bear, luxuriating on top of a freshly killed caribou about 200 yards away. Rick identified this bear as the three-year-old sister of "Little Stoney," the mischievous boar grizzly about whose eventful life and tragic death he wrote his popular book *Grizzly Cub*. Rick excitedly set up his heavy Bogen tripod and Minolta camera—with the enormous 600mm lens attached—and we prepared for a pleasant morning of bear watching. At intervals, the grizzly would either roll around on the carcass, or lightly nap, or pull off long pieces of delicious red meat and eat them with evident satisfaction. She was the very picture of worldly contentment, like one of those Pompeian frescoes depicting some extravagant first-century Roman feast.

After about forty minutes, the grizzly stopped feeding and looked off intently into a nearby willow patch. Rick soon located a large gray wolf sitting in the willows about a hundred feet from the grizzly and the carcass. I am not wholly certain, but I believe this was the same wolf—identifiable from the dark markings on his face like the war paint on the Pawnee and Comanche chiefs in George Catlin's nineteenth-century paintings—I had seen the previous night about ten miles to the west of Thorofare Pass. The wolves, Rick believed, were making nightly feeding trips all the way out to Thorofare Pass from their base of operations on the Toklat. He believed the wolves would eventually—and this was later confirmed—move the pups, one by one, to either the Toklat den site or to a nearby summer rendezvous location. For quite some time the wolf remained there, napping and yawning and scratching at the mosquitoes and flies. The bear went back about her business on the carcass, but with a nervousness that had not been evident before. After a while the wolf stood up, stretched, and walked in a large circle around the grizzly. This definitely got the attention of the bear. A three-year-old grizzly is not that big—about 175 or 200 pounds—and the wolf probably weighed in the neighborhood of 120 to 130 pounds, so the match was not as uneven as it might sound, although if it came to a fight, Rick and I realized that the bear would have the advantage of weight and weaponry—that muscular hump and those awesome foreclaws—over the speed, agility, and razorlike carnassials of the wolf. After circling the bear two more times—you could feel the tension in the air—the wolf made his move, creeping forward slowly but steadily on a direct path toward the bear. When the wolf got about twenty feet away, the grizzly charged out like a locomotive with all her guardhairs fully erect—making her appear significantly larger—and her lips curled to expose an impressive array of teeth. The wolf spun around and nearly fell over as he slipped down the steep hillside. Several times in the next hour the wolf attempted to dislodge the bear, but each time with the same results. After sitting down to further consider the matter—the bear appeared to become more self-confident with each confrontation—the wolf decided to leave. About ten minutes later, the irritated grizzly followed her challenger's scent trail for quite a distance over the tundra before returning to the carcass, where she concealed herself in the willows within charging distance of the prize.

The very next morning, within fifty yards of the now-devoured caribou carcass, Rick and I were startled to see a three- or four-year-old Dall sheep ram "treed," as it were, on a solitary rock outcropping about fifteen high by two adult wolves, one of which was the same wolf we had seen the previous day with the grizzly. It is quite unusual to see a sheep on a valley floor in the middle of nowhere. Apparently, the young ram had become indifferent to his protected life with the maternal bands in the foothills and had been attempting to cross over the valley to the immense peaks of the Upper Toklat, where the mature rams live in bachelor bands during the summer, when the wolves—cleaning up what the grizzly had left of the carcass—had discovered him. The two wolves tried every conceivable tactic to frighten the little ram. They attacked from above, from the sides, and even attempted to scramble up the vertical formation from below, but the animal had found the only secure place for two miles in any direction and would not be moved. Next the wolves pretended to leave, walking away in full view of the promontory, only to sneak back through the brush above the ram. Again, he refused to cooperate. At this point the wolves lay down in frustration and, apparently, decided to wait this one out. Things looked grim for the sheep, or so we thought.

With Rick McIntyre and myself that June morning was Bob Landis, a renowned Montana cinematographer whose first trips to Denali in the late 1960s corresponded with the last years of Ade Murie. It was Murie, Bob once confided, who had converted him from big game hunting to wildlife cinematography. Bob, who teaches high school in Billings, drives north every summer to work in the park. Despite having spent a quarter of a century in Denali, Bob still becomes excited as can be whenever he sees a wolf or a bear. He told Rick and I that, based on his experience, the standoff with the wolves could continue for several days before the sheep finally collapsed from hunger, thirst, and fatigue. As the three of us sat there on the hillside—it was a glorious morning with just the right combination of warm sun and cool breeze—we exchanged anecdotes about wolves. I started first, with the account of a radio-collared wolf that had been trapped the previous winter on Minto Flats near Fairbanks. When the trapper turned in the collar to state wildlife officials, they discovered the wolf had been fitted with the apparatus on the Kenai National

Wildlife Refuge—some 350 air miles south—the year before. We all agreed that persistent reports of wolf sightings in Washington, Oregon, North Dakota, Wyoming, and even Arizona and New Mexico should not be discounted. Wolves love to roam. Bob explained his current project—filming red foxes for a BBC documentary—and then related the account of a pair of radio-collared wolves—an alpha male and female—that were killed in an avalanche while leading their pack over a Denali snowfield. The two had sacrificed themselves in order to determine if the route was safe for the others. Rick McIntyre talked about the period from 1946 through 1951 when a misbegotten piece of congressional legislation forced park managers—despite howls of protest from Ade Murie—to kill wolves in order to increase the hoofed animals that the visitors preferred to see. He also reported that five wolves had been killed the winter before on the Lower Toklat, shot from the air by some misguided soul. At that point the two wolves got up and left the valley. We surmised they were going back to the den for reinforcements. Much to our chagrin, however, the ram leaped off the pinnacle, briefly collected himself on the valley floor, and then ran as fast as he could—which is much faster than any of us believed—all the way back to the high green slopes where his troupe no doubt waited for him. He would have to wait another year to join the mature rams—they leave the winter range together in large groups each spring—but for now he had outwitted the predators, and that, to a certain extent, was what his existence was all about. The two wolves returned shortly and appeared to be disappointed that the fresh mutton had gotten away.

September is a time of rapid change on the Alaskan tundra, as the first strong arctic fronts sweep in from the Bering Sea and Siberia beyond, carrying with them subfreezing temperatures, permanent snow, and the last of the migrating geese, ducks, and cranes. In many ways, this is the most beautiful season of the year, as the lowering termination line of the previous night's snowfall contrasts sharply with the rainbow colors ripening on the autumn tundra—the warm salmon reds of the blueberry patches, the soft yellows of the willow thickets, the orange stands of dwarf birch, the dark honey of the sedge hummocks, the bright green of the scattered spruce islands, and the worn saddle hue of the long, windswept grass hills. The stars return to the sky after a four-month sabbatical and some nights the northern lights are wonderful. In the high mountains the caribou pour through the passes by the hundreds, heading toward distant pastures on their strangely clicking hooves. The grizzlies are stunning in their shaggy winter coats, and so are the wolves, dressed in those thick capes so prized by native trappers, who sew the fur ruffs to their handmade parkas in order to keep the frost off at fifty below. The bull moose rub the velvet from their antlers and begin to drift out of the peaks into the valleys searching for cows. Down along the rivers, rafts of ice fall through the rapids and gather in pools. Withered stalks of fire-weed empty their feathered seeds to the wind, and merlins (*Falco columbarius*) fly low in mated pairs over the mosquito-less bogs, look-ing for one last mouse before turning south to Oregon. Sometimes you see a wolverine as it shuffles out on the sandbars and searches the bleached piles of driftwood for old salmon. The whole country is rest-less. For the wolves, this is a particularly difficult time, as resources begin to dwindle and competition within and between the packs increases. This is the time of highest mortality for the year's young.

My last trip of the season occurred in September. My partner for the week—Montana writer Rick Bass—proved a first-rate wilderness companion and all-around raconteur. We discussed everything from the poetry of Robert Penn Warren to the stories of Jim Harrison to Bass's boyhood in Texas and his years of football at Utah State University to the two wolves he had seen near his ranch, which is located in one of those wide, shining valleys up near the Canadian border. Rick has the arms, shoulders, and neck of a man who chops a lot of wood. He was working on a novel that has to do with wolves and was anxious to view Alaskan wolf country. On the third day, when I learned a major storm was coming in from the Yukon Delta and that shortly the west end of the park would be impassable, I decided to take a final hike on the Toklat. Rick opted that day for a long march in the rain across the Plains of Murie into some very wild country. I did not plan to see any wolves. I only wanted to get out on the hills and breathe the clean air and take one season-ending look at a place I love. Nineteen ninety had been a good year. I had finally shown my father a wolf in late August, and despite the smoke from the forest fires in the middle of the summer, I had seen many wonderful things.

I had not gone very far down the worn caribou trail—stopping to pick some seasoned blueberries and examine a shed moose antler that had been gnawed on by a porcupine—when a willow ptarmigan, still in its summer brown, flushed from an alder patch just ahead. As he flapped heavily downhill, flying with so much effort it would seem easier to walk, I was amazed to see a wolf about thirty feet away, the wolf with the dark markings on his face. I was so shocked that I spoke out loud. I said "What are you doing here?" The wolf looked at me impassively—I will never forget those yellow eyes—and then turned away into the alders. After an appropriate wait, I walked to where the wolf had been standing. The wolf was nowhere to be seen. From that point I had a view of the entire valley. There was a snowstorm in progress on the Toklat Glacier—a preview of the blizzard to come—and a wall of sleet was pouring over the high ridge to the west. The first pellets of sleet struck my face, but somehow they were not so much stinging as invigorating. Winter would arrive soon, in a matter of hours, and bring with it the great cold—not the cold where pan water freezes, but the cold where there is no water left to freeze, where the temperatures of outer space come down to Earth and death stalks everywhere looking for life. Somehow the wolves would endure all that. I spotted some caribou down on the Toklat, coming my way, and I took out my binoculars and brought them closer. There were five bulls, ranging in size from a spindly four-pointer to an old fellow with double shovels and so many tines I lost count. Two of the younger bulls broke from the others and galloped up the hill toward me. The large hanging flaps of white breast fur that squared the front quarters swayed loosely as they slowed to a canter. They stopped and locked antlers, then trotted off together, their racks held high over their shoulders. The wall of sleet steadily engulfed the caribou and, one by one, they dissolved into the storm. It was then, scanning the slopes, that I saw the wolf again, far below. The wolf was loping along, hidden by an intervening ridge, on an intercept course with the caribou. He moved rhythmically with visible strength, his head lifted and his tongue hanging out. His tail was up. He was a big, powerful animal, and he carried a weight on him that bespoke his success as a hunter. And then I saw the other wolves—three of them—closing rapidly on the other flank. They had targeted the caribou, and had the caribou right in between them and were accelerating to attack speed. At that moment I lost the wolves, as I had the caribou, to the wall of winter. The storm was on me, and it was like something from *King Lear*. I stood there for a long time on the side of the hill, trying to decide whether to hike deeper into the valley and risk disturbing the hunt, or to remain on the overlook as the storm obscured the view and forever wonder at the outcome.

Wolf country, I have learned, is a place where the sky is bluer, the trails are longer, the frosts are earlier, the moon is brighter, the streams are colder, and the good times are better than anywhere else. It is in these remote roadless areas that the roots of civilization ultimately draws their nourishment—in the fresh tracks along the river that proclaim a far-ranging pack passed through during the night, in the sudden scattering of the strong, healthy herds over the hills as they sense some peculiar disturbance of the summer calm, and in the resonant howls echoing down the rocky canyons as if the stones themselves had finally been liberated and were crying out with the accumulated vitality of the ages. This is the raw soil that sustains the rose of human culture, and no definition of freedom or progress can be complete without providing for the wolf. Even the Romans—hardly known as preservationists—had enough sense to allow the gray wolves and the brown bears a place of their own in the rugged fortress of the Apennine Mountains, just fifty miles from the Coliseum, where the two species still endure twenty centuries later. The wolf has much to teach the modern industrial world about survival: about the importance of hard work, tradition, loyalty to place, shared labor, and love of family. These are the stern old values—the creed of Epictetus, Zeno, Seneca, Diogenes, and Aurelius—and are the virtues first abandoned in times of plenty. Above all, the wolf teaches tolerance—the Aristotelian acceptance of diversity—and this is the most valuable lesson, for it is on tolerance that the foundations of the physical universe and human society rest.

I flew over Denali National Park in a jet aircraft recently, returning home from a mid-December trip to the Outside. The entire snowy park was laid out like a giant luminous relief map. There was Denali in the distance—still Mount McKinley to the federal cartographers—forever shrouded in snow and ice and monumental indifference. Only the northern lights touched the bright mountain, reaching out like some incorporeal intelligence from the cold, dark quarters beyond Polaris. Much closer, draining the Alaskan Range, were the five parallel rivers I know so well—the Savage, Sanctuary, Teklanika, and the two Toklats—each supporting its own resident pack. Wolf country, there. The realm I searched half my life to find. From the storm-blasted highlands of Glacier Gorge on the west to the owl-haunted woodlands of Riley Creek on the east. A land that as recently as 1906 had never been traversed by a Euro-American explorer. A land whose pristine character attests to the success of 10,000 years of Athapaskan stewardship. I located the grassy knoll where Dave Wallace and I knelt and glassed for wolves one fine June day, and the steep mountainside where Rick Bass and I scrambled like eager boys to get above the September clouds and walk among the wild sheep, and half a dozen other hidden places whose privacy is secure in this pen. The fine dry snow was deep over the whole territory, and I was glad the drifts denied the park to all but a few rime-coated dog-sledders for seven or eight moons out of twelve. As the massive backbone of the colossal range dropped away, I looked south and traced the high passes I would cross in the summer, seeking out those lost valleys where, it is possible, no man has slept since the beginning of time. There I would climb, when the grass was thick over the grave of winter, and camp with the wolves and the wild sheep, beside a stream as pure as the air washing down the glacier. Long days on the heather. Time to sit and watch the sun clear the ridge and the valley fill with light. Six miles beneath the starboard wing, a circle of log buildings marked Denali park headquarters, as remote an outpost of the conservation ethic as can be found. Other than that tightly clustered constellation of mercury vapor lights, the entire park—a sanctuary larger than the state of Massachusetts—was illuminated only by the distant candlelight of the Christmas stars and the gentle benediction of the aurora borealis. Just knowing that the wolves were down there, running wild and free across the frozen lakes and through the dark, radiant forests, and knowing that the wolves will be in the park so long as the rivers run, made me smile, and gave me faith that—despite the doubts that furrow my brow late at night—there may be some hope for the human race, after all.

EPILOGUE

WOLVES ONCE LEFT their tracks on the sand dunes of Cape Cod. In the limestone bluffs above the Ohio River they hid their whelping dens. Their well-worn trails stretched through the sunflower thickets of the Illinois prairie. All of the secret woodland clearings and deer runs along the central Mississippi Valley were familiar to them. Where Iowa silos bulge today with feedlot corn and market cattle doze in the sun, wolves once coursed through herds of wapiti and chased grunting bison to the horizon. Across the windblown homeland of the Pawnee and the Sioux, and the dark Yellowstone high timber, and the lost driftwood beaches of California, the mesmerizing howls of the far-roaming packs echoed. No more. Today there are only a few areas in the United States where *Canis lupus* still lives unharassed and regular pack activity is in evidence: the alplands of Glacier National Park, the Idaho Bitterroot country, the north Cascades of Washington, the lakes and forests of upper Minnesota, the Carolina swamplands, and the mosquito-filled outback of Alaska. With each passing year, more and more of this acreage disappears or is attenuated by development. Even in Alaska, with widespread fur trapping and aerial hunting, the status of the wolf is by no means permanently secure.

This is a book about those last parcels of innocence, with writings by naturalists who love wolves, who have seen the value of predators in the natural scheme of things, and who wish, above all, to build bridges of understanding between human nature and wild nature. Indeed, that increasingly global effort of reconciliation is one of the central themes of our age and may yet redeem it in the courts of history. All around the world, wolves are being thought of differently, in countries as diverse as Mexico, Spain, Italy, Greece, Israel, Iran, India, and China. Nowhere among those nations have wolves been historically more reviled and persecuted or, lately, more revered and protected, than in the United States. At the forefront of the movement to reverse five millennia of predator prejudice have been the nature writers, who can be nominally divided into two subgroups. In the first group are professional book authors such as Roger Caras, Barry Lopez, and Jan DeBlieu, who have acted as translators of more specialized technical discourse. The second band of practitioners consists of professional scientists such as Aldo Leopold, Adolph Murie, and David Brown, who have acquired the writing skills necessary to bring the public closer to the subjects of their study. Collectively their articles, essays, and books have had an enormous positive influence, as evidenced in public policy changes (the Endangered Species Act), reintroduction projects (the red wolf), and dramatic reversals in public opinion, as demonstrated in scientific polls commissioned by the National Park Service.

This anthology began with Aldo Leopold's "Thinking Like a Mountain" because the incident described—the killing of a Mexican wolf in the Apache National Forest in 1907—marked a turning point in the author's life and, as a result of the influential essay written in 1944, in the American consciousness. The frontier was closed by the time Leopold arrived as a young forester from Yale eager to clear-cut the old-growth ponderosa stands, but the wolves still persisted. This would not last much longer, as the large-scale persecution of predators by the U.S. Biological Survey would shortly devastate the region. This "American pogrom," as Barry Lopez aptly phrased it, eventually targeted nearly all predators in the western United States—from black-footed ferrets to black bears to bald eagles—and was carried out largely at the behest of private livestock interests, who were, then as now, abusing the public lands on a massive scale. When the wolfers were done, the species was extinct everywhere but northern Minnesota; even in Yellowstone National Park (formed in 1872) the wolves were gone. Aldo Leopold was so ashamed to have been associated with this debacle that he wrote the essay as a sort of apologia. Years later, after he had left government service for a professorship at the University of Wisconsin, Leopold was moved by a recently published study of the wolf to ask an obvious but long-overlooked question: "Why did the heavy wolf population of presettlement days fail to wipe out its own mammalian food supply?"

That question was answered by Adolph Murie, who was the first naturalist to undertake a comprehensive study of the wolf in the field. In 1939 Murie was directed by the National Park Service to determine the relationship between wolf predation and Dall sheep populations in Mount McKinley National Park. Murie was the perfect person to undertake this study, because he had just completed a groundbreaking analysis of the relationship of coyote predation and deer and elk populations in Yellowstone National Park. Following two years of observation, Murie published his wolf findings, *The Wolves of Mount McKinley*, in 1944. He came to the startling conclusion that "Wolf predation probably has a salutary effect on the [Dall] sheep as a species. At the present time [in Mount McKinley National Park] it appears that the sheep and wolves may be in equilibrium." This statement sent shock waves through the scientific community and through the National Park Service, which had been looking forward to eliminating the wolves in order to produce more caribou, moose, and sheep for tourists to watch. Unfortunately, Congress passed a special bill in 1946 authorizing the McKinley wolf eradication program; as a result, caribou populations burgeoned to more than 20,000 by the 1960s and then plunged to their present numbers (around 2,000). Half a century after its publication, Murie's impeccably researched monograph continues to influence managers and scientists. Barry Lopez has called it "a classic . . . the first unbiased ecological treatise on wolves."

A generation of gifted writers and scientists in the 1950s and 1960s built upon the foundation laid by Leopold and Murie in the 1940s. One thinks first of the venerable Durward Allen at Purdue University, who supervised L. David Mech's (pronounced *Meech*) doctoral work at Isle Royale National Park in Michigan, and who later authored *The Wolves of Minong*. Mech's dissertation was eventually released as *The Wolves of Isle Royale*, which is second only to Murie's work in importance and was, like Murie's monograph, published in the National Park Service's Fauna Series. Isle Royale, the largest island in Lake Superior (more than 500,000 acres), supports between 600 and 1,000 moose and represents an ideal natural laboratory for studying the interaction between predators and prey. During Mech's years of study in this region, flying in rickety old aircraft and fighting the mosquitoes and biting flies of summer, he accumulated an enormous amount of data and provided science with a comprehensive view of the species unlike any other offered before that time. After leaving Isle Royale, Mech went on to study wolves in Minnesota, Alaska, and, most recently, the Canadian Arctic.

During this same period a major popular work was written by Roger Caras, who served for many years as a special environmental reporter for ABC Television and who is currently president of the American Society for the Prevention of Cruelty to Animals and has written numerous books on animals. Caras's *The Custer Wolf* documents the life and death of perhaps the most famous of the plains wolves, an animal that was allegedly responsible for a number of live-stock depredations between 1915 and 1920 near Custer, South Dakota. Caras's 1966 book is distinctive in how far removed it is from the sentimental perspective found in Ernest Thompson Seton's 1926 *Lobo, King of the Currumpaw*. Caras writes with the compassion and out-rage of a conservationist but with none of the anthropomorphizing of earlier nature writers. Additionally, Caras thoroughly researched the scientific literature and integrated this material with the historical record and his own imaginative reconstruction of the events. As a result, the book was a landmark in the popular literature as much as Murie's monograph was in the scientific literature.

With passage of the Endangered Species Act of 1973 and the sub-sequent classification of various U.S. wolf populations as endangered, more attention than ever was focused on the species. Two important works were published in the 1970s: Edward Hoagland's "Lament the Red Wolf" (1976) and Barry Lopez's *Of Wolves and Men* (1978). Hoagland's lengthy essay is based on interviews with southeast Texas and southwest Louisiana ranchers, retired wolfers, and wildlife biolo-gists. Hoagland toured the country of the red wolf, which was being subdivided, parceled out among the oil refineries, transformed into farming plots, and generally degraded by industrial sprawl, and inquired as to whether what he saw constituted progress or not. The red wolf in his narrative became both a symbol for wild nature and a catalyst for a larger examination of civilization and its discontents.

Barry Lopez's work is arguably the most influential popular study of the wolf ever written. *Of Wolves and Men* has gone through more than a dozen printings and still sells briskly. Literary scholar Thomas J. Lyon of Utah State University has praised the book as a "significant synthesis, combining science reporting, lore collection, and an unsettling, unsparing historical critique." Lyon believes that Lopez "attempted something more comprehensive" than either Murie or Mech in that Lopez provides "not only a plausible behavioral description, but [also] an insight into what is being lost as the wolf declines—what kind of different, lesser world is evolving." Like Edward Hoagland, Barry Lopez directly linked the loss of the wolf to the loss of the wilderness and, ultimately, freedom. Like all books des-tined to endure, *Of Wolves and Men*—as a comprehensive treatment of a single species—has spawned dozens of imitations, few of which have done more than polish the reputation of the book they emulate.

The 1980s saw significant progress vis-à-vis the wolf as the 1973 Endangered Species Act received tough new enforcement language with the 1982 amendments, wolf restoration moved forward for the red wolf, the reintroduced Yellowstone wolf continued to advance, and several scientific studies in Minnesota, Canada, and Alaska helped to enlarge our understanding of the species. Some of the most important work was done in Minnesota, where wolf livestock depredations were finally proven to be almost inconsequential (less than one-fifth of one percent of the 12,000 farms in a given year suffered depredations). Wolf literature continued to enjoy great popularity with the masses, as evidenced in this volume with the five selections from that decade. The Thomas McNamee essay, "Trouble in Wolf Heaven," which appeared originally in *Audubon* magazine, provides a close examination of the wolf situation at Isle Royale, which deteriorated after his 1981 visit to the extent that almost all the wolves were lost. In "The Subarctic Wolf," cultural anthropologist Richard Nelson, who has spent a lifetime among the Native people of the Alaskan outback, documents the Athapaskan perspective on the subarctic wolf, a view that is significantly different from the Euro-American, biblically based outlook. The selection by Dan O'Brien returns to the South Dakota grasslands of Roger Caras's *The Custer Wolf;* O'Brien writes in his novel *Spirit of the Hills* about a large male wolf that returns to the Black Hills and is hunted down by an old wolf trapper. California naturalist David Rains Wallace presents a general overview of the historical conflicts between Western civilization and predators in his essay, "The Importance of Predators," which is one of the finest short treatments of the subject ever written. Lastly, former Alaskan poet laureate John Haines, who trapped wolves for years along the Tanana River, pays eloquent tribute to the species in his short sketch "Wolves," which follows a confrontation between a moose and wolves as recorded in the snow. What unifies these five essays is a growing understanding of and tolerance for wolves; great strides were made in a short ten years.

The current decade already has seen an astonishing proliferation of essays and books about wolves that directly parallels the rapid progress being made on preserving and/or restoring the gray wolf, red wolf, and Mexican wolf. North Carolina nature writer Jan DeBlieu paints a vivid picture of the red wolf restoration project in her state in "A Chorus of Wolves," and hails the return of these predators to the white-tailed deer habitat they once helped to superintend. Similarly,

Montana writer Rick Bass documents the arrival of gray wolves at a
valley near his home in "The Way Wolves Are" and offers a joyful
celebration of the event as well as a somber warning. Southwesterner
David E. Brown, of the pioneering study *The Wolf in the Southwest*, asks
whether the Mexican wolf might be restored to his native Arizona or
to adjacent New Mexico in "A Tale of Two Wolves," and Yellowstone
National Park manager Paul Schullery asks whether the same might
not happen for his park in "The Hyperbolic Wolf." Linda Hasselstrom
presents a final look at the plains wolf in her beautiful poem "Wolves,"
in which wolves figure both literally as predators and symbolically as
emblems of death. Alaska is featured in "Trails in the Snow" by Tom
Walker, "The East Fork Pack" by Rick McIntyre, and "Wolf Country"
by the editor, the latter two of which return readers to the East Fork
of the Toklat River pack, where the anthology began. Taken together,
the eight selections from the 1990s are full of hope and excitement, as
conservationists have reason to believe that red wolf restoration will
proceed successfully, that the gray wolf will be reintroduced to
Yellowstone, and that the Mexican wolf will be returned to at least one
location in the Southwest—all of this to occur before the year 2000.

What is the current (1993) status of the wolf in the United States?
The response depends on whether you speak of the red wolf, Mexican
wolf, or gray wolf; all three can interbreed with each other, domestic
dogs, or coyotes, but are distinct enough in terms of physical characteristics and geographic distribution to be thought of as unique
species. The red wolf has received most of the recent public attention
as several highly publicized restoration projects have been undertaken
in the Southeast. Originally the species inhabited the entire Old
South, from central Texas and central Oklahoma east to the Atlantic,
and from the Gulf of Mexico north to the lower Midwest; apparently
there was little overlap with the gray wolf, which inhabited most of the
rest of the continent. The red wolf appears in the wild as a much
smaller version of the more robust gray wolf, with shorter and more
noticeably red fur and a lighter bone mass. As a result of decades of
persecution, by 1970 the red wolf was found only in a few parishes in
southwestern Louisiana and a few counties in northeastern Texas
along the Gulf Coast. Jan DeBlieu has described the region as follows:

> The last stronghold of the red wolf in the wild, a sodden,
> forsaken flatland on the Texas and Louisiana coast, was

remarkable only for its proximity to the burgeoning cities of
the Sunbelt. It lay on a wedge of coastline surrounded by the
belching gray stacks of oil refineries and the outlying streets of
suburbia, the tentacles of Beaumont, Houston, and Galveston.
Composed mostly of low, poorly drained coastal marsh and
prairie, the land was split by earthen cattle walks elevated above
the brush through which wolves scouted for prey. Fields of culti-
vated rice gave way in gradients to cattails and rushes and finally
salt grass, as the land sloped to the Gulf of Mexico. Oil pumps
nodded methodically. A mongrel breed of cattle . . . grazed
in pastures turned black by their hooves and dung. . . . It was
in this last miserable corner of its range that *Canis rufus* waited
to die.

Following the granting of endangered status in 1973, a number of
these last holdouts were captured, checked for their genetic purity
(red wolves interbreed with coyotes), and then placed in several captive breeding programs. Since 1988 red wolves have been released at
Bulls Island, South Carolina; Horn Island, Mississippi; St. Vincent
Island, Florida; Alligator River National Wildlife Refuge, North
Carolina; and Great Smoky Mountains National Park (Cades Cove),
Tennessee. These successful release programs, which were undertaken with the support of local residents after a public education program, have positively influenced prospects for gray and Mexican wolf
restoration in the Rockies and Southwest, respectively.

Historically, the Mexican wolf was found across southern and
western Texas, southern New Mexico, southern Arizona, and northern Mexico. As with the red wolf, the Mexican wolf was listed as an
endangered species in 1973; currently there are about forty Mexican
wolves being held in captivity. Unlike the red wolf, which is believed
to be extinct in the wild, the Mexican wolf, according to some scientists, still persists in several locations in northern Mexico. Additionally,
there have been occasional reports of Mexican wolves in southeastern
Arizona (Chiricahua Mountains) and southwestern New Mexico
(Animas Mountains). The Mexican Wolf Recovery Team has recom-
mended restoration areas in Texas (Big Bend National Park) and New
Mexico (White Sands Missile Range). Although the Department of
Defense initially raised objections to the White Sands Missile Range,
these objections were withdrawn in 1990. Opposition still remains in

both states from the respective livestock associations. Other pos-
sibilities for reintroduction include the 900-square-mile Gila
Wilderness Area in southwestern New Mexico, the 500-square-mile
Gray Ranch (managed by the Nature Conservancy) in southwestern
New Mexico, the 300-square-mile Blue Range Primitive Area in
Arizona, and 1,200-square-mile Grand Canyon National Park, abutting
the Kaibab Plateau, in northcentral Arizona.

There were, Arizona wildlife biologist and nature writer Dave
Brown maintains, two ironies surrounding the extinction of the wolf
in the Southwest. The first "irony [was] that those who mourned the
wolf's disappearance were the wolf hunters themselves" and the
second was that "no [sportsmen or environmental] group opposed"
the destruction of the Mexican wolf by the livestock interests in collu-
sion with the Predatory Animal and Rodent Control branch of the
U.S. Biological Survey. A third irony may soon be added to that historical record, as the same federal agency that persecuted and
destroyed the species may be charged with reintroducing and preserving it across the Southwest, from the Madrean evergreen woodlands of the Animas Mountains to the oak- and juniper-studded mesas
of the Gila Wilderness.

The situation for the gray wolf in the United States is, while better
for the most part than that of the red wolf and Mexican wolf, certainly
not without cause for concern. For one thing, the gray wolf was once
the most widely distributed of the three wolf species in North America
and is today found only in northern Minnesota, northwestern
Wisconsin, the upper peninsula of Michigan, northern Montana,
northern Washington, and central Idaho. Reliable reports of wolf
activity also occasionally come from northwestern Wyoming and
North Dakota. In 1986, following extensive study, the U.S. Fish and
Wildlife Service proposed that gray wolf restoration and preservation
in the Rocky Mountains be concentrated in northwestern Montana in
and around Glacier National Park, in northwestern Wyoming in and
around Yellowstone National Park, and in central Idaho in and
around the Selway-Bitterroot Wilderness Area. Because it is unlikely
that natural recolonization will occur soon in the last two areas, plans
have been made to move captured or captive-bred wolves into them.
As is always the case, objections have been raised by cattlemen and
wool growers, but it now appears that the recovery in Yellowstone will
proceed over their objections by the mid-1990s. Should this project be

successful, it is possible that the Idaho population may be augmented. Also, managers in Rocky Mountain National Park have long called for wolf restoration in their park. Wolves in Rocky Mountain, as in Yellowstone, would help control the elk populations, which officials currently have no legal method of managing.

What happened in Yellowstone National Park earlier in this century—the systematic extermination of wolves by the agency charged with their protection—was a result of the most egregious management decision ever made by the National Park Service (followed by the decision in 1970 to suddenly close the garbage dumps to keep grizzlies from becoming accustomed to that food source). An indication of how far we've come, though, is found in the plan to return gray wolves to the region in the 1990s. In fact, the first one-acre wolf enclosure already exists at this writing behind the Lamar Ranger Station in the northeastern sector of the park; eventually the park will be home to about a hundred wolves. No one has been more active in this historic effort than U.S. Representative Wayne Owens (Democrat, Utah), who serves on the powerful Interior Committee and who has been instrumental in obtaining appropriations for Yellowstone wolf studies. Owens wrote in *Defenders* magazine (1988) that without wolves "Yellowstone . . . is no longer whole" and that "nature has a way of striking a balance between animals and their food sources; but, without wolves in Yellowstone, that balance has been disturbed." Although Owens concedes that "we must listen to the local people and make sure the livestock industry remains viable . . . we must also listen with equal concern to the millions of people all over the country who want a whole Yellowstone without pieces." Clearly, in this case, the broad national interests outweigh the narrow local interests, and, as with the Alaskan Lands Bill in 1980, the measures enabling wolf restoration to proceed should be implemented over the objections of the local congressional delegation. While earlier in this century naturalist/politician Theodore Roosevelt called wolves "the beast of waste and desolation" and considered predators as hunting trophies and livestock nuisances, we can see from Wayne Owens's comments and actions that the country and the federal government have evolved a healthier, more mature perspective on nature in general and predators in particular.

The Farley Mowat selection, "School Days," from his best-selling book *Never Cry Wolf,* offers readers the perspective of a well-known

Canadian nature writer on the wolves of his country. Farley Mowat writes in the tradition of Ernest Thompson Seton, who personalized and humanized the animals about which he wrote (most notably, *Lobo, King of the Currumpaw*). To a lesser extent, Mowat was influenced by Adolph Murie, who also spent a season in the north passively observing wolves in the wild. While wolves will probably always be secure in the Northwest Territories of which Mowat wrote, the species is beleaguered and losing habitat in other areas of Canada, particularly the eastern provinces. In their book *Wild Hunters: Predators in Peril,* British Columbian conservationists Monte Hummel and Sherri Pettigrew proposed that Canada establish several large Carnivore Conservation Areas designated specifically to protect the natural range of wolves and other predators. In these regions, wolf control projects and bounties, either public or private, would be outlawed. Any activity detrimental to the native carnivores—such as ski resort development, logging road construction, or oil and gas extraction—would be prohibited. Hummel and Pettigrew have called for such an extreme measure because only about one percent of the wolf range in Canada is currently protected. The same is also true for grizzly bears, wolverines, mountain lions, and other carnivores. Five Carnivore Convervation Areas have been tentatively proposed: Northern Yukon, Mackenzie Mountains (straddling the border of the Yukon and Northwest Territories), Thelon Game Sanctuary (Northwest Territories), Northern British Columbia, and the Rocky Mountain Park Complex (straddling the border of Alberta and British Columbia). A growing Canadian human population will increase development pressure on very finite wild areas; only vigilance and prudent planning will protect wolf habitat for posterity in the more temperate regions of Canada.

One of the finest views in North America can be found near the headwaters of the McKinley River in the far western reaches of Alaska's Denali National Park. If an epic poem is ever written of the Americas, it will begin there, with the first Siberians venturing deeper into the continent, amazed at the bounty of the land, reassured to find the plodding mammoths and familiar wolves sharing the steppe with them. The country unfolds from horizon to horizon like some Renaissance canvas of the first morning after creation. Denali, the tallest mountain on the continent, commands the scene. Scattered herds of caribou too numerous to count drift over the tundra foothills, cow moose and their calves forage in their ravines, and solitary grizzlies patrol the McKinley floodplain, their silver humps driving forcefully through the alder thickets. Look closely through your binoculars and you will find the wolves, half-hidden in the late afternoon shadows just below a river terrace, waiting for the thirsty Dall sheep to descend the cliffs a few yards upstream. Here is a drama that was already ancient when the ziggurats of Ur were just a dream. To gaze at the realm of the wolf is to behold a land as it was meant to be. To realize that here alone remains intact one small corner of a wilderness that once stretched from Alaska to Argentina is to experience a sadness not assuaged by the knowledge that our civilization has put men on the moon, the works of Darwin on library shelves, and the sculptures of Michelangelo in museum galleries.

This anthology about wolves is unlike any other, for the contributors have written out of reverence and understanding. Think of these selections not as a eulogy but as a prolegomenon, for the future of wolves will, we hope, be brighter than the past. Wolves have had, as all who have read Barry Lopez's writings know, a very hard time of it. Wolves have known the bone-crushing snap of a steel trap, the bitter quinine taste of poisoned bait, the mortal blast of a bullet through the lungs, the persistent roar of a bounty hunter's plane, and the sudden jolt of a head snare behind the ears. Yet through it all they have somehow endured, kept their dignity and their clans intact, held to the remote pockets of wilderness so rugged that even the most tormented men would not go there, and waited for their human allies to outnumber their human enemies. At last, it seems, in the closing years of a dark, violent century and on the eve of the third millennium, that human race has finally come to its senses. We have learned to see the wolf not as an adversary but as an integral part of our world. The German author Herman Hesse put it this way in *Steppenwolf,* a novel in which a man—a loner, an alienated intellectual—is quite literally compared to a wolf:

> Harry [Steppenwolf] finds in himself a human being, that is to say, a world of thoughts and feelings, of culture and tamed or sublimated nature, and besides this he finds within himself a wolf, that is to say, a dark world of instinct, of savagery and cruelty, of unsublimated or raw nature. In spite of this apparently clear division of his being between two spheres, hostile to one

another, he has known happy moments now and then when
the man and the wolf for a short while were reconciled with
one another.

Hesse is right. Humankind needs the wolf. We see in the wolf
those values and traits without which we as a species will perish. A
human being without a family, without roots, without work, a human
being without a sense of place, of location, of community, is like a
wolf without its pack, its home territory, its sense of belonging and
purpose and security. The person becomes alienated, fearful, oppor-
tunistic, amoral, and, above all, alone. A society—or worse, a world—
built of such people has lost its center, its heritage, and quite possibly
determined its downfall. The wolf—and the writings on the wolf gathered here—reminds us of what we cannot forget: that our origins are
out there, in the cold, windy outback of time, and that we are, despite
all of the tinsel and trappings of civilization, still very much a part of
that wild nature.

ABOUT THE CONTRIBUTORS

RICK BASS is the author of several acclaimed works of nonfiction, including *The Deer Pasture, Wild to the Heart, Winter: Notes from Montana,* and *The Ninemile Wolves.* His first novel, *Where the Sea Used to Be,* which is about wolves and a wolf biologist, will be published soon. Bass lives near Troy, Montana, with his wife, Elizabeth Hughes, and their infant daughter.

DAVID E. BROWN is one of the foremost experts on predators in the western United States. Formerly game branch supervisor with the Arizona Game and Fish Department, Brown is the author of such influential books as *The Grizzly in the Southwest: Documentary of an Extinction* and *The Wolf in the Southwest.* He has served as president of the Arizona Bear Society and has been actively involved in the Yellowstone wolf restoration effort.

ROGER A. CARAS, familiar to most readers from his work as a wildlife correspondent with ABC Television, is currently president of the American Society for the Prevention of Cruelty to Animals. His many books include *The Custer Wolf: Biography of an American Renegade; Monarch of Deadman Bay; Mara Simba: The African Lion; The Forest; Sarang: The Story of a Bengal Tiger;* and *The Endless Migrations.*

JAN DeBLIEU is the author of *Hatteras Journal* and *Meant to be Wild: The Struggle to Save Endangered Species Through Captive Breeding.* She lives in North Carolina with her husband, Jeffrey Smith.

JOHN HAINES, past poet laureate of Alaska, is the author of the personal memoir *The Stars, The Snow, The Fire* and six collections of poetry. For nearly twenty-five years Haines homesteaded along the Tanana River in northern Alaska.

LINDA HASSELSTROM, a rancher from South Dakota, is the author of the award-winning *Land Circle: Writings Collected from the Land, Windbreak,* and *Going Over East.*

EDWARD HOAGLAND, currently an English professor at Bennington College in Vermont, has been called "the Thoreau of our time" and has authored three novels, two travel books, and three essay collections, including *Red Wolves and Black Bears* and *The Courage of Turtles.*

ALDO LEOPOLD first encountered wolves while working as a forester in Arizona in the early twentieth century. The essay that resulted from that experience, "Thinking Like a Mountain," continues to influence the way Americans view predators.

BARRY LOPEZ is one of the foremost nonfiction writers of his generation and has authored such celebrated works as *Of Wolves and Men, Winter Notes, Desert Notes, Crossing Open Ground,* and *Arctic Dreams.*

RICK McINTYRE has one of the best collections of wild wolf photographs in the world, taken during fifteen years spent as a ranger at Denali National Park in Alaska. McIntyre currently works at Glacier National Park in the summer and spends his winters as a ranger at Joshua Tree National Monument in southern California. He is the author of *Grizzly Cub: Five Years in the Life of a Bear* and a forthcoming book on the wolves of North America.

THOMAS McNAMEE is the author of *The Grizzly Bear,* an acclaimed book on the Yellowstone grizzly, and has been active in the movement to restore wolves to Yellowstone and to manage the park according to ecosystem boundaries.

FARLEY MOWAT is the Canadian author of more than two dozen books that have been published in twenty languages in more than forty countries. His works include *Owls in the Family, No Birds Sang, People of the Deer, A Whale for the Killing,* and *Never Cry Wolf,* which became an international best-seller.

ADOLPH MURIE produced the first scientific study of wolves, *The Wolves of Mount McKinley,* in 1944. His other important monograph was a study of coyotes in Yellowstone National Park. Both books helped to transform the way the National Park Service viewed these wild canids.

RICHARD NELSON was awarded the John Burroughs Nature Writing Medal for his book *The Island Within*. He is a cultural anthropologist by profession and has lived and researched in several remote locations in Alaska. Nelson's many books include *Make Prayers to the Raven: A Koyukon View of the Northern Forest*, *Hunters of the Northern Forest*, and *Hunters of the Northern Ice*.

DAN O'BRIEN is the author of a prize-winning collection of short stories, *Eminent Domain*, and a highly praised novel, *Spirit of the Hills*. His memoir *The Rites of Autumn* describes a journey he undertook with his pet peregrine falcon across the American West. O'Brien lives in South Dakota.

SIGURD F. OLSON, for many years, was a professor and college administrator in Ely, Minnesota. He is the author of *The Living Wilderness*, now considered the classic nature book on the Superior-Quetico north woods.

PAUL SCHULLERY has published more than two dozen nature books. He currently works as a senior staff member at Yellowstone. His finest work is generally considered to be *Mountain Time*, a personal memoir of his early years at Yellowstone National Park.

TOM WALKER has photographed, hiked, hunted, and fished across Alaska for more than twenty years. He lives in a cabin he built himself near Denali National Park and has authored two books, *Shadows on the Tundra: Alaskan Tales of Predator, Prey, and Man* and *Denali Journal*.

DAVID RAINS WALLACE was awarded the John Burroughs Nature Writing Medal for his nature book *The Klamath Knot*. He has authored nine other works of nature writing, including *The Untamed Garden and Other Personal Essays*, and two novels. Wallace lives in Berkeley, California, with his wife Betsy.

THE WOLF: A CHRONOLOGY

20,000 B.C.—Cave drawings of wolves are made in southern Europe.

5000 B.C.—Early agricultural settlements in Southwest Asia come into conflict with wolves.

2300 B.C.—First reference to a wolf in Western literature occurs in the *Epic of Gilgamesh.*

800 B.C.—Numerous references to wolves are made in Homer's epic poem *The Iliad.*

500 B.C.—Aristotle describes wolves in his writings.

A.D. 30—Jesus Christ uses wolf parables to illustrate moral principles.

70—Pliny the Elder provides a detailed pseudoscientific account of wolves in his book, *Natural History.*

70—Plutarch describes the legend of Romulus and Remus, founders of Rome who were raised by wolves, in his *Putative Lives of the Noble Greeks and Romans.*

600—During the European Middle Ages, legends of werewolves and beliefs that wolves are associated with devils abound.

750—*Beowulf,* the oldest of the major narrative poems in English, is composed; the protagonist, named for a wolf, slays a monster named Grendel.

1600—William Shakespeare employs dozens of wolf references in his plays.

1630—First wolf bounty law passed by the Massachusetts Bay Colony.

1632—First wolf bounty law passed by the Virginia Bay Colony.

1697—New Jersey offers a wolf bounty.

1750—Wolves become extinct in the Scottish Highlands at the hands of Lochiel, a clan chieftain, because they "preyed on the red deer of the Grampians." Wolves are similarly persecuted in western Europe, but do not become extinct in France, Italy, or Spain as they do in other countries.

1758—Linnaeus recognizes the wolf as a circumpolar species and gives the species the Latin name *Canis lupus linnaeus.*

1790—Russian and German naturalists report wolves in Alaska.

1793—Wolf bounty is offered in Ontario.

1805—Explorers Meriwether Lewis and William Clark encounter wolves in the Far West.

1808—Zebulon Pike reports wolves in what is today Colorado.

1819—The government expedition of Major Stephen Long encounters wolves in large numbers in Colorado.

1823—As with earlier government expeditions, trapper/explorer James Ohio Pattie documents wolves living in close association with extensive prey populations.

1832—Artist George Catlin paints *Buffalo Hunt Under the Wolfskin Mask,* depicting two Pawnee warriors hunting buffalo disguised as wolves, and *White Wolves Attacking a Buffalo Bull,* which portrays two dozen wolves killing an old bull buffalo. These paintings are later exhibited in New York, London, and Paris.

1835—America's first internationally known writer, Washington Irving, describes wolves in what is today Oklahoma in his travel narrative *A Tour on the Prairies;* he is the first professional writer to do so.

1840s—Tens of thousands of settlers head west on the Oregon Trail and the Santa Fe Trail. Increasing settlements come into conflict with wolves and their prey species as the entire Great Plains ecosystem begins to be destroyed.

1860s—Western railroad expansion brings buffalo market hunters to the Far West, decimating the great buffalo herds.

1870s—First cattle drives introduce livestock into previously remote mountain habitat for wolves; sheep herds will come later, leading to even more destruction of wolves and other predators.

1872—Yellowstone National Park is established in northwestern Wyoming.

1880s—Theodore Roosevelt reports wolves are becoming scarce in the Dakotas.

1884—U.S. Biological Survey is formed (a precursor to the U.S. Fish and Wildlife Service).

1894—Nature writer Ernest Thompson Seton kills the Currumpaw wolf of New Mexico and his mate, Blanca. Seton will eventually write a book, *Lobo, King of the Currumpaw,* about this experience.

1897—Frederic Remington paints *Moonlight Wolf,* depicting a solitary Great Plains wolf (*Canis lupus nubilus*), a subspecies that would become extinct in a few years.

1899—Wolf bounty is offered in Alberta.

1909—Aldo Leopold kills a mother wolf and pups in the Apache National Forest of Arizona. This incident will later inspire his seminal essay "Thinking Like a Mountain," written in 1944 and published posthumously in 1949.

1909—Wolf bounty is offered in British Columbia.

1914—Congress designates U.S. Biological Survey as chief predator control agency.

1915—First professional trappers and hunters hired by U.S. Biological Survey; their heyday will run through 1942 as wolfers operate in Colorado, Wyoming, Montana, the Dakotas, Arizona, and New Mexico.

1915—Wolf bounty is offered in Alaska.

1916—National Park Service Act is signed into law, mandating protection of wildlife and maintenance of recreational opportunities.

1916—The American Far West is divided into control districts by U.S. Biological Survey, thus paving the way for the systematic extermination of all predators through the use of poisoned baits (strychnine; Compound 1080 after 1944) and steel leg-hold traps; eventually airplanes and helicopters will be used.

1925—Last wolf in South Dakota ("Old Three Toes") is killed.

1926—Since 1914 about 120 wolves have been killed in Yellowstone National Park; after 1926 there are no viable reports of wolves or wolf activity in northwestern Wyoming for a number of decades.

1927—Last wolf in eastern Montana is killed.

1929—German novelist Herman Hesse publishes *Steppenwolf,* a novel that links the impulsive, atavistic nature of man with the same quality in the wolf of the eastern European/western Asian steppes.

1929—Ernest Thompson Seton publishes *Lives of the Game Animals,* a seminal work of natural history.

1933—Wolf bounty law is repealed in Montana.

1934—Wildlife biologist Adolph Murie begins his study of the coyote in Yellowstone National Park and confirms the wolf is now extirpated. Murie also establishes that the coyote poses no threat to the major game species, most notably elk, that migrate out of the park into national forests, where they can be hunted.

1939—Adolph Murie begins a two-year study of the relationship between the subarctic wolf (*Canis lupus pambasileus*) and the Dall sheep (*Ovis ovis dalli*); Murie concludes that the wolf has a "salutary effect" on the prey species, a finding that stirs much controversy in the National Park Service.

1943—Last wolf in Colorado is killed on Upper Conejos River near Platoro Reservoir.

1944—Stanley Young's *The Wolves of North America* (a mixture of fact and folklore) is published. Adolph Murie's *The Wolves of Mount McKinley* is published; it is the first scientific treatise on the species. Murie is the first professional photographer to extensively document the wolf in the wild.

1948—Special Act of Congress permits wolf trapping in Mount McKinley National Park over the objections of Adolph Murie and other biologists. Murie later is forced to play a role in this eradication measure, which results in the artificially elevated numbers of caribou seen in the park in the 1960s and 1970s (before the caribou population collapse).

1950s—Aerial hunting of wolves in Alaska and Canada begins in earnest.

1960s—Persistent unconfirmed wolf sightings in Yellowstone National Park will continue until the present time. Radio-collared Alaskan wolves have covered up to 400 miles in one year, so the possibility that the Yellowstone wolves came from Canada cannot be ruled out (nor can the covert release of wolves by unknown parties).

1962—L. David Mech completes his doctoral dissertation on the wolves of Isle Royale National Park. (This wolf population will later be decimated by canine distemper in the late 1980s.)

1963—Canadian writer Farley Mowat publishes *Never Cry Wolf;* a highly successful film will later (1983) dramatize Mowat's adventures in the Canadian Arctic and for the first time portray wolves positively to the public in the cinema. Leopold report recommends predator restoration.

1964—Wilderness Act is signed into law; it protects former wolf habitat for future restoration projects (though not by design).

1970—Mexican wolf killed in Peloncillo Mountains of New Mexico.

1970—L. David Mech publishes *The Wolf: Ecology and Behavior of an Endangered Species.*

1970s—U.S. Fish and Wildlife Service captures Mexican wolves in Mexico for captive breeding.

1970s—U.S. Fish and Wildlife Service captures red wolves in Texas and Louisiana for captive breeding.

1970s—U.S. Fish and Wildlife Service extensively studies the Minnesota wolf population.

1971—Quebec ends wolf bounty.

1972—Ontario ends wolf bounty.

1973—Endangered Species Act is passed into law. The 1982 amendments will put enforcement strength into the act and provide further clarification on restoration issues.

1974—Yellowstone wolf search involves 1,800 hours of airplane overflights and reveals only one "wolf-like canid."

1976—Encouraged by National Park Service officials, Colorado State University graduate student Herb Conley writes a thesis on the restoration of wolves to Rocky Mountain National Park, where the burgeoning elk populations are destroying habitat, as in Yellowstone.

1976—Two red wolves are released on Bulls Island off the South Carolina coast.

1978—Barry Lopez publishes *Of Wolves and Men*.

1979—Mexican Wolf Recovery Team is appointed; recovery plans for the red wolf and the northern Rocky Mountain gray wolf are also institutionalized at this time. Durward Allen publishes *The Wolves of Minong: Their Vital Role in a Wild Community*.

1980—Alaska National Interest Lands Conservation Act (ANILCA) is signed into law. It doubles the National Park system and triples national wilderness acreage in Alaska.

1980s—Discussions of northern Rocky Mountain gray wolf recovery focus on Yellowstone, central Idaho, and northwestern Montana.

1982—Montana biologist Diane Boyd completes her thesis on a migrant wolf on the North Fork of the Flathead River near Glacier National Park; during the late 1980s several wolf packs will establish themselves in this region of the United States.

1982—Arizona wildlife manager David E. Brown publishes *The Wolf in the Southwest*, which documents the eradication by the federal government of the southern Rocky Mountain gray wolf and Mexican wolf in Arizona and New Mexico.

1983—Film version of *Never Cry Wolf* is released.

1985—Retired professor Alston Chase alleges in his controversial book *Playing God with Yellowstone* that the National Park Service secretly tried to restore wolves to Yellowstone.

1986—Eight red wolves arrive at Alligator River National Wildlife Refuge in coastal North Carolina; after acclimatization they will later be released, with mixed results in terms of adaptation and survivability.

1986—L. David Mech begins study of arctic wolves in Canadian high Arctic.

1988—Wolves killed in northwestern Montana by federal agents after livestock depredations.

1988—U.S. Fish and Wildlife Service report concludes White Sands Missile Range in southern New Mexico is a suitable location for Mexican wolf restoration. Army raises objections but drops them in 1991, while livestock interests continue to oppose this. Other sites discussed include Big Bend National Park in Texas, the Gila Wilderness Area in New Mexico, and several wilderness locations in Arizona.

1990s—Wolves are confirmed in Washington, Idaho, and North Dakota.

1991—Two red wolves arrive at Cades Cove, Tennessee, to be prepared for release in Great Smoky Mountains National Park. Red wolves have also been released by this time in Florida, Mississippi, South Carolina, and Alabama in various study projects. (A total of thirty-five red wolves are alive in captivity by 1991, including those in North Carolina.)

1992—U.S. Fish and Wildlife Service Director John Turner endorses a blue-ribbon report recommending restoration of the gray wolf to Yellowstone National Park; the environmental assessment process further studies the potential effects of reintroduction on other species, including the threatened grizzly bear (to be completed in May 1993).

1992—The film *Dances with Wolves* portrays wolves in a positive light and wins several Academy Awards.

1992—Rick Bass publishes *The Ninemile Wolves*, which examines the impact of a newly formed wolf pack near his home in northwestern Montana.

1992—Polls indicate two out of three Montanans favor natural recovery of wolves in the state.

FURTHER READING

Allen, Durward L. 1979. *The Wolves of Minong: Their Vital Role in a Wild Community.* Boston: Houghton Mifflin.

Bass, Rick. 1992. *The Ninemile Wolves.* Livingston, Mont.: Clark City Press.

Boyd, Diane. 1982. "Food Habits and Spatial Relations of Coyotes and a Lone Wolf in the Rocky Mountains." M.S. thesis, University of Montana, Missoula.

Brandenburg, Jim. 1988. *White Wolf: Living with an Arctic Legend.* Minocqua, Wis.: Northword Press.

Brown, David E. 1982. *The Wolf in the Southwest.* Tucson: University of Arizona Press.

————. 1984. *The Grizzly in the Southwest.* Norman: University of Oklahoma Press.

Caras, Roger A. 1966. *The Custer Wolf: Biography of an American Renegade.* Boston: Little, Brown and Company.

Carbyn, L. M. 1983. "Wolf Predator on Elk in Riding Mountain National Park, Manitoba." *Journal of Wildlife Management* 47(4): 963–76.

Chadwick, Douglas H. 1987. "Manitoba's Wolves: A Model for Yellowstone?" *Defenders* 62(2):30–36.

Conley, Herb. 1976. "Impacts of Reintroducing Gray Wolves into the Rocky Mountain National Park Area." M.S. thesis, Colorado State University.

Curnow, Edward. 1969. "The History of the Eradication of the Wolf in Montana." M.S. thesis, University of Montana, Missoula.

DeBlieu, Jan. 1991. *Meant to Be Wild: The Struggle to Save Endangered Species Through Captive Breeding.* Golden, Colo.: Fulcrum.

Despain, D. et al. 1986. *Wildlife in Transition: Man and Nature on Yellowstone's Northern Range.* Boulder: Roberts Rinehart.

Fischer, H. 1988. "Wolves for Yellowstone?" *Defenders* 63(2):16–17.

Fritts, S. H. 1990. "Management for Wolves Inside and Outside Yellowstone National Park and Possibilities for Wolf Management Zones in the Greater Yellowstone Area." In *Wolves for Yellowstone?* Yellowstone National Park et al., 1–3 to 1–88.

————. 1982. *Wolf Depredation on Livestock in Minnesota.* U.S. Fish and Wildlife Service Resource Publication 145. Washington, D.C.

Haber, Gordon. 1977. "The Socio-ecological Dynamics of Wolves and Prey in a Subarctic Ecosystem." Ph.D. diss., University of British Columbia.

Haines, John. 1989. *The Stars, The Snow, The Fire.* St. Paul, Minn.: Graywolf Press.

Hasselstrom, Linda. 1992. *Land Circle: Writings Collected from the Land.* Golden, Colo.: Fulcrum.

Hoagland, Edward. 1976. *Red Wolves and Black Bears.* New York: Random House.

Kaminski, T., and J. Hansen. 1984. "Wolves of Central Idaho." Unpublished. Montana Cooperative Wildlife Unit, Missoula, Mont.

Keiter, R. B., and P. T. Holscher. 1990. "Wolf Recovery Under the Endangered Species Act: A Study in Contemporary Federalism." *Public Land Law Review* 11:19–52.

Kerasote, Ted. 1989. "Getting to Yes on the Wolf." *Sports Afield* 202(1):45–47, 99–102.

Lawrence, R. D. 1986. *In Praise of Wolves.* New York: Henry Holt.

Leopold, Aldo. 1949. *A Sand County Almanac, with Essays on Conservation from Round River.* New York: Oxford University Press.

Lopez, Barry Holstun. 1978. *Of Wolves and Men.* New York: Scribner's.

Magoun, A. J. 1976. "Summer Scavenging Activity in Northeastern Alaska." M.S. thesis, University of Alaska, Fairbanks.

McClure, J. 1990. S. 2674. *A Bill to Provide for the Establishment of the Gray Wolf in Yellowstone National Park and the Central Idaho Wilderness Areas.* 101st Cong. 2d sess. May 22.

McIntyre, Rick. In press. *A Society of Wolves.* Stillwater, Minn.: Voyageur Press.

McNamee, Thomas. 1986. "Yellowstone's Missing Element." *Audubon,* January, 12–19.

McNaught, D. A. 1985. "Park Visitor Attitudes Towards Wolf Recovery in Yellowstone National Park." M.S. thesis, University of Montana, Missoula.

Mech, L. David. 1966. *The Wolves of Isle Royale.* Washington, D.C.: U.S. Government Printing Office.

———. 1988. *The Arctic Wolf: Living with the Pack.* Stillwater, Minn.: Voyageur Press.

———. 1991. *The Life of the Wolf.* Stillwater, Minn.: Voyageur Press.

———. 1991. "Returning the Wolf to Yellowstone." In *The Greater Yellowstone Ecosystem,* edited by R. B. Keiter and M. S. Boyce. New Haven: Yale University Press.

Mowat, Farley. 1963. *Never Cry Wolf.* Boston: Little, Brown and Company.

Murie, Adolph. 1940. *Ecology of the Coyote in the Yellowstone.* Washington, D.C.: U.S. Government Printing Office.

———. 1944. *The Wolves of Mount McKinley.* Washington, D.C.: U.S. Government Printing Office.

Murray, John A. 1987. "The Wolf in Colorado: Past and Future." *Colorado Outdoors.* March/April.

Murray, John A. 1987. *Wildlife in Peril: The Endangered Mammals of Colorado.* Boulder: Roberts Rinehart.

Nelson, Richard. 1983. *Make Prayers to the Raven.* Chicago: University of Chicago Press.

O'Brien, Dan. 1988. *Spirit of the Hills.* New York: Crown.

Olson, Sigurd F. 1956. *The Singing Wilderness.* New York: Alfred A. Knopf.

Owens, Wayne. 1988. "Crying Wolf at Yellowstone." *National Parks,* March/April, 16–17.

———. 1988. H.R. 3378. *A Bill to Require the National Park Service to Reintroduce Wolves into Yellowstone National Park.* 100th Cong. 1st sess. September 30.

———. 1989. H.R. 2786. *A Bill to Provide for a Timely Analysis of All Factors*

Relating to the Restoration of Gray Wolves in Yellowstone National Park and Surrounding Public Lands, and for Other Purposes. 101st Cong. 1st sess. June 28.

Peterson, Rolf. 1977. *Wolf Ecology and Prey Relationships on Isle Royale.* National Park Service Scientific Monograph Series No. 11. Washington, D.C.: U.S. Government Printing Office.

Schullery, Paul. 1986. "Drawing the Lines in Yellowstone: The American Bison as Symbol and Scourge." *Orion Nature Quarterly,* 5(4):32–45.

Serveen, C. W., and R. R. Knight. 1990. "Possible Effects of a Restored Wolf Population on Grizzly Bears in the Yellowstone Area." In *Wolves for Yellowstone?* Yellowstone National Park et al., 4–35 and 4–49.

Seton, Ernest Thompson, 1929. *Lives of Game Animals.* New York: Doubleday.

Steinhart, P. 1988. "A Wolf in the Eye." *Audubon,* January, 79–89.

Tucker, P. 1988. *Annotated Gray Wolf Bibliography.* Denver: U.S. Fish and Wildlife Service, Region 6.

U.S. Fish and Wildlife Service. 1982. *Mexican Wolf Recovery Plan.* Albuquerque: U.S.F.W.S., Region 7.

———. 1987. *Northern Rocky Mountain Wolf Recovery Plan.* Denver: U.S.F.W.S., Region 6.

———. 1988. *The Mexican Wolf: Biology, History and Prospects for Reestablishment in New Mexico, and An Evaluation of the Ecological Potential of White Sands Missile Range to Support a Reintroduced Population of Mexican Wolves.* Albuquerque: U.S.F.W.S., Region 7.

———. 1989. *Red Wolf Recovery Plan.* Atlanta: U.S.F.W.S., Region 2.

———. 1992. *Recovery Plan for the Eastern Timber Wolf.* Twin Cities, Minn.: U.S.F.W.S., Region 3.

Walker, Tom. 1990. *Shadows on the Tundra: Alaskan Tales of Predator, Prey, and Man.* Harrisburg, Pa.: Stackpole.

Wallace, David Rains. 1986. *The Untamed Garden and Other Personal Essays.* Columbus: Ohio State University Press.

Weaver, John. 1978. *The Wolves of Yellowstone.* U.S. National Park Service Natural Resources Report No. 14.

Weise, T. F. et al. 1975. *An Experimental Translocation of the Eastern Timber Wolf.* Audubon Conservation Report No. 5. Twin Cities, Minn.: U.S.F.W.S., Region 3.

Williams, Ted. 1990. "Waiting for Wolves to Howl in Yellowstone." *Audubon,* November, 34, 36, 38, 40.

Wolf Management Committee. 1991. *Reintroduction and Management of Wolves in Yellowstone National Park and the Central Idaho Wilderness Area.* A Report to the United States Congress.

Yellowstone National Park, U.S. Fish and Wildlife Service, University of Wyoming, University of Idaho, Interagency Grizzly Bear Study Team, and University of Minnesota C.P.S.U. 1990. *Wolves for Yellowstone?* A Report to the United States Congress. Vol. I, Executive Summaries. Vol. II, Research and Analysis.

Young, S. P. 1946. *The Wolf in North American History.* Caldwell, Idaho: Caxton.

Young, S. P., and E. A. Goldman. 1944. *The Wolves of North America.* New York: Dover.

INDEX

ABOUT JOHN A. MURRAY

JOHN A. MURRAY is Assistant Professor of English at the University of Alaska Fairbanks. He has published twelve other nature books, including *A Republic of Rivers: Three Centuries of Nature Writing from Alaska and the Yukon* and *Wild Africa: Three Centuries of Nature Writing from Africa*. His previous writings on the wolf can be found in *Wildlife in Peril: The Endangered Mammals of Colorado*. For the past five summers he has studied and photographed the wolves of Denali National Park and Preserve.